IRANIAN CULTURE

A Persianist View

Michael C. Hillmann

UNIVERSITY
PRESS OF
AMERICA

Lanham • New York • London

Copyright © 1990 by
University Press of America®, Inc.
4720 Boston Way
Lanham, Maryland 20706

3 Henrietta Street
London WC2E 8LU England

Library of Congress Cataloging-in-Publication Data

Hillmann, Michael C.
Iranian culture : a Persianist view / Michael C. Hillmann.
p.   cm.
Includes bibliographical references.
1. Iran—Civilization.   I. Title.
DS266.H55   1990   955—dc20   89–29018 CIP

ISBN 0–8191–7694–X (alk. paper)
ISBN 0–8191–7695–8 (pbk. : alk. paper)

The paper used in this publication meets the minimum requirements of
American National Standard for Information Sciences—Permanence
of Paper for Printed Library Materials, ANSI Z39.48–1984.

This book is dedicated to the memory of Carter Harrison Bryant II (1944-1986), an American Peace Corps Volunteer in Torbat-e Jâm, Director of the Iran-America Society in Mashhad, holder of a Ph.D. degree in Comparative Literature from The University of Texas at Austin, a literary critic, gifted translator, lover of Iran, and a good and kind man.

ACKNOWLEDGEMENTS

Research for this volume was supported by grants, hereby gratefully acknowledged, from the University Research Institute and the Department of Oriental and African Languages and Literatures at The University of Texas at Austin.

Among the many colleagues who have commented on drafts of individual chapters or have otherwise contributed to this study, special thanks go to Leonardo P. Alishan, Aziz Atai-Langroudi, Michael Beard, Hamid Dabashi, Dick Davis, M.R. Ghanoonparvar, Jerrold Green, Zjaleh Hajibashi, William L. Hanaway, Jr., J. Paul Luft, Heshmat Moayyad, A.R. Navabpour, Michael Phillips, Annette W. Pomeroy, Patrick Salmon, Diane L. Wilcox, and Ehsan Yarshater.

The volume has benefited also from the opportunity afforded me to lecture on Ferdowsi, Khayyâm, Hâfez, Sâdeq Hedâyat, Forugh Farrokhzâd, and Jalâl Âl-e Ahmad at the Unversity of Arizona, Columbia University, Harvard University, The University of Pennsylvania, Rice University, the University of Utah, and especially at the University of Durham during a term there as Visiting Fellow in the Centre for Middle Eastern and Islamic Studies.

In addition, I thank Three Continents Press and Mage Publishers for their invitations to write essays on Âl-e Ahmad (for *Lost in the Crowd*, 1985) and Hâfez (for *Hâfez, Dance of Life*, 1987) respectively, which grew into the treatments of those two literary giants in this volume.

Finally, thanks go as always to Sorayya.

Michael Craig Hillmann
Austin, Texas, U.S.A.
August 1989

CONTENTS

PREFACE

Iranian Culture: A Persianist View describes features of the culture of Irân through scrutiny of the most prominent Persian literary works and figures amenable to appreciation by readers not necessarily familiar with the Persian language.

Judging from reactions in the West to events in Iran from 1978 onward, one might suppose that Iran's is an internally confused culture. Judging from representations by Iranians themselves, one might conclude that almost as many Irans exist as there are Iranians describing their country. In contrast, the present study argues that in humanistic terms Iran's is a rich, coherent culture embodying as well the manifold, internal conflicts and contradictions one might expect in a traditional society as it deals with the contemporary world.

Iranian Culture: A Persianist View is the upshot of my attempt during the 1980s to define that culture for myself and to reconcile different personal perspectives on Iran. Seven years of living and working there left me with the strongest feelings of affinity for the place. A second perspective, involving reassuring appreciation of presumed cultural continuity as exhibited in Persian literature, derives from orientalist training in Persian studies at The University of Tehran and The University of Chicago and from academic activities as a professor of Persian literature and Iranian culture. A third perspective, involving doubts (described in due course) as to Iran's future viability as the cultural context for literary expression, has emerged in coming to terms with personal consternation at the dramatic civil upheaval which commenced in Iran in early 1978, which culminated a year and several months later in the establishment of the Islamic Republic of Iran, and which led to headlines on Iran in the world's press throughout the 1980s.

The issues raised and treated in this volume are my day-to-day concerns as an intellectual trying to understand Iran and as a Persianist expected in both teaching and research to deal not only with other persons who have a background in Persian studies, but also with colleagues and students lacking direct familiarity with Persian literature. The latter rightly expect me to be able to communicate much of what I am supposed to know to them. And from them, by means of such communication, I hope to learn more about what I study or about how to study it.

1

The chief subjects of the six chapters in this study are literary figures and works I regularly seek out for leisure reading and directly address in university courses on Persian literature. In another course I teach called simply "Iranian Culture," versions of the chapters comprise formal lectures. In fact, *Iranian Culture: A Persianist View* might serve as a supplementary textbook in courses on Middle Eastern cultures in general and on Iran in particular. The volume's primary purpose, however, is to offer non-specialist readers an alternative perspective, that of the Persian literature scholar, to more commonly represented views of Iran by historians, political scientists, sociologists, and anthropologists. Without at all implying that my analysis is more telling than any other, I hope readers come to agree that the heretofore unrepresented Persianist perspective is valid and fruitful.

The phrase "Iranian culture" seems straightforward enough at first glance. According to *Webster's Dictionary*, the word "culture" denotes "the body of customary beliefs, social forms, and material traits constituting a distinct complex of traditions of a racial, religious or social group." The word "Iranian" means "belonging to Iran," the Middle Eastern country whose 630,000+ square miles are bordered on the northwest by Turkey and the USSR, on the north by the Caspian Sea and the USSR, on the east by Afghanistan and Pakistan, on the south and southwest by the Persian Gulf, and on the west by Iraq and Turkey. The phrase "Iranian culture," then, should denote simply the aggregate of attitudes and customs of the people of Iran. However, the physical country of Iran is not paralleled by a single, homogeneous society. In other words, "Iranian" as an epithet for people merely identifies persons who hold Iranian identity cards, but who often do not share much else in common. This view even a casual look at Iranian living environments and groups substantiates.

Most of the 1985 estimated 45,000,000 inhabitants of Iran live on about ten percent of the land, because ninety percent of Iran is not arable. But even the consequent density of population does not result in close communication among various traditional sectors of the Iranian population because of the country's distinctive topography. Two forbidding mountain ranges loom across the country: the Alborz that run from west to east cutting the plateau region off from the Caspian littoral to the north, and the Zâgros mountains that run from northwest to southwest cutting off the plateau from the western Kurdish areas and the Iraqi Mesopotamian area beyond it. Then there are vast stretches of nearly impassable salt desert flats separating population centers that ring them. Because of such topographical barriers, different Iranian areas have developed different social, cultural, and linguistic patterns. Thus, the Irans experienced by the inhabitants of Rasht on the Caspian, Hamadân on the plateau, Zâhedân in the southeast, Ahvâz in Khuzestân, all of them major provincial cities, are very different in climate, language, diet, and customs. Or, for example, although the Qashqâ'i nomad in Fârs Province, the Baluch villager in Khorâsân, the Afshâr town dweller in

Kermân, and the Torkaman farmer in Gonbad-e Qâbus are all originally tribal people, each of them today lives in a different Iran.

In general geographical terms, desert, valley, mountain, plateau, Caspian littoral, and Gulf littoral Irans exist. In population terms, tribal, village, town, city, and Tehrân Irans exist. In linguistic terms, Âzarbâyjân, Arab, Caspian, Turkic (other than Azarbâyjâni), Armenian, Assyrian, Persian, and other Irans exist. But even "Persian" Iran is not a monolith insofar as some Persian dialects are almost mutually incomprehensible. More importantly, different groups of "Persian" Iranians have vastly different perceptions of Iran as a culture and as a society with traditions and a history.

As a region in which Indo-European Iranian peoples have lived and been influential, Iran has a history of 3,000+ years. Ever since the Achaemenid victory over the Medes in 559 BCE (= Before Common Era = B.C.), these Persian-speaking Iranian people have been culturally dominant in the region, even when conquering invaders and their successors have wielded the political power, as in the case of the Seleucids (330-150 BCE), the Arab Moslems (650-900 CE = Common Era = A.D.), the Ghaznavids (950-1030), the Saljuqs (1055-1157), the Il-Khânids (1258-1390), and the Timurids (1390-1450). Or when originally non-Persian elements long settled in Iran have exercised this power, such as the Turkish Safavids (1501-1736) and later the Qâjârs (1796-1925).

Because Iran is a region with a lengthy and continuous history, many Iranians define their Iranianness, in part, in terms of history. However, not necessarily included among these are the five to ten percent of the population still nomadic (thirty-five percent were nomadic in 1900, fifty percent in 1800), or the estimated sixty percent of the population that is illiterate, which includes almost half of the country's population still living in 65,000 or more villages.

But not only the fact of a lengthy history makes the Iran of educated Iranians so distinctive; it is also the fact that Iran's is a history punctuated with great events, glory, and richness. The Achaemenid Empire (559-330 BCE), the Zoroastrian religion that was the official faith then and later through the Sâsânid Empire (224-640s CE), the great Saljuq hegemony, Iranian contributions to Sufism which had its thirteenth-century golden age in the midst and aftermath of devastating Mongol invasions, and the great architectural achievements commissioned by Safavid Shâh 'Abbâs I (1587-1629) are just a handful of very different sorts of historical high points. Yet only that minority of Iranians with some formal education and exposure to the world beyond Iran's borders is likely to appreciate the significance of such achievements as Achaemenid imperial organization, Zoroastrian spirituality, Saljuq achievements in science, the world of ideas, and government, Sufism, and the aesthetic appeal and symbolic import of Esfahân's Royal Square. Therefore, the history of the region constitutes an aspect of Iranian identity only for those Iranians conscious of it, for whom their country today offers at every turn physical, architectural, ethnic, and religious reminders of the past. In contrast, the Qashqâ'i woman weaver who includes a representation of Persepolis columns and protoma in carpet field designs is probably unaware of what the Achaemenid shrine called Persepolis was or means, even though history in the form of experiencing the Persepolis platform on migrations affected her ancestors as surely as it does educated Iranians.

For these same educated Iranians, the Iran of Twelver Shi'i Islam has long been part of their Iranian legacy, regardless of how individually religious they are or were even before the Khomayni era. An especially fertile region for the development of religious ideas and systems, among them Zoroastrianism, Manichaeism, Mithraism, Mazdakism, and the Baha'i Faith, educated Iranians have looked at their own Iranian world and the world beyond with culturally Shi'i eyes at least from Safavid days.

A third essential aspect to the outlook of these educated Iranians is their command of the Persian language, regardless of possible non-Persian origin, for example, Kurdish or Azarbâyjânian. Again, as with self-consciousness with respect to the past, such competence in the Persian language makes these Iranians a special minority and the Iran open to them a special cultural environment. It is the only Iran, in fact, which *Iranian Culture: A Persianist View* explores.

In other words, this book examines literary dimensions of "Persian" Iranian culture manifested and experienced by educated, Shi'i Moslem Iranians who are thus considered both a national and a cultural group, and the dominant cultural force on the Iranian plateau. That historical records and literacy in the Persian language are essential features of this Iranian culture make it a suitable subject of study and reflection by a specialist in Persian literature. In fact, the Persianist could hardly study any Iranian culture besides this "Persian" culture with much confidence. In addition, because imaginative literature represents for many Iranians the most significant manifestation of their culture, the scrutiny of the chief works of such major figures as Ferdowsi (d.c.1020), 'Omar Khayyâm (d. 1131), Sa'di (d.c.1290), Hâfez (d.c.1390), Sâdeq Hedâyat (d. 1951), Jalâl Âl-e Ahmad (d. 1969), and Forugh Farrokhzâd (d. 1967) is a particularly relevant and potentially fruitful enterprise in coming to grips with Iranian culture.

Few, if any other, books better represent Iranian ideals in the literary past for many literate Iranians than Abolqâsem Ferdowsi's famous eleventh-century redaction of the epic narratives of Iranian mythology and history called *Shâhnâmeh* [Book of Kings]. Chapter 1 treats one of the most famous episodes in the *Shâhnâmeh*, the tragic story of Rostam and his ill-fated son Sohrâb. Called "Iranian Patriarchy, Its Victims, and Persian Sadness," this chapter calls into play Persianness, attachment to the Iranian homeland, the mystique of kingship, the omnipotence and justice of Allâh, and an arguably Iranian fatalism. But the chapter's most telling focus is on patriarchal values and the eventual defeat Iranian culture tells of itself again and again, and the defeat of sons at the hands of fathers, filicide accomplished in the name of the king or other patriarch.

But at least in the Iranian world of ultimate defeat in the *Shâhnâmeh*, Ferdowsi posits a providential God. With an unjust, unwise or otherwise imperfect god, or no god at all, Ferdowsi's Iranian world becomes 'Omar Khayyâm's. His ideas, which Edward FitzGerald's *Rubáiyát of Omar Khayyám* represented for the West centuries later, became and remain an influential cluster of themes in Persian literature and Iranian culture. In chapter 2, called "Perennial Iranian Skepticism, Individualism, and Dreams of Gardens," Khayyâm's life and famous quatrains together with Edward FitzGerald's famous poem are the chief focus of attention. The discussion aims to describe the specifically Iranian yet universal mood herein called "Khayyâmic" and then to contrast it very briefly with another perennial cultural attitude in Iran which is embodied in the work of Sa'di (d.c. 1290).

Chapter 3, called "Persian Classicism, Aesthetics of Decoration, and Ambivalence" mainly treats the fourteenth-century Hâfez, the most important lyric poet in the history of the Persian language, as the embodiment of Persian aesthetic ideals. Hâfez's poetry reveals him as an individualistic thinker, often Khayyâmic in tone and mood, but possessing an optimism or ambivalence toward things lacking in Khayyâm. From within mental, formal, and aural patterns of his inimitable *ghazal* poems, Hâfez's specific Iranianness emerges and with it something of Iranian aesthetic categories and ideals, particularly the long-standing tendency toward a culture-specific classicism.

As ensconced as Ferdowsi, Khayyâm, and Hâfez are in a pre-modern Iranian past, they nevertheless live as a vital heritage today for those Iranians who are both literate and self-conscious about their Iranianness. These national literary treasures from the medieval past remain, in fact, subjects of discussion and debate in Iran today and are acknowledged inspiration to modernist authors, among them the subjects of the second half of the study.

Chapters 4, 5, and 6 mainly treat the three most controversial contemporary Iranian literary figures, Sâdeq Hedâyat, Jalâl Âl-e Ahmad, and Forugh Farrokhzâd. Actually, the three are the most significant figures in their respective literary fields in the post-classical age, which is to say, since the fifteenth century.

Called "A Modernist Iranian Writer's Almost Inevitable Nightmare," chapter 4 analyzes Hedâyat's *The Blind Owl*, his famous 1941 novel of obsession with the past, confusion about its relation to the present, and fear of the future, as an Iranian reaction to today's world. In *The Blind Owl*, the voice of Khayyâm, a repudiation of Arab Moslem supplanting of pre-Islamic Iranian culture, and European intellectual notions of the 1920s and 1930s blend in the dramatic portrayal of an Iranian artist's failure to achieve harmony with the world in which he lives.

5

Chapter 5, entitled "Cultural Dilemmas of an Iranian Literary Intellectual," uses the biography and social content of the writings of Jalâl Al-e Ahmad, the most prominent non-establishment intellectual during the post-Mosaddeq pre-Khomayni era (1953-1978), to show deep-seated cultural tensions and conflicts which many thinking Iranians face in the contemporary world. First is Al-e Ahmad's advocacy of modernism and adoption of technology in the face of the realization that they are Western, alien, and potentially implicative of shortcomings or inadequacies in Iranian culture. Second is his rejection of religious superstitions and institutions in the face of an awareness that secularism for Iranians brings with it an almost inevitable rootlessness. Third is his uncompromising, non-establishment idealism vis-à-vis Iranian social and political institutions which demand flexibility and compromise of those who would work to improve them.

In chapter 6, called "An Iranian Finally Speaks as a Woman and as an Individual," the poetic personae of Forugh Farrokhzâd, Iran's most important poetess in history, are presented as the dramatic, cultural testimony of a middle class, mid-century, Tehrân woman in a male-dominated society. The results are significant revelations about contemporary Iranian individualism and individuality.

In short, this volume presents literary Iranians speaking through those of their chief writings available in published English translations. This fact, together with the fact that many Iranians likewise perceive the works and figures discussed herein as extremely important, are reasons enough for hoping that insidious ethnocentrism does not figure significantly in this study. Furthermore, because literary works and their authors are treated in their own terms as part of an Iranian self-view, even in the treatment of subjects the commentator's ethnocentrism should have only minimal effects.

This does not imply at all that my Persianist view embodies "scientific objectivity." It goes without saying that humanistic writers or observers of culture tend to see what they want to see and are limited in what they are capable of seeing. In addition, they may subconsciously seek to reaffirm previous notions or to interpret phenomena in terms of previous horizons. I admit such limitations in my approach in this study: what I write about Iranian culture is not directly about cultural truths, but only about the truth of my confrontation with cultural facts and my truthful impressions of their meaning and significance. Nevertheless, if I have here provided a forum for the voices of Ferdowsi, Khayyâm, Khâqâni, Rumi, Sa'di, Hâfez, Hedâyat, Nimâ Yushij, Al-e Ahmad, Farrokhzâd, Gholâmhosayn Sâ'edi, Mehdi Akhavân-e Sâles, and others, much cultural truth should remain in the pages, my presence notwithstanding. In the volume's "Epilogue," however, I offer an unabashedly personal view of these literary Iranian lives as embodying inevitable and irresolvable cultural tensions and conflicts.

A CHRONOLOGY OF IRANIAN CULTURE

1000+ BCE(=BC)	Medes and Persians enter the Iranian region.
600s BCE	Persian vassal state to the Medean empire. Concept of "king of kings" [*shâhanshâh*]. Zoroaster (between 1000 and 600) and Zoroastrianism.
559-529	Reign of Cyrus "the Great" begins the Achaemenid Empire. Old Persian language. The compendium of sacred Zoroastrian writings called *Avestâ,* compiled in the Avestan dialect, includes poems and poetic hymns called *Gathas* and *Yashts.*
539	Capture of Babylon and liberation of Jews in exile.
529-522	Reign of Cambyses. Invasion of Egypt. Emergence of Gawmata, claimant to the Achaemenid throne.
522-486	Reign of Darius. Bisotun inscription. Construction at Persepolis begins. Invasion of Greece, battle of Marathon (490).
486-465	Reign of Xerxes. Battle of Thermopylae (480). Burning of Acropolis. Battles of Salamis and Platea (479).
330	Alexander the Great destroys Persepolis and ends the Achaemenid empire. No written records survive of orally transmitted Old Persian poetry.
323	Alexander dies, and Iran is divided among Greek generals.
312	Seleucus Nicator begins the Seleucid dynasty.
250 BCE	Arcasid Dynasty and Parthian state. Zoroastrianism as a state religion. Parthian language and Pahlavi script. Revival of the title *shâhanshâh. Gosâns* [court poets/minstrels] transmit Kayâni legends.
1 CE (=AD)	Magi (=Zoroastrian priests) at Christ's birth.
63 CE	Treaty between Rome and the Parthians.
123-187	Reign of Mithridates II.
212	Inhabitants of Pârs rebel against the Parthians.
224-651	Sâsânid empire. Middle Persian language: Pahlavi dialect and script. Minstrel poetic tradition.
241-270	Reign of Shâpur I. Mâni (b. 215) begins preaching. Manichaeism. Poetic hymns, psalms, narratives.

260	Capture of Roman emperor Valerian.
272-273	Reign of Hormozd I.
273-276	Reign of Vahram (Bahrâm) I. Magi torture and kill Mâni.
310-379	Reign of Shâpur II. Constantine becomes a Christian.
420-438	Reign of Bahrâm "Gur," credited with composing a Persian poem. Middle Persian redaction of *Shâhnâmeh* sagas.
488-530	Mazdakism.
531-579	Reign of Khosrow I.
590-628	Reign of Khosrow II. Composition of *Khwadây Nâmag* [Book of Lords].
622	Mohammad (c.570-632) and his followers leave Mecca for Medina. "Revelations" later constituting the Koran had been communicated to him from about 610.
632-661	"Rightly Guided" caliphs after Mohammad's death: Abu Bakr (632-634), 'Omar (634-644), 'Osmân (644-656), and 'Ali (656-661).
640s	Moslem Arab occupation of the Iranian region.
651	Yazdgerd III, the last Sâsânid ruler, dies in Marv.
661-750	Omayyad Caliphate, whose capital is in Syria. Arabic becomes the official language of government.
680	'Ali's younger son Hosayn (third Shi'i Emâm) is killed at Karbalâ.
750-1258	'Abbâsid Caliphate, Baghdâd its capital from 762.
786-809	Caliphate of Hârun al-Rashid. Arabic literary traditions are formalized.
816	Death of Emâm Rezâ's sister Fâtemeh at Qom.
817-838	Movement of Bâbak.
818	Death of Rezâ, eighth Shi'i Emâm, in "Mashhad" (the word denotes "burial place of the martyr").
815+-1000	Autonomous regional dynasties in Iran: Saffârids,Tâherids, Sâmânids and Ziyârids.
873	Disappearance of the twelfth and last Shi'i Emâm.
900s	Emergence of New Persian [*Fârsi*] as a literary language. **Rudaki** (d. 940/1) is the first major Persian poet.
922	Martyrdom of the Sufi mystic poet Mansur al-Hallâj.
998-1030	Reign of Mahmud of Ghazneh. **Ferdowsi** (c.940-c.1020) finishes his *Shâhnâmeh*.
1037	The philosopher Avicenna [Ebn-e Sînâ] dies. Nâser Khosrow (1004-c.1088), Isma'ili propagandist and poet.
1055	The Saljuq leader Toghrel Beg enters Baghdad and is declared *soltân*.
1072-1092	Reign of Malekshâh. Careers of vizier Nezâmolmolk (d. 1092), the philosopher Ghazâli (d. 1111), and **'Omar Khayyâm** (1048-1131). Hasan Sabbâh and the Isma'ili 'Assassins."

1097	The First Crusade begins.
1157	Death of Sanjar, the last major Saljuq *soltân*.
1200-1205	Deaths of the poets **Khâqâni** and Nezâmi.
1220s	Mongols invade Iran.The Sufi poet 'Attâr dies. Mowlânâ **Jalâloddin Rumi** (1207-1273), the premier Sufi poet.
1258	Hulegu Khân captures Baghdad and ends the Caliphate. Il-Khânid dynasty rules Irân. Career of the poet **Sa'di** (c.1215-c.1290), including *Bustân* (1257) and *Golestân* (1258).
1294	Marco Polo spends nine months in Tabriz.
1380	Tamerlane (1335-1405) invades the Iranian plateau. **Hâfez** (c.1320-c.1390), the premier lyric poet in Iranian history.
1414-1492	The poet Jâmi, whose death marks the end of the "classical" period of Persian poetry.
1501-1736	Safavid dynasty. Esmâ'il Shâh (reigned 1501-1524) assumes the title of *shâhanshâh*. Hosayn Vâ'ez Kâshefi writes *The Garden of the Martyrs*. Beginnings of curvilinear Persian carpet designs. Poets emigrate to India.
1514	The Ottomans defeat the Safavids at Chalderon.
1587-1629	Reign of Shâh 'Abbâs "the Great." Esfahân becomes the capital in 1598, and the Royal Square is built.
1708, 1715	Commercial, capitulatory treaties are signed with France.
1720	Afghans invade Irân and occupy Kermân and Esfahân.
1736-1747	Reign of Nâder Shâh Afshâr.
1750-1779	Reign of Karim Khân Zand. *Ta'ziyeh* [Karbalâ drama] performances develop. Beginning of "Literary Return" style.
1771	**Sir William Jones** publishes "A Persian Song."
1796	Aghâ Mohammad Khân, founder of the Qâjâr dynasty, is crowned *shâhanshâh* in the new capital Tehrân.
1797-1834	Reign of Fath 'Ali Shâh.
1813-1828	Treaties of Golestân and Torkmanchây cede the Caucasus and Armenia to Czarist Russia.
1824	Publication of James Morier's *Hajji Baba of Ispahan*.
1848-1896	Reign of Nâseroddin Shâh.
1850s	Iran's first newspaper. The beginnings of Persian translations of European books.
1852	A Western-style secondary school opens in Tehrân.
1853	**Matthew Arnold** composes *Sohrab and Rustum*.
1859	The first edition of **Edward FitzGerald's** *Rubáíyát of Omar Khayyám* appears.
1863	The Bahâ'i Faith develops out of Bâbi Movement of the 1830s.
1864	The death of Shaykh Mortazâ Ansâri, who had consolidated Shi'i theologians.
1870	The London-Tehran telegraph line is set up.
1883	Diplomatic relations with USA are established.

1890	Tobacco concession and Talbot monopoly. Successful boycott of the concession.
1896	Assassination of Nâseroddin Shâh.
1906	A constitution is drafted and signed by the Mozaffaroddin Shâh (ruled 1896-1906).
1907-1909	Reign of Mohammad 'Ali Shâh.
1908	Discovery of oil near Masjed-e Solaymân.
1911	Constitutionalist cleric Mollâh Khorâsâni dies.
1912	Anglo-Persian Oil Company produces oil.
1914	Turkey invades Irân, as do England and Russia later.
1919	A convention makes Irân nearly a British protectorate.
1921	Rezâ Khân (1888-1944) executes a coup d'état. The Shi'i theologian Hâ'eri moves to Qom and stimulates its emergence as a center for Shi'i learning.
1921/2	Berlin publication of *Once upon a Time* by **Mohammad 'Ali Jamâlzâdeh** (b. 1892).
1922	*The Myth* by the first modernist Persian poet **Nimâ Yushij** (1895-1960) is published in Tehrân.
1925	Rezâ Pahlavi deposes Ahmad Shâh (ruled 1909-1925) and crowns himself *shâhanshâh* in 1926.
1926	Publication of E.G. Browne's four-volume *A Literary History of Persia.*
1927	Construction of trans-Iranian railroad begins.
1930	**Sâdeq Hedâyat** (1903-1951) returns from Europe and begins publishing writings in Tehrân. The first Iranian motion picture (silent) is shown. 900+ feature films are produced in Irân from 1930 to 1978.
1931	Anti-Communist legislation and banning of Communist party founded in 1921. *Ta'ziyeh* performances are banned.
1934	University of Tehrân is founded. **Hedâyat** publishes *Songs of Khayyâm.*
1935	Foreign states are directed henceforth to refer to the country as "Irân." Royal troops fire on a crowd of dissenters at the Mashhad shrine; over a hundred are killed.
1936	Wearing of the châdor veil by women is banned. In the first Persian talkie called *The Lor Girl,* an unveiled female face appears on an Iranian screen for the first time.
1939	Execution of traditionalist poet Farrokhi Yazdi (b. 1899).
1941	Allied occupation of Irân and abdication of Rezâ Pahlavi in favor of Mohammad Rezâ Pahlavi (reigns 1941-1979). Beginning of "Twelve Years" of freedom of the press and expression. Formation of the Tudeh Party of Irân. Publication of Hedâyat's *The Blind Owl.*
1942	American military forces arrive in Tehrân.

1945	USSR-supported republics are established in Kordestân and Azarbâyjân.
1946	Social reformer Ahmad Kasravi (b. 1890) is assassinated by a Devotee of Islam.
1949	Assassination attempt on Mohammad Rezâ Pahlavi by a Tudeh Party member. Ineffective ban on the Tudeh Party.
1951	Iranian Prime Minister 'Ali Razmârâ is assassinated by a Devotee of Islam. Hedâyat commits suicide in Paris. Premiership of Mohammad Mosaddeq (1880-1967) begins. Oil nationalization law.
1953	USA-organized coup d'état precipitates Mosaddeq's fall. Commencement of USA aid to Irân. Roger Lescot's French translation of *The Blind Owl* appears.
1954	Trials for leftist military. **Forugh Farrokhzâd** (1934/5-1967) composes **"The Sin."**
1955	Semi-official persecution of Bahâ'is takes place.
1956-7	**Mehdi Akhavân-e Sâles** (b. 1928) composes **"Winter"** and **"The Ending of the *Shâhnâmeh*."**
1957	Publication of *Fresh Air* by **Ahmad Shâmlu** (b. 1925).
1958	SAVAK secret police organization is established. **Jalâl Al-e Ahmad** (1923-1969) publishes *The School Principal*.
1960	Nimâ Yushij, the "father" of modernist Persian poetry, dies. Irân recognizes Israel.
1961	Leading Shi'i cleric Hosayn Borujerdi dies. 'Ali Mohammad Afghâni's 887-page novel *Ahu Khânom's Husband* is published.
1962	Al-e Ahmad publishes *Weststruckness*. The Pahlavi Land Reform Law is enacted.
1963	The White Revolution is promulgated, along with a women's suffrage act. Emergence of Ruhollâh Khomayni (b. 1902) as the chief anti-government voice leads to June riots.
1964	Farrokhzâd publishes *Another Birth*. **Sohrâb Sepehri** (1928-1980) composes "Water's Footsteps." Khomayni is exiled to Turkey and then Iraq.
1966	**Sâdeq Chubak** (b. 1916) publishes the novel *The Patient Stone*.
1967	Farrokhzâd dies. The Family Protection Law is enacted.
1968	Founding of the Association of Writers of Irân. Women accepted into the Literacy Corps. The writer and social reformer **Samad Behrangi** (b. 1939) dies.
1969	**Hushang Golshiri** (b. 1936) publishes the novel *Prince Ehtejâb*. Al-e Ahmad dies. **Simin Dâneshvar** (b. 1921) publishes the novel *The Mourners of Siyâvash*.

1970	A short story by **Gholamhosayn Sa'edi** (1935/6-1985) becomes the basis for a screenplay and a famous "New Wave" movie called *The Cow*.
1971	Thirteen members of a leftist group are executed after the Siyâhkal uprising.
1973	Oil prices rise dramatically. Sâ'edi is incarcerated until June 1975.
1974	Oppositionist poet Khosrow Golesorkhi is executed.
1976	The Pahlavi government institutes an "imperial" calendar based on the establishment of the Achaemenid dynasty.
1977	The social reformer 'Ali Shari'ati (b. 1933) dies in England. The *Ten Nights* readings take place at Tehran's Goethe Institute.
1978	Anti-Pahlavi sentiments surface in Irân. Civil upheaval ensues. 300+ moviegoers are trapped and die in Abâdân's Rex Threatre during a showing of *The Deer*.
1979	The Shâh flees Irân and Khomayni returns in triumph to establish Islamic Republic of Irân. **Shâmlu** (b. 1925) composes **"In This Deadend."** The American Embassy in Tehrân is seized.
1980	USA breaks diplomatic relations with Irân. The Iran-Iraq War begins. Universities close. Secular-minded intellectuals are under fire. Sepehri dies.
1981	Minor dramatist and poet Sa'id Soltânpur is executed.
1982	Sâ'edi escapes from Irân, settles in Paris, and revitalizes the journal *Alefbâ*.
1983	*Sorayyâ in a Coma* is published in Tehrân by **Esmâ'il Fasih**.
1984	**Nâder Nâderpur** (b. 1929) composes "Sohrâb and Simorgh" in Paris and **"Blood and Ashes"** in Nice. Iranian Tudeh Party officials, who had supported the Islamic Republic, are arrested.
1985	Sâ'edi dies in Paris. Sirus Tâhbâz publishes **Nimâ Yushij's** *Complete Poems* in Tehrân.
1986	In Tehrân, **Mahmud Dowlatâbâdi** (b. 1940) publishes a 2,836-page novel called *Klidar*.
1988	Irân and Iraq end hostilities. Publication of Ehsan Yarshater's *Persian Literature* in The States. UNESCO and Iran celebrate "The Year of Hâfez."
1989	American publication of Nâderpur's *False Dawn* and *Blood and Ashes*. Khomayni dies in Tehrân.

1

IRANIAN PATRIARCHY, ITS VICTIMS, AND PERSIAN SADNESS

Unhappy Persia, that in former age
Hast been the seat of mighty conquerors,
Have triumphed over Afric, and the bounds
Of Europe where the sun dares scarce appear
For freezing meteors and congealed gold.

To see our neighbors, that were wont to quake
and tremble at the Persian monarch's name,
Now sit and laugh our regiment to scorn."
Cosroe, *Tamberlaine the Great* (I.i.)
by Christopher Marlowe

After the emergence of the New Persian language in the ninth century, the first monumentally significant Iranian cultural event was the eleventh-century *Shâhnâmeh* [Book of Kings] composed by Abolqâsem Ferdowsi (d.c.1020). A loosely connected and chronologically ordered series of episodes, the *Shâhnâmeh* recounts the mythological origins and some of the history of the Persian Iranian people who had entered the Iranian plateau region before 1000 BCE. One of the longest verse compositions ever produced by a single poet, Ferdowsi's 50,000 closed couplets comprise the Iranian national epic and the most discussed and revered literary work in the 1,100-year history of Persian literature.(1)

In size and scope, the *Shâhnâmeh* seems a literary twin to Persepolis, the great Achaemenid shrine built some thirty miles northeast of Shirâz on the road to Esfahân.(2) Both monuments vividly testify to pride in Persianness, Iranian attachment to the homeland, and the grandeur and eclectic richness of Iranian culture and imperial traditions.

Darius I (ruled 522-486 BCE) chose the site for Persepolis sometime before 520. Successive Achaemenid emperors added buildings to it; but it was not yet finished when Alexander the Great and his Greek armies overran the region in 330 BCE. Yet even what remains of Persepolis today, the giant platform on which it sits, column bases and columns, capitals, stairway façades, doorways, and bas relief decoration, tell the story of a brilliant empire and reveal a self-confident culture at the world's crossroads, borrowing and adapting from Lydia, Greece, Egypt, and elsewhere, but arranging and orchestrating all of it in a characteristically Persian manner. Specifically, its location, its great size of over 1,300,000 square feet consisting of a platform of 900' x 1500' some 40' to 60' above ground, and its architectural decoration reveal cultural features relevant to an appreciation of modern Iran, among them internationalism, a tradition of imperial forms, and a penchant for pomp. Bas reliefs at Persepolis also depict the religious core of the Achaemenid culture: the all-knowing god of light called Ahurâmazdâ appears as superior to the king and responsible for royal success through bestowal of divine blessing. Persepolis likewise communicates confident self-awareness of Persian prosperity and hope for its continuity.

As for the *Shâhnâmeh*, it depicts a world with Iran at the very center possessed of a unique destiny resting on the shoulders of its quintessential figures, its kings. The battles are grand, the heroes larger than life. Its stories had passed from generation to generation from before the Arab conquest of Iran in the middle of the seventh century. By Ferdowsi's day, numerous prose versions of *Shâhnâmeh* episodes had been composed. A poet called Daqiqi (d. 978) of the generation before him had begun a redaction of the national epic in verse. Ferdowsi reputedly spent some thirty years completing his *Shâhnâmeh*.

The *Shâhnâmeh* and Persepolis are similar in another respect as well. Both bear witness to eventual Iranian defeat at the hands of peoples whom Iranians perceived as foreign barbarians. Alexander ravaged Persepolis, which marks the end of the Achaemenid dynasty (559-330 BCE) that had brought into being one of the first great world empires. However much life inheres on the Persepolis platform today, a walk through the place communicates an equally powerful sense of destruction and defeat. Few of its original 550 columns now stand. The conflagration ordered by Alexander destroyed the wooden roofs over the various halls and palaces. At some moments, backed up against a mountain on one side and overlooking a broad plain on the others, Persepolis appears desolate and in pieces. As for Ferdowsi's *Shâhnâmeh*, its account of Iranian history ends with the defeat of the Iranian army by the Moslem Arabs and the shameful flight and murder of Yazdgerd III, the last of the Sâsânids (ruled 224-651), who were Rome's equals two centuries earlier.

In the context of literary epics, Ferdowsi's *Shâhnâmeh* is thus an unusual work. Although the literary epic tradition generally implies or represents nostalgia for a bygone heroic age, epics themselves generally recount the story of victory in the heroic age of the people or nation whose history the story represents. The Greeks defeat the Trojans in the *Iliad*. Odysseus returns home to Penelope in the *Odyssey*. The *Aeneid* celebrates the founding of Rome. Hope for humankind is the final message in *Paradise Lost*. The future holds promise for the Joads of America at the end of *The Grapes of*

Wrath. But Ferdowsi composed his *Shâhnâmeh* as a national history culminating in disaster.

In these terms, the *Shâhnâmeh* is a document which attests to complexities and paradoxes of Iranian cultural identity. For example, national pride in the *Shâhnâmeh* would seem to imply pride in the institution and perpetuation of monarchy and in the storied efforts of such heroes as Rostam to defend and perpetuate the monarchy. Yet, the twentieth-century history of Iran has been one of chafing at the monarchical bit and the dramatic overthrow of the short-lived Pahlavi dynasty (1926-1979), whose name hearkens back to the days of the *Shâhnâmeh*(3) and whose two monarchs attempted to use pre-Islamic Iranian traditions and symbols as a legitimizing basis for their own rule and as a nationalizing and unifying aegis for Iran's heterogeneous population.

A second aspect of this complexity is Iranian sorrow and despair in the *Shâhnâmeh* at the historical invasion of "barbarian" Arabs with their strict, then new monotheistic faith, vis-à-vis post-Pahlavi national unity in the 1980s under the banner of Islam. As heirs to Indo-European clans and traditions, many Iranians have always been quick to distinguish themselves from Arab and other Moslem neighbor peoples. But with its fervent latterday religious nationalists reacting against both Iranian monarchy and secular westernization, the Twelver Shi'i sect of Islam, which became the formal state religion of Iran at the beginning of the sixteenth century, has become Iranian or, in other words, has become a basis for Iranianness. This cultural dilemma which many Iranians see themselves facing today is imbedded in the warp and woof of Ferdowsi's work as well. As described by one Iranian scholar: "The overriding tragic fact of the poet's life is that the glory of which he sings is no more. But this is not to say that the *Shâhnâmeh* is a defiant nostalgic lament. The intellectual horizon of Ferdowsi is that of a rational and devout Moslem . . . [therefore] the cumulative emotional tensions of his 'history' are unresolved."(4)

In one way or another, as much as any other single Persian document, the *Shâhnâmeh* embodies or evokes values which many secular-minded, literary Iranians hold essential to their culture and their Iranianness. Interestingly, the *Shâhnâmeh* may be equally significant for many unlettered Iranians for whom, having heard its episodes recited by professional story-tellers time and again, it is their only ethnic history. (For that matter, even educated Iranians in pre-modern times took *Shâhnâmeh* legends as history.) But these values and this history are not necessarily comforting, precisely because the *Shâhnâmeh* immortalizes defeat. A popular proverb, a famous modernist poem, and a classic Iranian novel illustrate this.

The proverb translates as "the ending of the *Shâhnâmeh* is joyful" and is used in situations where someone is suggesting that an enterprise which has begun well is likely to conclude favorably. In response, a pessimist will comment to the effect that "[You'll see--]the end of the *Shâhnâmeh* is the happy part!"

15

The poem is "The Ending of the *Shâhnâmeh*" (1957) by the prominent modernist poet Mehdi Akhavân-e Sâles (b. 1928). Also the author of "I Saw Susa" (1972), a poetic tour de force in which the personified Achaemenid ruins at Susa condemn today's Iranians as a "spineless generation,"(5) Akhavân-e Sâles utilizes historical images and symbols more than most other contemporary Iranian poets. Yet many secular-minded Iranians share the outlook he voices in "The Ending of the *Shâhnâmeh*." The poem reads:

[1]This harp, broken and out of tune,
tame in the pale, old harpist's hands,
sometimes seems to dream.
It sees itself in the Sun's luminous court
[5]as the rare beauty and beloved of Zoroaster
or a coquettish intoxicated fairy
in the pure, bright meadows of moonlight.
It sees false lights--
the caravan of dead flames in the swamp on the *mehrâb*'s holy brow.
[10]In memory of the days of glory and pride and innocence
it sings joyfully the sad tale of exile:

"O, where is the capital of this mad century of false faith
with its nights bright like day,
its stark and dark days like nights in the depths of fairy tales,
[15]with its strong, dreadful, impenetrable fortresses,
with the mean smiles of its gates, cold and alien?

O, where is the capital of this turbulent century of evil faith,
the crooked-faced century
which has surpassed the moon's orbit,
[20]but remains so far from the pivot of the sun,
the bloodthirsty century,
the century of the most frightening message,
in which, with the fantastic excrement of a far-flying bird
the four pillars of God's seven climes are instantly rocked
[25]and whatever there is of existence, depth, and height
is struck down, is swept clean?

O, where is the capital of this shameless, faithless century
in which, without the slightest respite,
every new blossom is a plaything of the wind,
[30]just as respect for the aged, having born their fruit,
is sacrificed to rejection, ridicule, treachery, and injustice?

The capital of such a century is where,
on which nameless peak, in which direction?

16

Warn the watchmen lest sleep deceive them,
[35]alert and intent, atop their sentry,
lest the star's spell or
the charm of the city of the silver moonlight deceive them.
On ships of rage with bloody sails
we are coming toward the century's capital to conquer,
[40]to open wide the wide, nine-folded nothingland
of this insensitive dusty place
with the dreadful clashing of our sharp swords,
the frightening thunder of our dreaded drums,
the stone-splitting flight of our swift arrows,
[45]to snatch demons' life bottles
from the spell of the hidden fortress
from the hands of their sorcerer guards,
to smash them on the ground.
And if the earth--that decrepit cradle of the world's horizons--
[50]offers the soft hand of its greenness
to hide stones from us,
we shall gash its face.
We are the conquerors of fortresses of history's glory
and witnesses of each century's cities of splendor.
[55]We are mementos of the sad innocence of the ages.
We are narrators of cheerful, sweet tales,
tales of clear skies, flowing light, the water,
dark cold earth, the tales of the most joyous message
from the limpid luminous streams of the ages,
[60]tales of deep woods, behind it the mountain, the river at its foot,
tales of a friend's warm hand on cold city nights.
We are the caravan of the cup and harp,
gypsies our harp, strumming our lives, our lives poems and fables,
intoxicated cupbearers in a drunken state.
[65]O, where is the capital of the century?
We are coming to conquer,
to open up its nothingland . . ."
This broken harp, heartsore and impossible dreamer,
the singer of imagination's empty sanctuary,
[70]eternally cloaked with secrets,
what stories it tells itself day and night.
O helpless, delirious one! Change the tune.
Zâl's son Rostam cannot escape his step-brother's will.
He is dead. He died. He died.
[75]Begin the story of Farrokhzâd's son Rostam,
the one whose groan seems to come from a deep well's depths.
He moans and weeps,

he weeps and says:
"Oh, from now on we resemble hunchbacked, old conquerors.
[80]On ships of waves with sails of foam,
our hearts bound by the memory of the lambs of splendor,
in the fields of empty days,
our blades rusty, worn out, and weary,
our drums, forever silent,
[85]our arrows with broken feathers.
We are conquerors of cities gone with the wind.
In a voice too weak to come out of the chest,
we are narrators of forgotten tales.
Nobody pays us heed or spares a copper for our coins,
[90]as if they were of a foreign king
or of a prince whose dynasty has been overthrown.
At times we hope to awaken from this spell;
like from the cave companions' sleep,
we will rub our eyes and say:
[95]There it is, the golden rare palace of charming morning.
But, Daqyânus is immortal, o, o, alas."(6)

"The Ending of the *Shâhnâmeh*" depicts an old harpist's out-of-tune harp which plays only dreams of the pre-Islamic past and of "itself in the sun's radiant court as . . . the beloved of Zoroaster." Its "tale of separation" involves a search for "the capital of this perverted mad century" in which manned space capsules are launched and atomic bombs dropped. The harp dreams of conquering the sterile, modern, technological world. But that is possible only in a dream. In Akhavân's view, Iranians today, or at least Iranian poets--who are harpists, their imagination their harps--are dreamers in a world they cannot control and do not understand. Their past was grand and noble. But nobility and heroism are as mortal as the great hero Rostam, son of Zâl, who singlehandedly protected the mythological Iranian monarchy for centuries. One needs to remember that in real life another Rostam, Farrokhzâd's son and the Sâsânid military commander, led the Iranian army to ignominious defeat at the hands of the Moslem Arabs. The Iranian poet now can relate only tales of the past.

Akhavân, in short, tells readers to face the facts of their present lives and not to fall prey to futile dreams of the past. The first fact needing admission is that the legendary hero Rostam has given way to the ill-starred general ironically also called Rostam. That fact has changed Iranian culture for all time. Nevertheless, Akhavân may imply a glimmer of hope in telling the harp to "change the tune." Perhaps Iran's poetry today can play a tune which may inspire Iranians to a new future of possibilities. One of those poets, Forugh Farrokhzâd (the subject of chapter 6), seems to have done just that. As for Akhavân, despite his warning to others, he seems to have spent much of his adult artistic life engaged in those futile dreams of the past, a more typical Iranian literary stance than Farrokhzâd's.

The weight of the cataclysmic defeat of Iran at the hands of the Moslem Arabs lies heavy on the heart of many Iranians, the thirteen intervening centuries notwithstanding. Sâdeq Chubak's (b. 1916) masterful novel called *The Patient Stone* (1966) provides another excellent illustration.(7) Its chief character Ahmad Aqâ relates in numerous monologues the desperate situations of the people around him in a lower-class, multi-family dwelling in Shirâz in the 1930s. A teacher, would-be writer and the one intellectual among the main characters in the novel, Ahmad Aqâ attempts to find meaning and significance in the pathetic lives of those around him as well as a point to his own existence. Suddenly, with no forewarning and instead of a report of some recent series of events, he recites the ending of the *Shâhnâmeh*, the defeat of the Iranians at the hands of the Arabs. He thus telescopes time in a characteristically Iranian way and implies that the plight of Iranians today derives from or resembles the plight of the Sâsânids, after whom many Iranians have always felt after their time and fated to a hellish existence.

Ferdowsi lived during an age in which some Iranians still thought about Sâsânid glory. After the Iranian defeat, Arab Moslem governments ruled the Iranian region, including Khorâsân, the eastern province in which was situated Ferdowsi's native city Tus, now a town and ruins near Mashhad. Then came the 'Abbâsid Revolution in which a leader in Khorâsân called Abu Moslem played a role in the "Persianizing" of the caliphal central government which moved from Damascus to Baghdâd in 762. In the next century, a native Iranian dynasty called the Sâmânids ruled Khorâsân and revitalized Persian literary culture. But their rule came to an end at the hands of a Turkish clan from the East called the Ghaznavids from their capital at Ghazneh in today's Afghanistan. Their most famous leader was Soltân Mahmud, "a world conqueror" in the Iranian perspective of the day, who ruled Khorâsân during Ferdowsi's lifetime. In fact, Ferdowsi composed his *Shâhnâmeh* for submission to Mahmud in hopes of a suitable reward for his labors from that age's most powerful patron of the arts. No doubt Ferdowsi as a Persian sensed the irony of his seeking patronage from a Turkish ruler, just as his *Shâhnâmeh* exhibits the cultural conflict between the poet's Iranian cultural nationalism and his Arab Moslem religious beliefs.

Ferdowsi's *Shâhnâmeh* begins with the invocation of God's name. The poet praises wisdom as the best guide in life and as the heart's enlivener, as one's helper in both worlds, and as the source of all human happiness and welfare. He then describes creation of matter as God's production of the elements of earth, air, fire, and water as a demonstration of divine power. The appearance of humankind is described as the key to the rest of creation: humans are creatures with sense and reason whose lives have meaning. The poet then contrasts light and dark, declares man's preeminence in nature, and proceeds to speak of the Moslem prophet Mohammad (c.570-632) and the

19

four rightly guided caliphs Abu Bakr, 'Omar, 'Osmân, and 'Ali, asserting 'Ali's special status among them.

Within the context of faith in Allâh, Ferdowsi turns to the legends held by Zoroastrian priests, the histories of the Iranian kings, and popular stories of ancient heroes, which he asserts a Persian noble had gathered as the foundation of a great book. This Persian noble's first question, the answer to which begins the *Shâhnâmeh* proper, was: who invented and first wore the crown of royalty?

It was Kiyomars whose son was killed by the Black Demon, the son of Ahriman (the Zoroastrian embodiment of darkness and evil). Kiyomars and his grandson Hushang thereafter attacked the Black Demon. For slaying it, Hushang was rewarded after Kiyomars's death with the royal crown and the refulgence, nimbus, or blessing called *farr*, which symbolized divine favor and portended greatness, invincibility, and good fortune. Hushang was succeeded by his son Tamuras, succeeded in turn by his son Jamshid, who was the first great king of Iranian legend.

During Jamshid's reign social classes were established, and the Iranian New Year, celebrated at the beginning of spring, was first commemorated. Jamshid is also associated by name with Persepolis, which is known in Persian as "Takht-e Jamshid" [Throne of Jamshid]. But Jamshid's pride led him to associate himself with the Creator and thus lose the divine *farr*. Consequently, he was susceptible to evildoers.

There was a man at this time named Merdas whose son Zahhâk was corrupted by the devil Eblis and persuaded by the latter to commit patricide. Zahhâk then became king of the Arabs and was eventually proclaimed king of Iran as well, because of popular discontent with Jamshid. For a thousand years, evil reigned in the world under Zahhâk's leadership. Then Faridun appeared, a rightful successor to the throne and who possessed *farr*.

Faridun, who captured and imprisoned Zahhâk, had three sons: Salm to whom he entrusted the kingdom of Greece, Tur who ruled the East, thereafter called Turân or Turânzamin [Land of Turân], and Iraj who ruled Iran. But, out of fraternal jealousy Tur killed Iraj, whose death was avenged by his son Manuchehr. During the latter's reign an important family emerged from the southeastern Iranian region of Sistân. The progenitor was called Nariman, whose son was the warrior Sâm. Then came Zâl, an albino raised by a phoenix-like bird called Simorgh. From Zâl's union with Rudâbeh came Rostam, destined during a lifetime of centuries of service to the Iranian monarchy to be Iran's greatest mythological hero.

At one point in his career, Rostam defeats the Turânian king Afrâsiyâb and en route back to Iran spends an evening in the kingdom of Samangân with a princess named Tahmineh and fathers Sohrâb. Ferdowsi's story usually entitled "Rostam and Sohrab" in Persian begins right before Rostam meets Tahmineh and ends with Rostam's grieving, momentary thoughts of suicide, and subsequent resignation to the awful tragedy of his son's death coupled with the realization that his life and duty to uphold the Iranian monarchy must go on.(8) As a cultural parenthesis to the context of Ferdowsi's redaction of the story of Rostam and Sohrâb, in the light of which the later discussion of Forugh Farrokhzâd as almost the first feminine voice in Iranian culture may seem even more pointed, the evening which Rostam spends with Tahmineh is the only romantic interlude in his long life.

Ferdowsi's story of Rostam and Sohrâb is the one *Shâhnâmeh* episode familiar to a wide audience in the West, that because Matthew Arnold was inspired by a résumé he read in a review of a translation of the *Shâhnâmeh* to compose "Sohrab and Rustum" (1853), one of the most important mid-nineteenth century English poems, and, after Edward FitzGerald's *Rubaíyát of Omar Khayyám*, the second most famous English literary work based on a Persian model.

Arnold's narrative of 892 unrhymed lines of iambic pentameter begins with the word "and," which communicated to his Victorian readers the sense that his story was an episode or self-contained section of an epic. In fact, "Sohrab and Rustum" is about as long as individual books in the *Iliad*. In addition, echoes of Homeric and Miltonic techniques abound in Arnold's poem, such as repeated references to tents at the beginning of the poem, numerous lengthy similes throughout it, and features of various characters' speeches, all of which are naturally of limited relevance to a reading of the poem in Iranian terms. Nevertheless, Arnold's poem is a convenient and telling starting point in discerning cultural facets of the legend of Rostam and his son.(9) It begins:

> And the first grey of morning filled the east,
> And the fog rose out of the Oxus stream.
> But all the Tartar camp along the stream
> Was hushed, and still the men were plunged in sleep;
> Sohrab alone, he slept not; all night long
> He had lain wakeful, tossing on his bed;
> But when the grey dawn stole into his tent,
> He rose, and clad himself, and girt his sword,
> And took his horseman's cloak, and left his tent . . .

Sohrab proceeds to the tent of an elder warrior to whom he confides:

> I seek one man, one man, and one alone--
> Rustum, my father; who I hoped should greet,
> Should one day greet, upon some well-fought field,
> His not unworthy, not inglorious son.
> So I long hoped, but him I never find.
> Come then, hear now, and grant me what I ask.
> Let the two armies rest to-day; but I
> Will challenge forth the bravest Persian lords

To meet me, man to man; if I prevail,
Rustum will surely hear it; if I fall--
Old man, the dead need no one, claim no kin.

The Tartar (=Turânian) elder does not like Sohrab's suggestion, but acquiesces. The Persians, to whose camp Rustum has just last night come, accept the challenge. Because Rustum is in a bad mood, a Persian leader has to approach him to persuade him to take up the challenge. This leader tells Rustum:

. . . from the Tartars is a challenge brought
To pick a champion from the Persian lords
To fight their champion--and thou know'st his name--
Sohrab men call him, but his birth is hid.
O Rustum, like thy might is this young man's!
He has the wild stag's foot, the lion's heart;
And he is young, and Iran's chiefs are old,
Or else too weak; and all eyes turn to thee.
Come down and help us, Rustum, or we lose!'

Rustum replies:

The young may rise at Sohrab's vaunts, not I.
For what care I, though all speak Sohrab's fame?
For would that I myself had such a son,
And not that one slight helpless girl I have--
A son so famed, so brave, to send to war,
And I to tarry with the snow-haired Zal,
My father, whom the robber Afghans vex,
And clip his borders short, and drive his herds,
And he has none to guard his weak old age . . .

The Persian leader then appeals to Rustum's sense of pride, and the latter finally agrees to combat with Sohrab, but with a condition: . . . I will fight unknown, and in plain arms; / Let not men say of Rustum, he was matched / In single fight with any mortal man." So Rustum prepares for battle, but only the Persians know who Sohrab's rival is. The poem continues:

And Rustum came upon the sand, and cast
His eyes toward the Tartar tents, and saw
Sohrab come forth, and eyed him as he came . . .,
And a deep pity entered Rustum's soul
As he beheld him coming; and he stood,
And beckoned to him with his hand, and said:--

'O thou young man, the air of Heaven is soft,
And warm, and pleasant; but the grave is cold!
Heaven's air is better than the cold dead grave . . .
O Sohrab, wherefore wilt thou rush on death?
Be governed! quit the Tartar host, and come
To Iran, and be as my son to me
And fight beneath my banner till I die!
There are no youths in Iran brave as thou.'
So he spake, mildly; Sohrab heard his voice, . . .
And he ran forward and embraced his knees,
And clasped his hand within his own, and said:--
'O, by thy father's head! by thine own soul!
Art thou not Rustum? speak! art thou not he?'
But Rustum eyed askance the kneeling youth,
And turned away, and spake to his own soul:--
'Ah me, I muse what this young fox may mean!
False, wily, boastful, are these Tartar boys.
For if I now confess this thing he asks,
And hide it not, but say: **Rustum is here**!
He will not yield indeed, nor quit our foes,
But he will find some pretext not to fight,
And praise my fame, and proffer courteous gifts,
A belt or sword perhaps, and go his way.
And on a feast-tide, in Afrasiab's hall,
In Samarcand, he will arise and cry:
"I challenged once, when the two armies camped
Beside the Oxus, all the Persian lords
To cope with me in single fight; but they
Shrank, only Rustum dared: then he and I
Changed gifts, and went on equal terms away."
So will he speak, perhaps, while men applaud;
Then were the chiefs of Iran shamed through me.'
And then he turned, and sternly spake aloud:--
'Rise! wherefore dost thou vainly question thus
Of Rustum? I am here, whom thou hast called
By challenge forth; make good thy vaunt, or yield!
Is it with Rustum only thou wouldst fight?
Rash boy, men look on Rustum's face and flee!
For well I know, that did great Rustum stand
Before thy face this day, and were revealed,
There would be then no talk of fighting more.
But being what I am, I tell thee this--
Do thou record it in thine inmost soul:
Either thou shalt renounce thy vaunt and yield,
Or else thy bones shall strew this sand, till winds

Bleach them, or Oxus with his summer floods,
Oxus in summer wash them all away.'
He spoke; and Sohrab answered, on his feet:--
'Art thou so fierce? Thou wilt not fright me so!
I am no girl, to be made pale by words.
Yet this thou has said well, did Rustum stand
Here on this field, there were no fighting then.
But Rustum is far hence, and we stand here.
Begin! thou art more vast, more dread than I,
And thou art proved, I know, and I am young--
But yet success sways with the breath of Heaven.
And though thou thinkest that thou knowest sure
Thy victory, yet thou canst not surely know.
For we are all, like swimmers in the sea,
Poised on the top of a huge wave of fate,
Which hangs uncertain to which side to fall.
And whether it will heave us up to land,
Or whether it will roll us out to sea,
Back out to sea, to the deep waves of death,
We know not, and no search will make us know;
Only the event will teach us in his hour.'

At this point, the combat begins, and Rustum strikes a blow and falls to
his knees afterwards.

And now might Sohrab have unsheathed his sword,
And pierced the mighty Rustum while he lay
Dizzy, and on his knees, and choked with sand;
But he looked on, and smiled, nor bred his sword,
But courteously drew back, and spoke, and said:--
'Thou strik'st too hard! that club of thine will float
Upon the summer-floods, and not my bones.
But rise, and be not wroth! not wroth am I;
No, when I see thee, wrath forsakes my soul.
Thou say'st, thou art not Rustum; be it so!
Who art thou then, that canst so touch my soul?
Boy as I am, I have seen battles too--
Have waded foremost in their bloody waves,
And heard their hollow roar of dying men;
But never was my heart thus touched before.
Are they from Heaven, these softenings of the heart?
O thou old warrior, let us yield to Heaven!
Come, plant we here in earth our angry spears,
And make a truce, and sit upon this sand,
And pledge each other in red wine, like friends,

And thou shalt talk to me of Rustum's deeds.
There are enough foes in the Persian host,
Whom I may meet, and strike, and feel no pang;
Champions enough Afrasiab has, whom thou
Mayst fight; fight **them**, when they confront thy spear!
But oh, let there be peace 'twixt thee and me!'
He ceased, but while he spake, Rustum had risen,
And stood erect, trembling with rage; . . .
His breast heaved, his lips foamed, and twice his voice
Was choked with rage; at last these words broke way:--
'Girl! nimble with thy feet, not with thy hands!
Curled minion, dancer, coiner of sweet words!
Fight, let me hear thy hateful voice no more!
Thou art not in Afrasiab's gardens now
With Tartar girls, with whom thou art wont to dance;
But on the Oxus-sands, and in the dance
Of battle, and with me, who make no play
Of war; I fight it out, and hand to hand.
Speak not to me of truce, and pledge, and wine!
Remember all thy valour; try thy feints
And cunning! all the pity I had is gone;
Because thou hast shamed me before both the hosts
With thy light skipping tricks, and thy girl's wiles.'. . .

The combatants battle again:

. . . first Rustum struck the shield
Which Sohrab held stiff out; the steel-spiked spear
Rent the tough plates, but failed to reach the skin,
And Rustum plucked it back with angry groan.
Then Sohrab with his sword smote Rustum's helm,
Nor clove its steel quite through; but all the crest
He shore away, and that proud horsehair plume,
Never till now defiled, sank to the dust;
And Rustum bowed his head; but then the gloom
Grew blacker, thunder rumbled in the air,
And lightnings rent the cloud; and Ruksh, the horse,
Who stood at hand, uttered a dreadful cry; . . .
The two hosts heard that cry, and quaked for fear,
And Oxus curdled as it crossed his stream.
But Sohrab heard, and quailed not, but rushed on,
And struck again; and again Rustum bowed
His head; but this time all the blade, like glass,
Sprang in a thousand shivers on the helm,
And in the hand the hilt remained alone.

25

Glared, and he shook on high his menacing spear,
And shouted: **Rustum**!--Sohrab heard that shout,
And shrank amazed; back he recoiled one step,
And scanned with blinking eyes the advancing form;
And then he stood bewildered; and he dropped
His covering shield, and the spear pierced his side.
He reeled, and staggering back, sank to the ground;
And then the gloom dispersed, and the wind fell,
And the bright sun broke forth, and melted all
The cloud; and the two armies saw the pair--
Saw Rustum standing, safe upon his feet,
And Sohrab, wounded, on the bloody sand.
Then, with a bitter smile, Rustum began:--
'Sohrab, thou thoughtest in thy mind to kill
A Persian lord this day, and strip his corpse,
And bear thy trophies to Afrasiab's tent.
Or else that the great Rustum would come down
Himself to fight, and that thy wiles would move
His heart to take a gift, and let thee go.
And then that all the Tartar host would praise
Thy courage or thy craft, and spread thy fame,
To glad thy father in his weak old age.
Fool, thou art slain, and by an unknown man!
Dearer to the red jackals shalt thou be
Than to thy friends, and to thy father old.'
And, with a fearless mien, Sohrab replied:--
'Unknown thou art; yet thy fierce vaunt is vain.
Thou dost not slay me, proud and boastful man!
No! Rustum slays me, and this filial heart.
For were I matched with ten such men as thee,
And I were that which till to-day I was,
They should be lying here, I standing there.
But that belovéd name unnerved my arm--
That name, and something, I confess, in thee,
Which troubles all my heart, and made my shield
Fall; and thy spear transfixed an unarmed foe.
And now thou boastest, and insult'st my fate.
But hear thou this, fierce man, tremble to hear:
The mighty Rustum shall avenge my death!
My father, whom I seek, through all the world,
He shall avenge my death, and punish thee!'
. . . Rustum knew not his own loss, but stood
Over his dying son, and knew him not.
But, with a cold incredulous voice, he said:--
'What prate is this of fathers and revenge?

The mighty Rustum never had a son.'
And, with a failing voice, Sohrab replied:--
'Ah yes, he had! and that lost son am I.
Surely the news will one day reach his ear,
Reach Rustum, where he sits, and tarries long,
Somewhere, I know not where, but far from here;
And pierce him like a stab, and make him leap
To arms, and cry for vengeance upon thee.
Fierce man, bethink thee, for an only son!
What will that grief, what will that vengeance be?
Oh, could I live, till I that grief had seen! . . .
He spoke; but Rustum listened, plunged in thought.
Nor did he yet believe it was his son
Who spoke, although he called back names he knew;
For he had had sure tidings that the babe,
Which was in Ader-baijan born to him,
Had been a puny girl, no boy at all--
So that sad mother sent him word, for fear
Rustum should seek the boy, to train in arms.
And so he deemed that either Sohrab took,
By a false boast, the style of Rustum's son;
Or that men gave it him, to swell his fame.
So deemed he; yet he listened, plunged in thought:
And his soul set to grief, as the vast tide
Of the bright rocking Ocean sets to shore
At the full moon; . . .
. . . And he saw that Youth,
Of age and looks to be his own dear son,
Piteous and lovely, lying on the sand, . . .
Lovely in death, upon the common sand.
And Rustum gazed on him with grief and said:--
'O Sohrab, thou indeed art such a son
Whom Rustum, wert thou his, might well have loved.
Yet here thou errest, Sohrab, or else men
Have told thee false--thou art not Rustum's son.
For Rustum had no son; one child he had--
But one--a girl; who with her mother now
Plies some light female task, nor dreams of us--
Of us she dreams not, nor of wounds, nor war.'
But Sohrab answered him in wrath; for now
The anguish of the deep-fixed spear grew fierce,
And he desired to draw forth the steel,
And let the blood flow free, and so to die--
But first he would convince his stubborn foe;
And, rising sternly on one arm, he said:--

'Man, who art thou who dost deny my words?
Truth sits upon the lips of dying men,
And falsehood, while I lived, was far from mine.
I tell thee, pricked upon this arm I bear
That seal which Rustum to my mother gave,
That she might prick it on the babe she bore.'
He spoke; and all the blood left Rustum's cheeks, . . .
And in a hollow voice he spake, and said:--
'Sohrab, that were a proof which could not lie!
If thou show this, then art thou Rustum's son.'
Then, with weak hasty fingers, Sohrab loosed
His belt, and near the shoulder bared his arm,
And showed a sign in faint vermilion points
Pricked; . . . the sign of Rustum's seal . . .
And Sohrab bared that image on his arm,
And himself scanned it long with mournful eyes,
And then he touched it with his hand and said:--
'How say'st thou! Is that sign the proper sign
Of Rustum's son, or of some other man's?'
He spoke; but Rustum gazed, and gazed, and stood
Speechless; and then he uttered one sharp cry:
O boy--thy father!--and his voice choked there.
And then a dark cloud passed before his eyes,
And his head swam, and he sank down to earth . .
And his sobs choked him; and he clutched his sword,
To draw it, and for ever let life out.
But Sohrab saw his thought, and held his hands,
And with a soothing voice he spake, and said:--
'Father, forbear! for I but meet to-day
The doom which at my birth was written down
In Heaven, and thou art Heaven's unconscious hand.
Surely my heart cried out that it was thou,
When first I saw thee; and thy heart spoke too,
I know it! but fate trod those promptings down
Under its iron heel; fate, fate engaged
The strife, and hurled me on my father's spear.
But let us speak no more of this! I find
My father; let me feel what I have found!
Come, sit beside me on this sand, and take
My head betwixt thy hands, and kiss my cheeks,
And wash them with thy tears, and say: **My son!**
Quick! quick! for numbered are my sands of life,
And swift; for like the lightning to this field
I came, and like the wind I go away--

But it was writ in Heaven that this should be.'
So said he, and his voice released the heart
Of Rustum, and his tears broke forth; he cast
His arm round his son's neck, and wept aloud,
And kissed him.

Arnold's poem concludes with a description of the Oxus, echoing its opening lines and the image in the middle of the poem of a wave on which Rostam and Sohrab were suspended:

But the majestic river floated on,
Out of the mist and hum of that low land,
Into the frosty starlight, and there moved,
Rejoicing, through the hushed Chorasmian waste,
Under the solitary moon . . .
A foiled circuitous wanderer--till at last
The longed-for dash of waves is heard, and wide
His luminous home of waters opens, bright
And tranquil, from whose floor the new-bathed stars
Emerge, and shine upon the Aral Sea.

As Arnold's title implies, his poem is the story of a father and a son who represent two conflicting environments and views of life. Their conflict is to be resolved by the competing personalities suspended together as it were on a wave of fate in the river of life. Rustum represents age, autumn, martial values, desert spartanness, and gloom. Sohrab represents youth, spring, aesthetic values, joy, and a springtime garden life, perennial images in the Iranian vision of the ideal world. Sohrab is overcome in his single-minded search for his own father and the latter's approval, in part because he naively carried his quest to the alien, desert, battlefield environment. There, in Arnold's version, his opponent cries out the name "Rustum" to strike fear in his youthful adversary. Sohrab, however, responds with filial emotion at hearing his father's name and momentarily drops his guard, which gives Rustum the opportunity to land the fatal blow.

Although Arnold perhaps saw the generational conflict in his story as an analogue to Victorian conflicts in general and to his own relationship with his father in particular, much about his narrative seems familiar from an Iranian perspective in terms of theme and outcome. The affinities exist even with respect to details Arnold presents that differ from Ferdowsi's account. For example, in Arnold's narrative Rustum thinks that his only child is a girl, whereas Ferdowsi's Rostam knows his child is a boy, but thinks he is too little and too young even to think about battlefield matters. Both versions fit the Islamic view which imbued Ferdowsi's age and is today the official contemporary Iranian outlook. As the chapter in the Koran called "Women" presents it in the words of Allâh, women and children are in one and the same category of persons who must obey men. In Arnold's narrative, Rustum's repeated characterization of Sohrab as girlish emphasizes the gap between childhood and femininity, on the one hand, and manhood, on the other, or between fatherhood and any other status in Iranian culture.

Of course, Sohrab could wait until he no longer behaves in a "girlish" manner or is no longer a child, and then be accepted as a man. But he seeks now to prove his worth through his deeds and not merely to wait for the approval that age bestows on a man. His efforts go against the grain of the traditional cultural order. He strives to be known as a person, as his father's son, in his own right in youth.

Ferdowsi's Sohrâb has a further, different aim, which is to place his father on the Iranian throne because he feels Rostam is more deserving than the actual king. This aim of Sohrâb's receives further attention in due course.

An additional contrast between Arnold and Ferdowsi is that in the redaction of the former the conflict between Rostam and Sohrâb ends as it does given the personality of the combatants, whereas Ferdowsi's narrative is a tragedy of fate in which only Sohrâb has an explicitly motivated personality. In addition, Ferdowsi's Rostam is a man whose personal views and values are not, at least on one thematic level, at issue: he serves the Iranian king whose authority and position he is obliged to preserve. That the king whom Rostam serves is selfish or stupid merely intensifies the irony which the final tragedy embodies.

Ferdowsi's story "Rostam and Sohrâb" depicts the tragic fruitlessness of a young man's dedication and persistence vis-à-vis an inexorable, intractable fate that destines him for death at the hand of a father whom he craves to meet, with whom he seeks to enjoy a father-son relationship, and whom he is determined to help attain his just desserts. Breathing his last on the battlefield, Sohrâb finally recognizes the invincibility of the forces pitted against him and adds his fatalism to that which permeates Ferdowsi's narrative from its famous exordium.

The exordium itself illustrates how greatly Ferdowsi's cultural context differs from Arnold's. For it clearly reiterates an Islamic backdrop to the whole *Shâhnâmeh* and introduces the dirge of fatalism which imbues the narrative. In a very popular variant, the poet says:

Hear now the battle of Rostam with Sohrâb.
You have heard other tales, hear this as well.
It is a story full of tears, and sure
to fill tender hearts with anger at Rostam.
If a harsh wind should blow from somewhere
and knock an unripe citron to the ground,
shall we call it oppressive or righteous,
ingenious and worthy, or the opposite?
If death is just, what can injustice be?
If just, why all this weeping and wailing?

Of this secret your soul has no clue;
beyond this curtain you cannot view.
Everyone has approached desire's door,
but to no one has it ever opened wide.
One may in departure find a better place,
resting at last in another abode.
If death does not devour one of the aged,
but a youth is buried instead,
then why should youth revel in this world,
in which old age is not the cause of death?
In this place of departure, not a place to tarry,
should death tighten the cinch about the steed of transience,
know that it is just and not unjust.
Since you're meted justice, why weep and wail?

As for the story itself, whereas Arnold recounts only the combat between
Rustum and Sohrab and related preliminary and subsequent events,
Ferdowsi's tale traces Sohrâb's life from birth to his fatal encounter with his
father, paralleled by an account of Rostam's exploits during the same period.

It is fate which brings together Rostam, searching for his lost horse
Rakhsh, and Tahmineh, daughter of the king of Samangân. Fate also brings
their son Sohrâb into a world where he must shield his identity from the
enemies of his warrior-father, especially from the Turânian king Afrâsiyâb.
Once told by his mother who his father is, it becomes Sohrâb's lot in a
martial age to feel obliged to choose a career in arms to find, prove himself
worthy of, and assist the legendary Rostam. He promises his mother:

Now from among the warlike Turânians
I shall raise an army with no bounds . . .
I will remove Kâvus from his throne
and blot out all trace of Nowzar's son Tus from Iran.
On Rostam I'll bestow mace and crown
and seat him on Shâh Kâvus' throne.
From Iran I will march against Turân
and confront Afrâsiyâb face to face.
I shall seize that king's throne
and raise my lance's tip above the sun.
Since Rostam is the father and I the son,
the world needs no other crown-wearer.

Afrâsiyâb soon becomes apprised of Sohrâb's identity. This sets into
motion a sequence of military exploits by Sohrâb, aided by Afrâsiyâb,
which lead eventually to Sohrâb's fatal encounter with his father. Afrâsiyâb
connives in the following words:

31

The son must not know who his father is . . .
When the two are brought face to face,
Rostam will doubtless seek the upper hand.
The aged hero then may find death
   at the hands of this lion-man.
When we seize Rostam-less Iran into our clutches,
we will make the world a narrow abode for Kâvus.
Then later we can deal with young Sohrâb
and overwhelm him with eternal sleep.
And if he's slain by his own father's hand,
that famous hero's heart will burn with grief.

It is at this point that the reader begins to sense the finely spun web in which Sohrâb, through no fault of his own, is entangled merely by virtue of his birth. The atmosphere of foreboding and fatalism that the narrator's comments and Tahmineh's misgivings create seems to make unnecessary any explanation of how Afrâsiyâb comes to know of Sohrâb's identity. It is fate, as is everything else.

Sohrâb's sudden rise to fame and military success prompt a desperate letter from Gazhdah(a)m to the Iranian king Kâvus:

A warrior-hero has come into our midst
who cannot be more than twelve years old.
He exceeds straight cypress trees in height,
and is like the shining sun under Gemini.
His torso is like a lion's, his shoulders splendid.
Among Turânians I never saw such hands or mace.
. . . In Irân and Turân, there is no such man.
He is without rival in the world.
He is the brave champion called Sohrâb,
who does not shy from devils, elephants or lions.
You would think he was Rostam himself,
or a warrior of the race of Nayram.

Through such partial recognitions of Sohrâb's identity, both the force of destiny and the disposition of the reader to eventual tragic emotions are effected. Even Rostam, when he hears of this young warrior of unknown origins in a letter from King Kâvus, reflects:

. . . a horseman has appeared in the world
resembling the great warrior-hero Sâm,
It is no wonder if he is of the blood of noble people;
but such a one could not be Turânian.
With the daughter of the king of Samangân,
I have a boy, who is still a child . . .

32

Rostam's subsequent days of drinking, his argument with King Kâvus, and Achillean sulking merely postpone what seems an inevitable confrontation between father and son. And, as powerful as Rostam supposes he is, the fact of man's total dependence upon his creator and powerlessness to alter the course of events is not lost on him, as when, during an angry outburst at Kâvus, he admits, even if his point is to remind Kâvus that the latter has no claim on him, that "My strength and victories spring from the Judge / not from armies and not from the king . . . / A servant of the Creator, that is who I am." Later, after his first combat with Sohrâb, Rostam says: "I'll strive, not knowing whose the victory will be, / Let us see for what God has cast his vote."

The reader finally discovers that in Ferdowsi's predetermined world, one man achieves victory over another only through divine intervention or fate. In a popular variant of the story, the narrator relates shortly before the third combat between father and son:

> I've heard that from the start, Rostam
> had been endowed by God with strength
> such that his feet sank into any rock he stepped on.
> Because of this he had constant problems . . .
> so he implored the Maker of the world
> and, weeping, expressed the desire
> that He might remove part of his strength
> so that he might be able to walk upon the roads.
> In accordance with this petition,
> God diminished the strength in that mountainous body.
> However, with this new task facing Rostam,
> his heart was troubled now for fear of Sohrâb.
> So he cried out to God, "O Creator,
> watch over your servant in this enterprise.
> I want again that first strength
> which you gave me, o holy Provider."

The world of Ferdowsi's "Rostam and Sohrâb" wants merely time till the proper pieces fall into their ordered places. Again and again, on the brink of a discovery which would constitute a reversal and victory over destiny, Sohrâb is thwarted in his single-minded search for his father. For example, when Sohrâb questions the captured Iranian warrior Hojir about the identity of the Iranian heroes on the battlefield, the latter says to himself:

> "If I reveal the sign of the elephant-bodied hero
> to this noble, lion-hearted youth . . .
> Rostam may be suddenly overcome . . .
> No, my best course is to keep secret his name,

to remove it from the roll of warriors."

So he tells Sohrâb that a Chinese warrior whose name he does not know is the only unidentifiable hero in camp. The reader is then told: "Sohrâb grew sad at heart at the fact / that there was no trace of Rostam." Later, meeting his father for the first time, Sohrâb says: ". . . let me ask you a question, / . . . It is my belief that you are Rostam, / and of the race of renowned Nayram." Rostam's answer is a flat denial.

The next morning, despite the danger of the impending renewal of hand-to-hand combat and despite Rostam's earlier denial, Sohrâb is still primarily concerned with finding his father. He says to a Turânian warrior called Humân:

> . . . This lion of a man battling me
> has a stature not less than mine;
> and in combat his heart never quails . . .
> My feeling is that he is Rostam,
> since few warriors in the world are like him.
> I must not battle my father
> and confront him shamelessly.

Human, who is actually a spy for Afrâsiyâb, responds by saying that neither the mysterious warrior nor his horse closely resemble Rostam and Rakhsh, respectively. Undaunted, Sohrâb proceeds again to plead with Rostam that they not fight. "O ambitious youth," Rostam replies,

> we had no such conversation yesterday.
> Yesterday our talk was all of wrestling.
> Your tricks will not work with me.
> Do not attempt to enter by that door.
> You are young, but I am no child.
> I have girded myself for combat. Let us fight,
> and let the outcome be whatever
> the Lord of all the world ordains.
> I've travelled high and low throughout my life
> and am not a man of words and deceit.

To the final, belated recognition scene, Ferdowsi consistently portrays Sohrâb as a noble young man with a single, noble mission from which neither his own fame nor the fear of death can distract him, a youth neither as rash and impetuous as Shakespeare's Hotspur, nor as consummately calculating as Prince Hal--honor is at stake here, too--but true, youthfully sincere, and trusting. Sohrâb accepts Afrâsiyâb's aid unquestioningly and has no reason to suspect the veracity of Hojir's remarks or to question Humân's misleading comments. Sohrâb even releases Rostam from certain death during their second combat when the latter deceitfully argues that Sohrâb would be violating Iranian military custom by not giving a fallen foe a second chance. In addition, Sohrâb holds no grudge at the end despite Rostam's deception and denial of his identity. In short, Sohrâb is the noble protagonist in a narrative tragedy of fate, in which the balanced plot of combat between father and son is one of the most convincing sequences. The first encounter is a draw, as it ought to be between "matchless" warriors of the same stock. On the second day, Rostam is brought low, credibly enough, since Sohrâb is younger and has greater reserves of energy. Then, Rostam escapes death through deceit, to which Sohrâb responds plausibly with mercy, since he, young and idealistic, is likely not to be on guard against duplicity, which Rostam, cagy and older, naturally includes in his arsenal of weapons. In their third and final encounter, Rostam, by means of the prayed-for return of preternatural strength (one version) or by fate (another version)--he could never defeat Sohrâb otherwise--, slays Sohrâb, giving his son no quarter in circumstances similar to those that prompted Sohrâb to release him the day before.

In contrast with Sohrâb, Ferdowsi's Rostam seems static and one-dimensional. Ferdowsi does not delineate or bring to life facets of Rostam's personality that, like the use of Homeric epithet, are mentioned in passing only. However, as a flat character, Rostam is hardly a stereotype whose personality might be capsuled in a phrase. It is possible that Ferdowsi, whose basic task in composing the *Shâhnâmeh* was to versify stories available to him in oral and written prose versions, faced such a firm and larger-than-life legend in Iran's greatest mythological hero that he did not dare to whittle Rostam down to size and, by motivating him consistently, bring him into sharp focus and thus to life in the "Rostam and Sohrâb" episode. Of course, facing a similar problem in *Paradise Lost*, which retells the most famous story in Western civilization, Milton succeeds in bringing the story to life by, among other things, inverting the chronological order, commencing *in medias res*, delineating Satan dramatically, and investing his tale with the anachronism of the theological and social concepts of his own day. Ferdowsi, on the other hand, chooses to tell his *Shâhnâmeh* in a straightforward, chronological manner, not tampering with the personalities which oral and literary traditions had transmitted through earlier generations.(10)

If Rostam were a character of peripheral importance, his lack of delineation and definite motivation would not matter. However, the story of "Rostam and Sohrâb" explicitly concerns the drama of "the one marked with age, the other fresh with youth," involving an attempted development of tension between the disparate worlds of father and son as they rush unwittingly toward each other and toward union in Sohrâb's death. Ferdowsi's cited juxtaposition of events is a conscious means of developing this tension. At the same time, because the basic conflict emerges as the moving drama of Sohrâb versus fate, that Rostam remains a mere name would not be so problematic were it not he who seals Sohrâb's fate in two strange couplets. The scene is Sohrâb's initial questioning of his opponent's identity, to which, in Ferdowsi's words:

> He answered thus that: "I am not Rostam,
> nor am I of the race of Sâm son of Nayram.
> For he is a champion and I am a lesser man:
> I have no throne, no majesty, no crown."

Ferdowsi offers no explicit character motivation or explanation for this reply to Sohrâb, which contrasts markedly with Rostam's previous behavior. This renders the crucial answer more than unexpected, more than something that the sense of fate in the *Shâhnâmeh* story can justify. Rostam's reply seems, in short, improbable in light of his earlier behavior: his threat to the king of Samangân, his response to Kâvus' letter and outburst at the king's court, and his reaction to Gudarz's entreaty to him to engage Sohrâb in single combat, all of which lead the reader to judge that here is a man always ready to recount his own heroic exploits, augment his fame, and protect his name. Then, on this one occasion when he has much to gain and apparently nothing to lose by proudly identifying himself and putting the fear of God into his youthful adversary, he suddenly denies his identity. It is an action that seems out of character for Rostam.

In contrast, Arnold's character never really denies his identity to Sohrab, but rather only implies that he is not Rustum by shrugging off Sohrab's question and trying to antagonize the latter. It is as if Arnold senses that a code of honor and avoidance of blatant prevarication must prevail on all sides for his heroic episode to evoke appropriate reader response. Moreover, Arnold's Rustum has a reason for not revealing his identity: he fears that his young opponent will find a pretext not to fight once he discovers who his adversary is and that he will later boast of having been on the same battlefield with the great Rustum.

As a resolution of these literary critical problems which Ferdowsi's characterization of Rostam seems to raise, one Iranian reading of the poem uncovers a texture of implied motivation on Rostam's part that offers insights into several characteristics of Iranian culture. These implied factors in Rostam's motivation relate to Iranian patriarchal politics.

According to Gerda Lerner in *The Creation of Patriarchy* (1986), "Patriarchy in its wider definition means the manifestation and institutionalization of male dominance over women and children in the family and the extension of male dominance over women in society in general."(11) As Lerner shows, patriarchy in the ancient Near East antedates the establishment of the Achaemenid dynasty, which means that the whole history of Persian Iranian culture has taken place in a patriarchal context.

In Iranian culture, male elders have a special place relinquished only in death. Sons are not named after fathers. In his own domain as head of the household or khân of the tribe or monarch of the nation, the male elder or father figure need answer to no one. He has proved his worth by becoming an elder in a world where it is not easy to live long enough to be old. The great father figures of twentieth century Iran have been Rezâ Shâh Pahlavi (1878-1944) who established the short-lived Pahlavi dynasty in 1926 and ruled until 1941, Mohammad Mosaddeq (1880-1967) who served as prime minister from April 1951 until he was ousted in a CIA-aided coup d'état which brought Rezâ Shâh Pahlavi's son and heir Mohammad Rezâ (1919-1980) back to the throne in August 1953, and Ruhollâh Khomayni (1902-1989) whom his followers in the Islamic Republic of Iran established in 1979 regarded as the paternal figure *par excellence* in both spiritual and political spheres.

In the patriarchal world of Iranian culture, boy children attempt to establish themselves as sons in their fathers' eyes, as Sohrâb tried to do. In the case of the reign of Mohammad Rezâ Pahlavi, the expected posture of other males in his government was that of sons, that is, children obeying the father of their nation. During the 1960s and 1970s, the first grade Persian school text in Iran described Mohammad Rezâ Pahlavi as the father of the country and a person children were to obey as unquestioningly as they would their own fathers.

In the case of Ruhollâh Khomayni, the figures of Abolhasan Banisadr and Sâdeq Qotbzâdeh exemplify patriarchal politics. Both politicians attempted to gain and maintain power through representation of themselves to Khomayni and fellow Iranians as sons of Khomayni, only to suffer eventual disinheritance. Khomayni's rejection of Banisadr and Qotbzâdeh provides a glimpse at the other side of this patriarchal order: the threat to the elder and his place comes not from his natural enemies, but from the next generation. The much revered Shâh 'Abbâs the Great (ruled 1587-1629) blinded two sons and had one executed, and blinded a grandson, all in the name of protecting his crown.

Ferdowsi's episode of "Rostam and Sohrâb" fits into this cultural context and explicitly depicts generational conflicts. The poet at one point calls it a battle between two heroes, one worn with age and the other blessed with youth. It may ring true for some Iranian readers because they have experienced in the traditional order of their culture the eventual victory of the patriarch or the father figure. In Rostam's case, it is not malicious filicide, but paradoxically worse than that: it is cultural inevitability that Rostam kill his own son to protect the monarchy, the ultimate fatherhood, as well as to protect his own patriarchal fiefdom.

As for the specific motivation behind Rostam's behavior and actions, questions persist in the reader's mind because of the unlikelihood that Rostam cannot discern the identity of his youthful adversary. Ferdowsi intimates that Sohrâb closely resembles Rostam in his youth through repeated references to Sâm. Rostam himself has strongly resembled his grandfather from youth. Then, everyone on the periphery in Ferdowsi's tale

37

immediately sees the resemblance between Sohrâb and his great grandfather, including Rostam when he first hears of this young warrior. All along, Tahmineh has been in contact with Rostam and has informed him of their son's martial proclivities. Rostam knows that Sohrâb is at least twelve and can recall his own size, strength, and abilities at that age.

After his three days of drinking and subsequent acquiescence to Gudarz's entreaties that he fight Sohrâb, Rostam surreptitiously enters Sohrâb's camp and slays the man whom Tahmineh has sent to make certain that Rostam and Sohrâb become acquainted should they meet. Upon returning to the Iranian camp, Rostam again remarks that Sohrâb seems a reincarnation of Sâm. He admits that no one except for himself in all of Iran is a match for this newcomer, an observation that should surely lead to a surmise about Sohrâb's paternity. Finally, when the two warriors approach the battlefield for their fateful encounter, Ferdowsi relates that Rostam there saw Sohrâb, armed and Sâm-like on horseback.

Ferdowsi implies that Rostam cannot have failed to recognize his own son. At the very least, such a physically special father would recall how he himself looked in youth. But, while Sohrâb has done all he could to find his father, Rostam does all he can to avoid acknowledging Sohrâb's identity. Ferdowsi, in turn, uniformly blames Rostam alone for the tragic outcome. He calls the episode "a story sure to fill tender hearts with anger at Rostam."

Consequently, as the critic Mostafâ Rahimi suggests, it may be that Rostam wants Sohrâb to remain unrecognized.(12) Rostam refers to "deceit" when Sohrâb proposes peace on the second morning. Self-deception may be the perfect label for Rostam's behavior from the moment his youthful adversary appears on the scene. During the course of their combat Rostam uncharacteristically deceives Sohrâb. And, at the end, with his attempted suicide he may be deceiving others. Rostam's self-deception has involved intense inner conflict, a reason perhaps for his uncharacteristic days of joyless drinking.

As to why Rostam feels the need to deceive himself and thereafter to confront his own son in combat, Sohrâb's plans provide the answer. The latter has attracted a considerable following in his revolutionary quest to destroy the existing political order in Iran and Turân and to replace it with a new order in which he would share power with his father who would be the new king. The new order would bring peace to the world as well.

But, even though Rostam would be king in Sohrâb's revolutionary order, he would not have attained that status on his own through his own initiative. For the first time in his career, he would have accepted the ideas and superior aid of another, someone with his own, independent base of popularity. Throughout his career, Rostam has never had such revolutionary thoughts himself. He is conservative and has a preeminent place and stake in the existing order. Moreover, in a realm without war, Rostam would not be a giant among men. In short, Sohrâb is suggesting a fundamental change both in the family structure--children bestowing power and glory on fathers--

and in the political order. Sohrâb is suggesting that fathers and sons will be equals, in effect destroying the traditional patriarchal domination of the former.

Ferdowsi implies that a sort of "lust" or "greed" (*âz* in Persian, translated as "desire" in the phrase "desire's door" in the quotation at the top of page 31, above), for perpetuation of his status the reader assumes, interferes with Rostam's expression of paternal love. This power-lust is great enough that Rostam attempts to deny the truth through self-deception. He wants to make himself believe that his young adversary is not his son. After all, he cannot relinquish his power and station in life--that would be shameful. And he cannot kill a youth he acknowledged as his son--that would be even more shameful. Therefore, combat undertaken with self-deception is the only answer. Rostam cannot afford to wait either: eventually the truth of his adversary's identity would become known and/or Sohrâb would continue to attract people to his cause. Rostam cannot be certain of the outcome of the combat. But it is his only choice as a warrior-hero thinking in traditional patriarchal terms.

As it turns out, fate (or the return of preternatural strength) causes Rostam to emerge victorious and put an end to this revolutionary threat to the order he is dedicated to preserve. But in so doing, Rostam also destroys the possibility of a new Iran. If Sohrâb had succeeded in making Rostam king, that would have inaugurated a new order through making succession to the throne not a matter of inheritance, but a matter of merit. In other words, right would be might, and persons of non-royal blood could aspire to the throne. The point is no less significant merely because Rostam's behavior marks him as undeserving to be king--his son naturally perceives his father from a distance as an ideal figure. At close hand, Sohrâb learns otherwise, but his filial love fills the gap.

Sohrâb's death, then, is the prototypical example of "son-killing," which Iranian critics note as a common theme in contemporary Persian literature alongside related issues of Iran's masculine history. As an illustration of both, Hushang Golshiri's brilliant 1969 novel called *Prince Ehtejâb*(13) tells the story of a middle-aged Tehrân man whose great great grandfather was Nâseroddin Shâh Qâjâr (ruled 1848-1896). His great grandfather was the famous Zellossoltân who with legendary cruelty, avarice, and meanness ruled several provinces, most notably Esfahân, up to the Constitutional Movement. Prince Ehtejâb's grandfather continued in Zellossoltân's footsteps as an equally cruel, self-centered man although with less power. Prince Ehtejâb's father abandoned the family landowning business and joined the Pahlavi army, performing his cruelty in the name of "upstarts." Then comes the last of the line, the title character who is himself dying of hereditary tuberculosis, i.e., is being physically destroyed by the disease of his fathers just as he has died spiritually as a result of inheriting their meanness. He cannot live with the memories of the past of his forebears; and his genes make it impossible for him to change. Golshiri, of course, is reminding his readers in the late 1960s that Iran cannot turn to its aristocracy for its political salvation, for the fathers of the aristocracy have polluted their heirs, i.e., have spiritually destroyed their sons.

A more direct analogue to son-killing as depicted in Ferdowsi's "Rostam and Sohrâb" is Gholâmhosayn Sâ'edi's 1973 short story called "The Game Is Over."(14) Set in a slum of huts on the outskirts of south Tehrân, it is the story of the narrator and his friend Hasani, whose mean, tyrannical father beats him almost every evening after coming home from work. Hasani wants revenge. So he and the narrator try to overpower the father one night, but the latter proves too strong. Then Hasani comes up with the idea of faking his own death to make his father grieve. They stage the death by pretending that Hasani has fallen into one of the many tar-pit wells nearby. The trick works, and Hasani's father displays grief at the memorial service. The narrator returns to where Hasani is hiding to tell him that he has finally gotten his revenge. The two boys run around the tar pits in joy, planning to go home shortly and make everybody happy that Hasani is still alive. But this time Hasani really falls into a well, and dies. The narrator races back to the cluster of hovels, screaming again, this time for real, that Hasani has fallen into a well. The elders treat the narrator as if deranged for still being so hysterically upset. On the morrow, in that poverty-stricken community fathers will continue to terrorize the next generation, which, it is seen, faces death or madness should it dare to challenge patriarchal authority. The socio-political twist here--Sâ'edi is as despairing of lower classes as Golshiri is of the aristocracy--is that the tyranny of Hasani's father is his response, in the microcosmic family environment in which he has power, to the oppression and tyranny to which he is subjected in the Tehrân workaday world over which the shâh rules.

Of course, non-establishment Iranian writers imply that the whole atmosphere of Pahlavi Iran exuded metaphysical son-killing or, better put, the enforced perpetuation of boyhood by the monarch and his representatives upon the Iranian male population. The literary scholar 'Abdolhosayn Zarrinkub recognized the seriousness of the situation when he wrote in the late 1970s: "The truth is that if our generation, the generation of the fathers, does not endeavor to know intimately the world of its sons, it is possible that this generation will unwittingly sacrifice its sons as Rostam did."(15)

Pahlavi Iran presumably failed to get to know and appreciate its sons, which, along with a sense of ignominious emasculation vis-à-vis the monarchy, led to a popular view in 1978 that almost any successor regime would be preferable. The Islamic Republic of Iran which came into being in the spring of 1979 was welcomed by part of the Iranian population not unlike the acquiescence Iranians exhibited in the face of the Arab Moslem invasion of Sâsânid Iran in the 640s. Those Iranians of nearly 1,400 years ago saw in Islam a possibly non-patriarchal salvation from the despotic hierarchy of the Sâsânid monarchy. Then in the recent past, Shi'i Islam, which had become the state religion at the beginning of the Safavid Era

(1501-1736), became the banner for the oppressed in the face of Pahlavi monarchy and secularization, with Ruhollâh Khomayni's emergence in the 1970s as the leading anti-monarchical voice. But obviously patriarchal in posture and attitudes toward the Iranian population, Khomayni seemed to his opponents or, better put, Shi'i Islam has seemed to them, to perpetuate son-killing as well, on a scale unprecedented in Iranian history.

During the eight years of the war between Iraq and Iran, which began with Iraq's invasion of Khuzestân in September 1980, thousands upon thousands of Iranian sons died as "martyrs" fighting for Islam against the "infidel" Iraqis allegedly fronting for the Satanic American superpower. Throughout the war, Khomayni stated his readiness to sacrifice all of Iran's young men in Islam's cause (while he and other Iranian elders did their best personally to avoid Iraqi missiles and bombs). If Ferdowsi's Sohrâb must die so that the order of Iran's patriarchal monarchy might be maintained, thousands upon thousands of Sohrâbs died in the Iranian 1980s to preserve the patriarchal order of the national theocracy. In this cultural sense, therefore, the Islamic Republic of Iran may not represent a revolutionary movement vis-à-vis the Pahlavi monarchy, but rather a coup d'état in which one patriarchal, son-killing force replaced another. Accordingly, a true cultural revolution in Iran would mean a victory for the Sohrâbs or a compromise by which their values would play a part in the social order, something that has yet to take place in Iranian history.

A final and ironic note is that today's Iranians may be fatherless in one sense as well. Although they once had fathers, for example the Achaemenid monarchs in history and the Kayâni and other mythological royal dynasties in Ferdowsi's *Shâhnâmeh*, who could protect them and conquer non-Iranians, those powerful patriarchs went to the grave forever with the "ending of the *Shâhnâmeh*" and their successor fathers conquer and control only their own sons, the Iranian nation. This is another aspect of the senses of loss and separation which contribute to the sadness that seems part of the warp and weft of Iranian literary culture.

2

PERENNIAL IRANIAN SKEPTICISM, INDIVIDUALISM, AND DREAMS OF GARDENS

> Oh, come with Old Khayyám, and leave the Wise
> To talk; one thing is certain, that life flies;
> One thing is certain, and the Rest is lies;
> The Flower that once has blown forever dies.
>
> *Rubaíyát of Omar Khayyám*, 1859(16)

The invitation which Edward FitzGerald's "Old Khayyám" extends to his readers contrasts markedly with Ferdowsi's encouragement to Iranians to accept an Arab God's omniscience as justification of the world's otherwise inexplicable ways to men and to take pride in their pre-Islamic Iranian past despite the ignominy of the Iranian present with its caliphal and Ghaznavid authorities. Nevertheless, the Khayyâmic invitation has special appeal for many of the same Iranians who have accepted the messages of Persepolis, Islam, and Ferdowsi as well.

Such acceptance seems per se reflective of a characteristic capacity in many Iranians to weigh, balance, and oscillate between paired extremes or opposites, resulting in a palpable ambivalence toward contrasting, even mutually exclusive goals, values, ideas, and ideals. In recent history, the Iranian pendulum has swung from enthusiastic Westernization and involvement in international affairs during the Pahlavi era to the xenophobic isolationism of the first years of the Islamic Republic. In the distant historical past, Ferdowsi had to weigh Islamic values of foreign origin against pre-Islamic Iranian culture, arriving at a compromise of nostalgic pride in the pre-Islamic Iranian grandeur and past, balanced by an acceptance of the wisdom of the Arab Allâh. Ferdowsi also expresses great sympathy and feeling for Sohrâb in that *Shâhnâmeh* episode, balanced by a belief that fate demanded the fulfillment of Rostam's destiny even at the cost of Sohrâb's life, the reader's sorrow to be assuaged by the belief that Allâh knows all and is all-just or that Iranian kingship must survive at all costs if Iran is to survive. Such cultural tension nowhere more clearly reveals itself than in sympathy for the Khayyâmic view on the part of Iranians otherwise engaged in lives and mirroring values inconsonant with that view.

The Khayyâmic view is a prototypical and influential stance of non-establishment individualism, echoes of which find their way into the attitudes of such leading twentieth-century literary figures as Sâdeq Hedâyat and Forugh Farrokhzâd. Those echoes make the Khayyâmic view a cultural bridge from Saljuq (1055-1157) to post-World War II Irans. In addition, the Khayyâmic view happens to be a most significant cultural bridge from pre-modern Iran to the modern world. Most importantly, this Khayyâmic view is today a significant component of the cultural attitudes of many Iranian writers and other literary intellectuals.

However, the very phrase "Khayyâmic view" and its relation to 'Omar Khayyâm (1048-1131) are not unproblematic. For example, the much studied historical figure 'Omar Khayyâm was not a professional poet and left no manuscripts containing any poems he authored. As for "his *rubaíyât*," no such thing as a single composition called *robâ'iyât* (which is the plural of the word *robâ'i* [quatrain]) existed in traditional Persian literature, much less a composition of connected *robâ'is* by 'Omar Khayyâm. In other words, in traditional Persian poetry *robâ'is* were composed as separate, self-contained, four-line poems. Furthermore, Edward FitzGerald's *Rubaíyât of Omar Khayyám* is by no means a translation of any single Persian work, much less a work by the historical figure of 'Omar Khayyâm.(17)

Paradoxically, FitzGerald's *Rubaíyát* is very close to the mood, imagery, and themes popularly associated in Iran with 'Omar Khayyâm. In addition, FitzGerald's poem fairly reflects the range in images and ideas represented in pre-modern Persian quatrains thought of as Khayyâmic. For these reasons, the parallel consideration here of the Persian *robâ'is* attributed to Khayyâm and FitzGerald's *Rubaíyát* seems a legitimate procedure for defining the Khayyâmic view. Glimpses of Khayyâm's life and times, as well as a brief review of Khayyâm scholarship, will add to the intended appreciation of that view. The upshot is the asserted significance of a culture-specific skepticism, together with a Perso-Moslem cultural nationalism and a vision of the perfect life as a spring-time garden as three other traditional characteristics of Iranian culture alive today for many literary Iranians.

Now, the study of the Khayyâmic view does not begin with Khayyâm or his age or Iran, but rather with Edward FitzGerald (1809-1883),(18) who introduced Khayyâm as a poet to England and the world, including Iran.

Edward FitzGerald first looked at a manuscript of Persian quatrains attributed to 'Omar Khayyâm in the latter part of 1856. Less than two years later, he submitted thirty-five "translated" quatrains to *Frazer's Magazine* for publication. When they did not appear, FitzGerald retrieved his manuscript, added forty more quatrains, and in March 1859 published 250 copies of the *Rubaíyát of Omar Khayyâm*. This first edition was followed by a second, expanded to 110 quatrains. A third edition of 101 quatrains appeared in 1872.

These three editions appeared anonymously, FitzGerald not formally acknowledged as the "translator" until 1876. A fourth edition, again including 101 quatrains, appeared in 1879. Although the literary world, including Thomas Carlyle, Gabriel Rossetti, A.C. Swinburne, John Ruskin, and C.E. Norton (who was the first American critic to review the *Rubáiyát*), had by the time FitzGerald's authorship was acknowledged recognized the poetic achievement of the *Rubáiyát*, the Khayyâm "craze" and worldwide acclaim of FitzGerald's poem, which has included hundreds of editions and translations and persists to the present day, did not commence until after FitzGerald's death in 1883.

From the moment FitzGerald's *Rubáiyát of Omar Khayyâm* began achieving its singular status in world literature as the most famous English language poem ever based on a foreign language model, scholars directed primary attention to its relationship to its Persian sources viewed either as literary inspiration or, at the other extreme, as Persian texts merely translated and arranged by FitzGerald in a particular order. At the turn of the century, Edward Heron-Allen investigated the issue in a book called *Edward FitzGerald's 'Rubáiyát of Omar Khayyám' with their Original Sources* (1899). There he conclusively demonstrated that FitzGerald's *Rubáiyát* is an original work inspired by Persian quatrains mostly attributed to 'Omar Khayyâm. But Heron-Allen also highlighted the intriguing and persisting problem of the authorship of the Persian quatrains attributed to 'Omar Khayyâm. Begun early on as an inquiry into "wandering quatrains" or poems which appeared in different manuscripts of poems by different Persian poets, the investigation of the authorship of the quatrains attributed to 'Omar Khayyâm has continued to the present day, with important studies undertaken by a series of Iranian scholars.(19)

The first of these is *The Songs of Khayyâm* (1934), compiled by Sâdeq Hedâyat, whose masterful novel *The Blind Owl* (1941), the subject of chapter 4, clearly exhibits Khayyâmic echoes. At the outset of his study, Hedâyat observed that Khayyâm the poet is an enigma because of the confusion wrought by the innumerable manuscript collections of quatrains attributed to him: "If for fun we flip through and read one of these manuscripts of quatrains, we will be confronted with contradictory ideas, diverse topics, and subjects that could not possibly be the mind set of one human being." In an attempt to limit attribution of *robâ'is* to Khayyâm to those not mutually contradictory in thematic terms, Hedâyat proposed to collect a handful of philosophical quatrains attributed in reliable fourteenth-century sources to the historical figure of Khayyâm. After an examination of the older anthologies, Hedâyat chose fourteen separate quatrains attributed to Khayyâm in two works written before the mid-fourteenth century that are stylistically and thematically consistent and consonant with the figure of Khayyâm the philosopher. These poems, here presented in translation, served Hedâyat as "the key and touchstone for recognition of other quatrains of Khayyâm."

From the hidden emerged this sea of life,
its essence no one has ever pierced.
Everyone has had something to say,
but not about things as they really are.

* * *

In the cycle of our coming and going,
neither beginning nor end is visible.
No one in this world has uttered the truth
as to whence we come and where we go.

* * *

When the elements were combined in creation,
why did the Maker endow them with transience?
If it did not work out well, fault is whose?
And if it turned out well, why destroy it?

* * *

As one can never add to days and lives,
one should not try the heart with more or less.
Our affairs, to where it is ours to choose,
cannot be shaped as wax by hands.

* * *

O you, who are the result of four and seven
and are always disturbed by seven and four,
drink wine; I've told you a thousand times:
there is no second coming--once gone, you're gone.

* * *

There was a drop of water, it merged with the sea.
There was a speck of dirt, it merged with the earth.
Your coming into the world is what?
A fly appearing and disappearing.

* * *

Should the world be arranged for your sake,
do not incline toward what the learned reject.
Many such as you go and many come.
Steal your own share because you will be stolen.

* * *

O wise elder, rise early and
look carefully at the child sweeping.

45

Advise him, tell him to sweep ever so gently
the brains of Kayqobâd and the eyes of Parviz.

* * *

Spring clouds have cleansed the tulip's cheek,
So rise and fill your cup--the time is right.
This lawn of grass, your scenery today,
will spring tomorrow from your dust.

* * *

Last night I dropped and broke my drinking bowl.
I did this foolish thing while I was drunk.
The bowl then mutely said to me:
Like you was I--and you will be like me.

* * *

Since I will not be in this world for long,
to be without my wine and love is wrong.
Till when will I hope or fear that the world is eternal or created,
which will mean nothing when I am gone?

* * *

It's dawn--so rise, o lovely one.
Slowly pour wine and play the lute,
because those here will not for long endure,
and none of those departed will return.

* * *

The fateful days hold in disgust that man
who sits upset in sorrow of the days.
From the crystal cup, drink to the lute's wail,
before your cup lands on a stone.

* * *

Drink wine: the universe means your demise,
intends the death of your pure life and mine.
Be seated on the grass and drink bright wine,
for here will blooms bloom from your dust and mine.

Altogether, Hedâyat presents 129 Khayyâmic quatrains in his collection,
grouped under such headings as *carpe diem*, life's tribulations, life's futility,
and the enigma of creation. Hedâyat's choices, almost all of them effective
quatrains, are thematically consonant with his fourteen "key" quatrains. At
the same time, from the quatrains he attributes to Khayyâm, Hedâyat derives
a very specific Khayyâmic personality and view. Hedâyat's Khayyâm rejects

Islam and the Semitic conception of God, holding instead that fate is this world's sole god. This leads him to the views that both the universe and humankind came into existence accidentally through the fortuitously appropriate combination of molecules, that human beings have only corporeal reality and lack spiritual souls, and that death is the total end to individual human existence. In light of these views, Hedâyat's Khayyâm believes that the only recourse for humankind is to live for the moment, with only romantic love and wine offering some pleasure and consolation. Wine is preferable because its intoxication brings forgetfulness along with its pleasure.

Hedâyat's view that Khayyâm rejects Semitic myths and notions of God leads to the assertion that:

> Perhaps we can count Khayyâm as among such anti-Arab Iranians as Ebn-e Moqaffa', Beh'âfarid, Abu Moslem, Bâbak, et al. Khayyâm refers to earlier Iranian monarchs with a sad, wistful tone. Perhaps this grief grew in him as a result of reading Ferdowsi's *Shâhnâmeh*. In his own quatrains, there are constant reminders of the decline and trampled splendor and grandeur of those kings, who have become one with the earth and in whose ruined palaces foxes have made their lairs and owls have built nests. From his angry cachinnation and his allusions and references to pre-Islamic Iran, it is apparent that from the bottom of his heart he despises the Arab highwaymen and their base thoughts. His sympathy lies with Iran which had been trapped in the mouth of this seventy-headed dragon and which flayed its arms and legs convulsively.(20)

Hedâyat also argues that Khayyâmic allusions in several quatrains to the now ruined "palace where Bahrâm took cup in hand" and which "used to be next to the heavens" are references to the Sâsânid palace at Ctesiphon, which Hedâyat thinks Khayyâm might have visited on the way to Mecca.(21) This would make Khayyâm a cultural nationalist feeling a deep-seated nostalgic sadness at Iran's loss of pre-Islamic grandeur and link him in that regard with Ferdowsi and such twentieth-century intellectuals as Akhavân-e Sâles and Hedâyat himself.

To be sure, a characteristic historical outlook that seems a pervasive piece of cultural luggage can be traced to Ferdowsi's *Shâhnâmeh*, which as a national epic is unusual in its depiction of ultimate Iranian defeat, not just defeat of a new Iran symbolized by Sohrâb, but the destruction of pre-Islamic Iranian life and the continuity of Iranian monarchy by the invading Moslem Arabs in the middle of the seventh century. This invasion was a cataclysmic historical fact, as were the destructive invasions of Alexander the Great and the Mongols in two waves in the thirteenth century, of which Iranians are reminded on a day-to-day basis. As they see it, the Iranian historical experience teaches that what Iranians build and what Iran becomes are eventually destroyed and that in defeat Iranians are forced to change religion, art forms, systems of writing, eating habits, clothing and the like. And they live thereafter with visual reminders of their defeat.

Some Iranian intellectuals often point to Iranian resiliency and adaptability in the face of periodic domination by foreign forces as essential aspects of the culture. They even argue that Iran's distinctiveness lies in its eventual cultural conquest of its military conquerors. For example, the Baghdad caliphs ruled the Islamic empire with a Sâsânid sort of governmental system. Or, by the time the Turkic Ghaznavids and Saljuqs conquered Iran, they had become Persianized and subsequently great patrons of Iranian arts. Or, for example, the Il-Khânid descendants of the Mongols ruled Iran in a Persian fashion.

But in the case of the Arab Moslem invasion, the most consequential event in Iranian history subsequent to the establishment of the Achaemenid empire in 559 BCE, this view is just not true. Iranian society was changed deeply and permanently by the invasion, through the imposition and subsequent development of Islam in Iran. For nearly fourteen centuries, Iranian eyes have looked to Mecca, that is to a foreign land, for spiritual leadership. In their Persian language, Arabic vocabulary accounts for a majority of the words. Arabic given names are more common in Iran than Persian given names. For over a thousand years, the basic system of prosody in Persian verse has been Arabic in origin. Arab art forms, or art forms originally Arab in inspiration, have dominated Iranian art and architecture. All of these and numerous other facts testify to the pervasive influence of Arab culture in Iran. The very existence of the Islamic Republic of Iran would be sufficient evidence even without these other apparent influences.

The cultural point is that, as the proverb about the end of the *Shâhnâmeh* goes, many Iranians assume that things turn out for the worse in Iran. Good times and prosperity end in disaster. Perhaps more important is the sense that Iran's glory was in the past, that some Iranians may think of themselves as living after their time: tomorrow is not all that worth struggling for communally, because nothing can ever match Achaemenid or Sâsânid achievements. These views lead to a pessimism and the already noted, perennial sadness of Iranian literary expression.

If such sadness seems only implied in Ferdowsi's *Shâhnâmeh* because of the poem's explicit Islamic framework, in the view of Hedâyat and other Iranian scholars it appears directly in such other classics of Persian literature as Khayyâmic quatrains and Khâqâni's (d. 1202) "Ode on the Palace at Ctesiphon." This extremely famous and beloved poem reads:

> [1]Take care, o heedful heart, to mind the eye's lesson:
> see the palace of Ctesiphon as a mirror of admonition.
> [2]Once along the Tigris, stop at Ctesiphon,
> and let a second Tigris flow onto Ctesiphon's soil.

[3]The Tigris itself so weeps a hundred bloody streams
that its lashes drip fire from the heat of these blood-red tears.
[4]Do you see how the Tigris shore foams at its mouth?
It is as if its feverish sigh blistered its lip.
[5]See the Tigris' liver scorched by regret;
did you ever hear of water that fire could scorch?
[6]Weep anew for the Tigris and give it your eyes' alms,
even though the shore takes alms from the Tigris.
[7]If the Tigris mixes cold sighs and fiery heartache,
one half will become ice, the other a furnace.
[8]Once the palace chain at Ctesiphon broke,
the Tigris went awry and twisted like a chain.
[9]From time to time call out to the palace in the tongue of tears
to hear with the heart's ear its reply.
[10]Each palace battlement gives advice time and again:
heed that advice from those heights in the depths of your heart.
[11]It says: You are of earth, and we now the earth beneath your feet;
trod upon us, and scatter two or three tears.
[12]Our head truly aches with the wailing of the owl;
weep rose-water tears and ease that pain.
[13]Yes, why do you marvel that in the world's meadows
owls follow nightingales, and lamentation song?
[14]We were the court of justice, and this injustice befell us;
what privation must await palaces of the unjust?
[15]This heavenly palace the decree of the turning heaven
or that of the heaven-turner seems to have overturned.
[16]Do you laugh at my eyes that they weep here?
O, weeping is for eyes not weeping here.
[17]Ctesiphon's white-haired woman is no less
                    than the old woman of Kufeh,
nor her narrow room less than the latter's oven.
[18]Do you know how to equate Ctesiphon with Kufeh?
Make a furnace of your breast and summon a storm from your eyes.
[19]This is the same palace where from imprints of faces
the threshold dirt became a portrait-gallery wall.
[20]This is the same royal court where among monarchs
the king of Babylon was but a slave, and
                    the Shâh of Turkestân a doorman.
[21]This is the same splendid pavilion where
the lion woven into the tapestry would attack Leo.
[22]Imagine it is that age: with your mind's eye
see the court's chain, the throng in the square.
[23]Dismount, put your face to the chess cloth ground,
see No'mân checkmated under the Sâsânid elephant's foot.
[24]No, no, see the No'mân-like elephant-slaying shâhs

49

the elephants of night and day have killed under the feet of ages.

[25]O, many an elephant-slaying shâh a regal chess elephant cornered,
checkmated by fate on the square of hopelessness.

[26]The earth is intoxicated, having drunk, instead of wine,
Anusharvân's heart's blood from Hormoz's skull.

[27]Counsel enough was visible then on his crown,
a hundred pieces of advice now hidden in the pith of his head.

[28]Anusharvân and his gold citron, Parviz and the golden quince
are gone with the wind, become one with dust.

[29]Parviz brought his golden fruit to every nation
and made of the gold cloth a golden garden.

[30]Of Parviz, now gone, speak no more.
Where are the golden fruit on the cloth? Remember the Koran says:
    "How many gardens did they abandon?"

[31]Where, you ask, have those crown-wearers gone?
The earth is ever pregnant with them.

[32]Yes, the pregnant earth gives birth late;
giving birth is difficult, conception easy.

[33]That wine the vine gives is the blood of Shirin;
of Parviz's remains the village gentleman shapes the vessel.

[34]However many tyrants it has devoured,
this hungry-eyed earth never becomes sated.

[35]This white-browed mother with black sagging breasts
makes her rouge with children's heart's blood.

[36]O Khâqâni, beg counsel from this palace door
so that henceforth the Khâqân will beg at yours.

[37]If today a vagabond seeks provisions from the Sultan,
tomorrow the Sultan will seek provisions at his door.

[38]If Meccan provisions serve every city along the way,
take provisions from Ctesiphon, a travel gift for Sharvân.

[39]From Mecca everyone takes prayer-beads of Hamza's clay,
so you take prayer-beads of Salmân's clay from Ctesiphon.

[40]Observe this sea of insight, do not pass it by without a drink.
One cannot depart such a sea thirsty.

[41]Friends returning from travels bring gifts--
this poem is a gift for friends.

[42]Heed the secret repeated herein by this friend, apparently dead but
with a Christ-like heart, apparently mad but with a wise soul.(22)

In Khâqâni's poem, the speaker reflects aloud on his thoughts at visiting
the Sâsânid ruins at Ctesiphon near the Tigris River, which itself has
weeped, as the speaker encourages his heart to do, ever since Anusharvân's
famous chain of justice was there broken. The battlements, halls of justice,
the porticos, and pavilions at Ctesiphon, are now all in ruins, while
Anusharvân, his father Hormoz, his grandson Parviz, and the latter's

Armenian consort Shirin, and all of Sâsânid civilization have been carried away by the wind and become one with the earth, whose belly is forever more pregnant with them. The speaker admonishes his audience to see this sea of inspiration, which Ctesiphon is, and not pass it by without a drink. In short, Khâqâni shows his Iranian readers why they are obliged to live with cultural sadness: their past was o so great and o so irretrievable.

Such a mood is pervasive in Iranian culture, manifesting itself in attitudes toward hospitality, leisure time, and much else. But perhaps its most significant manifestation reveals itself in the mythologized personality of 'Omar Khayyâm. Hedâyat goes so far as to ask, "Did not Khâqâni derive inspiration for the whole of his 'Palace at Ctesiphon' *qasideh* [panegyric ode] from this [following] Khayyâmic quatrain?"

> From that royal palace which once rose to the sky
> monarchs in splendor faced the world.
> But on its turrets I have seen a ring-dove seated,
> cooing, cooing over and over: where, where?(23)

Hedâyat's characterization of the Khayyâmic view will strike a chord of familiarity for anyone familiar with *The Blind Owl* and other Hedâyat fiction, which implies a scholarly difficulty with his selection and characterization of Khayyâmic quatrains. In other words, Hedâyat's own predilections, rather than a dispassionate research conclusion, prompt his characterization of the historical Khayyâm as strictly anti-religious and anti-Sufi, and his use of this characterization as a criterion for attribution of quatrains to Khayyâm. Nevertheless, Hedâyat makes the important point in *The Songs of Khayyâm* that attribution of Persian quatrains to Khayyâm must be based on some limitation of possible thematic range since one cannot easily assume that Khayyâm composed many quatrains embodying mutually exclusive world views. Further, Hedâyat's use of "key" poems seems a sensible approach in sifting through the many sorts of quatrains that have passed for Khayyâm's.

Some eight years after the publication of Hedâyat's *The Songs of Khayyâm*, the scholars Mohammad 'Ali Foroughi and Qâsem Ghani collaborated on another critical edition called *The Robâ'is of Khayyâm of Nishâbur*, basing their selection of quatrains on an expansion of Hedâyat's concept of "key" poems to sixty-six quatrains which the editors assumed could with confidence be deemed Khayyâm's.(24) Many of the 178 quatrains in the Foroughi-Ghani edition do not appear in Hedâyat's earlier *Songs of Khayyâm* mainly because the editors held the view that Khayyâm's ideas were wholly in accord with the orthodox Sunni religious sentiments of their day and that, for example, Khayyâm's use of wine imagery was symbolic, and not a literal verbalization of a *carpe diem* theme. Such a view affected the Foroughi-Ghani choice of quatrains as much as Hedâyat's equally subjective opinions affected his.

In the West, Persianist scholarship has not only failed to resolve the contradictory images of Khayyâm emerging from work in Iran, but has even added to the situation a generation of hoaxes and frauds, an intriguing, tangential dimension to Khayyâmic lore.(25) On the other hand, in Iran, 'Ali Dashti's *A Moment with Khayyâm* (1969) has proved a satisfactory culmination to earlier scholarship, as shown below after a thumbnail sketch of Khayyâm's life,(26) which is Dashti's initial focus as well.

'Omar Khayyâm was born in 1048 in Nishâpur, now a small city in the northeastern part of today's Iran. His birth took place as the great Ghaznavid dynasty's rule over the province of Khorâsân, in which Nishâpur was the chief city, was ended by the Saljuqs, an even greater dynasty. From the name 'Omar, it is obvious that Khayyâm was a Sunni Moslem by birth. 'Omar was the second Caliph, much despised by Iranian Shi'ites who still today curse his memory. Since the word *khayyâm* means "tentmaker," perhaps 'Omar Khayyâm's forebears practiced this trade.

In 1055, the Saljuq leader Toghrel Beg occupied Baghdâd, thus gaining control over the Moslem Caliphate and Empire. At his death, his nephew Alp-Arslân succeeded to the Saljuq throne, in part through the machinations of Nezâmolmolk, another famous man from Nishâpur, who was to serve the Saljuqs for over thirty years as a vizier. Alp-Arslân, who ruled from 1063 to 1072, was succeeded by his son Malekshâh who ruled until 1092.

Under Saljuq rule, Khayyâm studied first in Nishâpur and then in Balkh, a major eastern city in today's Afghanistan. From there, he went farther northeast to Samarqand, now in the U.S.S.R., where he wrote a treatise in Arabic on quadrilateral equations, available in Daoud S. Kaser's translation entitled *The Algebra of Omar Khayyâm* (1921). It is the most important of Khayyâm's extant works, ten or so short treatises, none of which offers glimpses into his personality, except to affirm his importance as a mathematician and astronomer whose public views were orthodox.

In Samarqand, Khayyâm was in the employ of a local magistrate and later the ruler of Bokhârâ, which led to his association with Malekshâh's court. Two of the projects on which Khayyâm worked were the construction of an observatory in the Saljuq capital at Esfahân in 1074 and the reform of the existing Persian calendar called "Maleki" after the monarch. The latter project is the autobiographical point to Stanza 57 of FitzGerald's *Rubáiyát*, in which the speaker Khayyâm says:

> Ah, but my Computations, People say,
> Reduced the Year to better reckoning?--Nay,
> 'Twas only striking from the Calendar
> Unborn tomorrow, and dead Yesterday.

Khayyâm was one of Malekshâh's favorite courtiers, but after the latter's death apparently never held important positions under other Saljuq rulers. In the mid-1090s Khayyâm made a hajj pilgrimage to Mecca and then returned to private life and teaching in Nishâpur. According to the next news of him, he was in Balkh around 1112. Several years later, he was in Marv where the Saljuq sultan had summoned him to forecast the weather for a hunting expedition. After 1118, when Sanjar became the sultan, no record exists of anything Khayyâm did. He died in 1131 at some eighty-three years of age.

Besides these few known facts about Khayyâm's life, one can learn a bit more about the man through examining his reputation as recorded by his contemporaries and his personality and views as revealed in his non-poetic writings. As to the former sources, although one can glean some information from contemporary accounts about Khayyâm's scientific reputation, no contemporary record exists of him as a poet. In fact, his acquaintance Nezâmi 'Aruzi, who visited his grave in Nishâpur around 1135, makes no mention of Khayyâm in the biographical-historical section on Persian poets in the famous prose work called *Four Discourses*, although he does relate two anecdotes about Khayyâm in the section on scientists.(27) The first record of Khayyâm as a poet does not come until nearly fifty years after his death in a chronicle of Islamic world poets in which an Arabic composition is attributed to him.

On the question of Khayyâm's personality as revealed in his non-poetic writings, Dashti presents an appealing, idealized portrait that goes beyond inferences from documentary evidence. In Dashti's view, Khayyâm was a scholar who, beyond special expertise in mathematics and philosophy, was well acquainted with all disciplines that played a part in his society; e.g., medicine, astronomy, Koranic Exegesis, Traditions of the Prophet, and Arabic and Persian literatures. He was a quiet, serious, introspective, scholarly man, who avoided philosophical disputation and open expression of opinion. A man totally without ambition, whose circle of acquaintances must have been limited to a small group of similarly exceptional, kindred spirits, Khayyâm was, in Dashti's view, one of those intellectual individuals who cannot be characterized in terms of popular beliefs, but rather who perforce face problems such as philosophical doubts which ordinary people do not come to face. His private doubts and literary taste seem to have led him to produce for his friends the *robâ'i*s under scrutiny.

In *A Moment with Khayyâm*, after describing the poet's personality, Dashti chooses thirty-six quatrains as "key" poems to serve as the basis of his edition of seventy-five quatrains attributed to Khayyâm. All fourteen of Hedâyat's "key" poems are among Dashti's "key" poems. Similarly, thirty of Dashti's key poems are included in the larger Forughi-Ghani list of sixty-six "key" poems. Thus, although only fifty of the some 250 quatrains these three Iranian editors attribute to Khayyâm are identical, still Hedâyat, Forughi-Ghani, and Dashti agree on a basic, core group of quatrains that appear in the most reliable collections and anthologies. In other words, there seems to be little reason to question the likelihood that 'Omar Khayyâm composed most of the thirty-six quatrains Dashti attributes to him. However, the wide discrepancy beyond the limits of the "key" poems makes impossible confident attribution of other poems to Khayyâm until less subjective grounds for supposing that Khayyâm is the author are found, such as real clues that critical editions of Khayyâm's non-poetic writings might provide. Until such time as definite authorship is established or until it becomes definite that authorship can never be established, the satisfying literary fact is that all of the poems in question exist in manuscript from pre-Safavid days: they are authentic products of a self-conscious literary tradition of which Khayyâm was neither founder nor zenith, but merely one of the less prolific and most successful practitioners. This fact ought to be enough to encourage literary critics of traditional Persian poetry to pursue serious study of these quatrains in terms of the aesthetic, an obviously more important issue, that obtained at the period of their composition and in terms of the aesthetic which reader-critics today espouse. Although the last word about what poems Khayyâm actually composed may never be said, the first word on the poems qua poems remains unsaid.

The upshot of Iranian scholarship is that the name 'Omar Khayyâm in conjunction with Persian quatrains has meaning only with reference to a small group of philosophically oriented poems which Khayyâm, never a professional poet, may be presumed to have composed. In view of this, it makes sense to use the name 'Omar Khayyâm in another sense in relation to Persian quatrains, somewhat in the sense that the names of Horace and Juvenal delineate kinds of satire. Assuming that Khayyâm is the actual author of some few poems, one can characterize the sort of quatrain that Iranian scholars attribute to Khayyâm as "Khayyâmic," as opposed to Sufi and romantic love quatrains, for example.

In cultural terms, such Khayyâmic quatrains depict mosques, houris, and the cities of Tus, Baghdâd, and Balkh. Temporally, their setting must lie some time between the middle of the seventh century when Arab Moslems invaded Iran and brought to an end the Sâsânid empire and the middle of the thirteenth century when Mongol invaders from the east conquered the region and put an end to the Baghdâd caliphate. That the setting is Iran specifically and not other regions of the Islamic world becomes apparent with allusions to Jamshid, Bahrâm, Kay Kâvus, Kay Qobâd, and Parviz, all of them legendary or actual rulers in pre-Islamic Iran. The further allusions to the four elements, the hand of fate, chess, caravanserais and the phoenix are all culturally consonant with the same time and place. Of course, the mere fact that the poems are in Persian further defines the setting because the New Persian language used in the poems attributed to Khayyâm did not become a vehicle for literary expression until the middle of the ninth century. In short, Khayyâmic quatrains internally reflect time in the Iranian plateau from the tenth through the twelfth centuries when it would have been possible for such poems to have been composed. Culturally, they reflect the following assumptions, conditions, and attitudes which were facts of life for Khayyâm and his audience at the end of the eleventh century: belief in a single, all-powerful Allâh, acceptance of an all-powerful ruler as a natural political

ondition, the merging of Arab Moslem and pre-Islamic Iranian traditions and mythologies, a religio-cultural inclination to see individual effort and struggle as fruitless in the face of fate, and a thoroughgoing sense of pessimism combined with a realization that the best must be made of the moment because tomorrow is an unknown quantity determined by divine or royal design or caprice.

According to Dashti, the Khayyâmic quatrain is distinctive in the context of traditional Persian lyric verse in numerous ways. First, it exhibits simplicity of style, unmarked by artificiality, tautology, or excessive use of rhetorical devices. Second, its basic posture is reflection on the puzzle of being and the final cause of creation, and confusion at the successive states of being and nonbeing. It features concern with the constant and continuous transformation and evolution characteristic of existing forms and the view that after a form ceases to exist and elements which composed that form return to their source, it seems unlikely that that form will appear again with exactly the same characteristics which it first had. Nature is at work and creates new forms from the elements of old forms which have passed away. Third, its message is that life is a unique and incomparable blessing which, since it comes to a person only once, ought not to be misused or wasted. This leads to obvious sensitivity to the beauties of nature and to other pleasurable aspects of life. Fourth, because human beings are without power or choice, as the manner of creation and the nature of human destiny prove, the quatrains argue that striving for success and searching for answers, or nurturing feelings of sadness and regret are useless and unproductive. Fifth, the Khayyâmic quatrain gives voice to indifference or, at least, doubt with respect to what is held indisputable in society. Thus, the Khayyâmic voice does not express fear of the outcome of things and consequent repentance and supplication.

The following two very popular Khayyâmic quatrains, together with the already quoted fourteen quatrains in Hedâyat's collection, clearly embody the poet's view of the role of the individual human being in the scheme of things.

> This ancient caravanserai called the world,
> home of the multicolored steed of night and day,
> is where a hundred Jamshids feasted, and
> a hundred Bahrâms ruled in splendor, and left.

* * *

> This jar was once a sad lover too,
> caught in the tangles of a loved one's hair.
> This handle that you see upon its neck
> once, when a hand, caressed a loved one's throat.(28)

55

As Khayyâm sees it, if the all-powerful Iranian emperors Jamshid and Bahrâm were unable to remain in the world for longer than their appointed time, then more ordinary mortals should be that much more certain of their own mortality and insignificance. The second quatrain restates the transience of human life, but focuses primarily on a sort of physical continuity in the natural order. The piece of pottery to which the speaker draws attention has been literally fashioned out of earth and clay to which the decomposed body of a lover of yore has contributed: the handle at the throat of the jar may well have been once the hand of the lover around the beloved's neck. This Khayyâmic sense of continuity, of the relationship of the past to the present, may not be a great consolation. But it becomes an integral part of the stance which FitzGerald's Khayyâm assumes in trying to make sense of life.

A comparison of Persian Khayyâmic quatrains with Edward FitzGerald's *Rubaíyát of Omar Khayyám* reveals that thematic and stylistic features of the former are further delineated and defined during the course of FitzGerald's 404 lines of verse, divided into 101 quatrains. Examples are: the nostalgia for a simpler, better, heroic past, the individualist's search on his or her own for answers, the straightforward, unflowery style of inquiry, and the dignity of the persona of Khayyâm in maturely and realistically accepting his obvious fate.

It is significant that such thematic and stylistic features are important Iranian cultural phenomena. Khayyâmic individualism parallels Iranian hesitance to accept institutional answers. Khayyâmic fatalism and pessimism seem a distinctive aspect of twentieth-century intellectual life in Iran. Khayyâmic calm in the face of the recognized plight and realization that all that humans can do is live while they still can and take advantage of what is available to them now seems the intuitive and distinctive choice of many Iranian intellectuals who reject traditionalist, past-oriented wishful thinking, the other worldly focus of the Sufi tradition, and the future-oriented "American" view of life as progress.

From the title of his poem, FitzGerald expects readers to be familiar with the life of Omar Khayyâm and with the poem's form: *robâ'iyât*, "Rubaíyát" for FitzGerald, a sequential poem composed of a series of quatrains. The 101 quatrain stanzas, each of them consisting of four lines of iambic pentameter with an aaba end rhyme scheme, present a day in the life of this fictional title character, who is the poem's speaker. FitzGerald's poem opens at dawn and closes at dusk on this particular day, which the speaker spends brooding about things in the tavern outside of whose doors he stands impatiently at the poem's beginning.

FitzGerald's representation of a day in the life of its title character exhibits four moods or phases. The first section of the poem (stanzas 1-24) establishes the setting and voices both *carpe diem* and *eheu fugaces* themes. In the much quoted stanzas 11 and 12 appears Khayyâm's most positive statement of possible earthly happiness for human individuals:

proved for him, there can be no afterlife, just as there has never been a just
God:

96

Yet Ah, that Spring should vanish with the Rose!
That Youth's sweet-scented manuscript should close!
   The Nightingale that in the branches sang,
Ah whence, and whither flown again, who knows!

97

Would but the Desert of the Fountain yield
One glimpse--if dimly, yet indeed reveal'd
   To which the fainting Traveller might spring,
As springs the trampled herbage of the field!

98

Would but some wingéd Angel ere too late
Arrest the yet unfolded Roll of Fate,
   And make the stern Recorder otherwise
Enregister, or quite obliterate!

99

Ah Love! could you and I with Him conspire
To grasp this sorry Scheme of Things entire,
   Would not we shatter it to bits--and then
Remould it nearer to the Heart's Desire!

Khayyâm expresses these regrets maturely, almost courageously as an
individual willing to stand alone without false hopes, props or opiates. In a
sense, he accepts the view that he expressed toward the end of the first
section of the poem (stanza 24), now better understood by himself and
through him by the reader. Of course, Khayyâm's reflections as the poem
proceeds are not without confusion. He is naturally hard put to find a
satisfying answer to his questions about life's meaning especially under the
pressure of the fact that his own individual bird of time has long since
begun to flutter (stanza 7). The reappearance and restatement of issues and
questions throughout the poem, as well as its meandering qualities as a
monologue, may persuade the reader that Khayyâm will face the same
questions again tomorrow, and the day after. This does not make him less of
an individualist standing on his own; but it does imply that in the cultural
history of individualistic Iranians, there are no final or permanent answers.
Such individualists are likely to struggle throughout life with the dilemmas
posed once they reject material progress and religion. Of course, in
FitzGerald's *Rubaíyát*, Khayyâm would really like to be able to forget
everything, to be relieved of his anxieties. He drinks not with the classic
carpe diem purposes of enjoying a transient life to the fullest at the moment
and of finding a love with whom to enjoy that moment, but rather to escape

from the present, to deaden his perceptions and senses, and to drown out the thought of death.

This Khayyâmic escape from the present through the reduction of one's capacity to feel may be philosophical in its inspiration, but it seems to parallel the reaction to the facts of the political present in the case of a startling number of modernist Iranian literary figures. Sâdeq Hedâyat (1903-1951) tried to find forgetfulness in opium both in *The Blind Owl* and in real life. Nimâ Yushij (1895-1960), the 'father' of modernist Persian poetry, took opium three times a day during his later adult years.(29) The major poets Ahmad Shâmlu (b. 1925) and Mehdi Akhavân-e Sâles (b. 1928) are described by friends and acquaintances as having gone through periods of dependence upon narcotics. Gholâmhosayn Sâ'edi (1935/6-1985), a leading writer of fiction and his age's premier dramatist, is thought by some to have drunk himself to death.(30)

The long-time expatriate writer Bozorg 'Alavi (b. 1904) appears to sense the significance of Khayyâmic drinking in the contemporary world when he responded in 1973 to an interviewer's question about his opinion of Jalâl Al-e Ahmad (1923-1969). 'Alavi observed: ". . . he apparently never stopped smoking and drinking. This drinking is a form of numbing a person . . . Those who drink, those who smoke opium, those who rely on narcotics . . . want to prevent their senses from being fully aroused. They want . . . not to think any more, not to feel any more. And this kind of temperament I find in Al-e Ahmad."(31)

Whether or not similar cultural circumstances have prompted such similar "fleeing the day" from the age of Khayyâm to that of Khomayni remains to be seen. Khayyâm obviously seems to fail in his attempts to avoid facing the facts of life; but still he is honest about his failure, and will presumably begin to struggle anew on the morrow. It also remains to be seen how successful and honest Hedâyat, Al-e Ahmad, Sâ'edi, and other twentieth-century Iranian literary artists have been in the same regard.

As individualistic as Khayyâm is in FitzGerald's *Rubaíyát* and even in his rejection of religious and other establishment values associated with Iranian culture, he nevertheless sees and represents things in Iranian terms. For Ferdowsi, the Iranian homeland is *Irânzamin*, the physical and geographical region over which the Persian Iranians held sway, their native region, in contrast with the Arab and Greek worlds to the west and the legendary *Turânzamin* or land of Turkic peoples to the east. The Iranian monarchy in Ferdowsi's *Shâhnâmeh* is charged to protect this homeland of the Persians. For Khayyâm, the physical *Irânzamin* is transmuted into a cultural homeland of the imagination of the medieval Persian intellectual. In that mental homeland live David, Moses, Jamshid, Bâhram Gur and Mahmud of Ghazneh, Zoroastrian priests and Sufi *pirs* [elders], Iranian mountains, plains, salt deserts, caravanserais, bazaars, Islamic schools, and the like. He may reject Zoroastrianism and Islam as faith systems, but he is sensitive to them as images bound together distinctively in his Persian Iranian culture of the Saljuq era. When the contemporary Iranian intellectual and social critic Jalâl Al-e Ahmad argues that the bases of Iranianness in the latter half of the twentieth century are Shi'i Islam, the Persian language, and Iranian cultural traditions, he may mean them as literal, narrowly construed facets of Iranianness. But even the Iranian Zoroastrian or Turkish-speaking Azarbâyjâni deals today with Iranian life in terms created and maintained through Islam and the Persian language. Khayyâm's Iranian world was that of Islam and what preceded it, with Arabic and Persian elements, in a physically distinctive Iranian environment. And the cultural nationalism that he displays toward the features of this environment as evidenced by the images used in FitzGerald's *Rubaíyât* remains true of educated Iranians today, even those who are secular-minded. The texture of imagery in Hedâyat's *The Blind Owl* is a good example.

The influence of the physical environment in this Khayyâmic cultural nationalism is also Iranian. It is the nature of the Iranian plateau region, with its difficult terrain and harsh climate of cold winters, hot summers, and general aridity, but with a springtime whose greenness gives Iranians a glimpse of an ideal which prompts Iranian poets to attempt to see the world in garden terms. After all, that would make Iran perfect, heavenly in fact. But the lessons of the physical environment offered through avalanches, earthquakes, springtime floods, and the brown barrenness make the poet wary of claims that human endeavor can change the environment into a "sown" field. On the other hand, the land naturally has been a hotbed for the development of religions because its inhabitants seem easily disposed to think of their world as a desert, as a desolate environment prompting them to put faith in a god to save them or at least to provide for them or to repay them in a hereafter for suffering in the desert.

The special appeal of Iranian springtime as the ideal moment in the year is not lost on FitzGerald's Khayyâm. In stanza 7, he urges that the "winter-garment of Repentance" be flung "in the fire of Spring," while he observes, in stanza 4, "the New Year reviving old Desires." Khayyâm's point in the latter allusion has to do with the fact that the Iranian new year, called *nowruz* [new day] in Persian, occurs each year on the vernal equinox, the very beginning of spring, March 21st usually.

The Iranian New Year is the most joyous moment in the Iranian calendar. Preparations for it begin with spring house cleaning and the purchase or sewing of new clothes. On the last Tuesday evening of the old year, a ceremony is held at which people jump over small fires, imploring as they do so that the yellow sallowness of the old year be drawn from them and that the red life of the new year become theirs. On New Year's eve, there is a formal dinner, with a special fish platter not served at other times during the year. Throughout the New Year celebrations, a special collection of objects, seven of them whose names begin with the letter 's,' is displayed on a table or mantlepiece. *Nowruz* is a time for family togetherness, visits to friends, and vacation trips. Traditionally, employees are given a special bonus at this time. Schools and offices close for a week or two. The last official event in the celebration occurs on the thirteenth day of the New Year, when everyone makes an effort to leave their homes and get to the the countryside for a picnic. They take with them on this excursion the greens they have grown at home during the holiday which are now thrown away, presumably absorbing all of the old atmosphere in the home.

The relevance of spring and the Iranian New Year for the Persianist is manifold. Spring happens to be the most popular aspect of nature depicted in Persian verse throughout history. In addition, spring is the season of romantic love, the most depicted emotional state in Persian poetry. The two images coalesce in the following typical poem by Qatrân, an eleventh-century Azarbâyjâni poet:

> [1]The New Year's festival comes once each year for one day;
> in seeing you I have a perpetual New Year's.
> [2]The rose bush is full of roses for one day;
> in your face a rose ever blooms for me.
> [3]I can pick violets from the garden for one day;
> your thick tresses are violets always.
> [4]The narcissus appears on the plains one week only;
> your eyes are narcissus visible all year long.
> [5]The narcissus is not fresh if not wide awake;
> your black narcissi are ever fresh asleep or awake.
> [6]Nature's jasmine appears in spring only; while
> on the hyacinth of your hair are jasmine night and day.(32)

In addition, spring and the Iranian New Year become images in Persian literature for social, political, and psychological states. Hedâyat provides a graphic example in *The Blind Owl*. Finally, one can view such conflicts as that between Rostam and Sohrâb as between winter and spring. Spring is youthful, promising, and evanescent, representing the garden life which is an unrealizable cultural ideal.

Because Khayyâm himself realizes that he cannot maintain his springtime garden life, what is ultimately most significant about the Khayyâmic view for Iranian intellectuals today is the individualistic, non-establishment skepticism it voices. Throughout Iranian history, literary Iranians have seemed to feel special appreciation for other Iranians who refuse to accept the view of the powers that be or who live their own lives. In twentieth-century Iran, Khayyâm has been mythologized into a figure quite different from what the known facts about his biography imply. But no matter, the view is that he bucked the tide of religious orthodoxy and dared to say what many Iranians feel in their heart of hearts: that answers which governments give about human and social progress buttressed with technology and science and the answers offered by religion neglect to account for that occasional or perhaps frequent flash of insight to the effect that the only meaning to human life lies in the individual lives of human beings. 'Omar Khayyâm remains a hero for many secular-minded Iranian intellectuals for this reason.

Over a century after Khayyâm's death appeared a literary work which presents an opposite Iranian stance, that of the literary intellectual who survives by adjusting to the powers that be and living personally and artistically within existing social and political constraints. In addition, the work, which is called *Golestân* [The Rose Garden] (1258), represents another and contrary Iranian view of the ideal garden and human mortality.(33) *The Rose Garden* is the most famous and imitated work of Persian prose in history. Its author Sa'di (c.1215-c.1290) is the acknowledged master stylist of Persian prose and verse in the classical period. More about Sa'di as a poet appears in the next chapter, while here a brief description of his *Rose Garden* and its cultural significance seems an appropriate balance to the already represented Khayyâmic view and stance.

Sa'di lived in a particularly violent and difficult age. Shortly after his birth the first wave of Mongol invasions devastated much of the Iranian plateau, although his home town of Shirâz was spared because of an accommodation between a regional dynasty and the Mongols. Sa'di travelled widely in youth and became a court poet and writer. He chose his pen name "Sa'di" in honor of a royal patron to whom he dedicated his *Rose Garden*. A second Mongol wave led by Changiz Khân's grandson Hulegu brought the Baghdad Caliphate to its end in 1258, the year in which Sa'di completed *The Rose Garden*. In every regard, Sa'di's was an age in which survivors had to be realistic, make compromises, and espouse a utilitarian ethics and in which the death and destruction wreaked on much of Iran inevitably encouraged literary Iranians to turn to religion, either for an explanation of such inexplicable events or surcease from them.

Sa'di's stylistic brilliance and practical outlook make him a perhaps more representative literary Iranian than the mythologized, individualistic and heterodox Khayyâm. But a consequence in modern times has been mixed feelings on the part of some readers, much impressed by Sa'di's mastery of Persian but somewhat disappointed at his accommodating attitude toward authority.

As for *The Rose Garden*, a work which brought Sa'di popularity abroad during the Age of the Englightenment and special appreciation on the part of such American Transcendentalists as Emerson and Thoreau, it presents an Iranian world with monarchy at its center and, through anecdotal prose tales interspersed with apposite verses, advocates a commonsensical dervish life style. Both its recognition of the centrality of the patriarchal monarch in Iranian life and its didactic tone are significantly typical of pre-modern Persian literature. But what is more significant in the context of the Khayyâmic view of the ideal life and world and his concomitant skepticism is Sa'di's vision of the organizing image and metaphor of his work, the rose garden.

63

Sa'di's *Rose Garden* promises to bloom forever, to offer its readers permanent springtime throughout the year and a refuge from the harsh climate and facts of life beyond the book. In this light, *The Rose Garden* serves purposes similar to other important Iranian art forms and monuments, among them the paradise garden in stone represented by the Apadana at Persepolis, the heavenly garden depicted in many traditional, Persian pile carpet patterns, the decorative elements in many pre-modern illuminated manuscripts, and actual formal Persian gardens with their distinctive communication of perfect order, rationality, and tranquillity, qualities which Iranian life beyond those walled enclosures presumably did not often offer. It is no exaggeration to suggest that almost every work in imaginative Persian literature needs at least momentary appreciative consideration as a reflection of its author's views about the ideal Iranian world as a paradise garden, as a potentially enduring *nowruz* [new year]. At the same time, Sa'di sees his *Rose Garden* as a means by which he might endure. In other words, he expects to live through his art and the good name it will give him forever.

3

PERSIAN CLASSICISM, AESTHETICS OF DECORATION, AND AMBIVALENCE

> O, if only I could compose poetry like Hâfez and like
> him possess the sensitivity to establish a relationship
> with all of the intimate moments in the lives of all
> future humankind.   Forugh Farrokhzâd(34)

The most frequently owned book in Iran after the Koran may well be the
Divân [Collected Poems] of Hâfez (c.1320-c.1390), the premier lyric poet in
the history of Persian literature. Iranians still turn to Hâfez's *Divân*, open it
to a random page, and choose a verse, couplet, or whole *ghazal* poem at
random as an augury. They quote Hâfez in everyday conversation, allude to
him in writing of all sorts, and recite his verses in social situations.
Scholars almost yearly publish new editions of his *Divân*, and argue
heatedly about verbal variants and the authenticity of individual couplets and
whole ghazals. Since World War II, scores of books and hundreds of articles
on the poet have appeared, their authors including a government minister, a
provincial governor, a senator, a university library director, Shi'i Moslem
clerics, popular writers, and assorted academics.(35) UNESCO designated
1988 as "The Year of Hâfez," which led to a spate of publications in Iran,
many of them naturally interpreting the poet as philosophically in tune with
the Islamic Republic.(36)

Hâfez was a kindred spirit and poetic ideal for Forugh Farrokhzâd in her
epoch-making career. The expatriate, leftist writer Bozorg 'Alavi (b. 1904)
recalls reading Hâfez regularly in prison after being incarcerated in 1937 by
the Pahlavi authorities for alleged Communist activities. 'Alavi's biographer
reports that on his first visit to 'Alavi's home in East Berlin in 1973, the
author insisted on reading aloud some Hâfez as entertainment.(37) For the
theatre director, dramatist, and minor poet Sa'id Soltânpur whom the Islamic
Republic of Iran executed in June 1981 for "warring against God," Hâfez
was an often cited model of national ideals. The moderate modernist poet
Nâder Nâderpur (b. 1929) consciously reflects on Hâfez for inspiration in his
own verse and has even conducted private seminars on Hâfez's poetry.(38)
Leading modernist poet Ahmad Shâmlu (b. 1925), a steadfastly *engagé* and

opposé voice, devoted years to editing Hâfez's poems, publishing his efforts in a 1975 volume, twice reprinted since. As for Hâfez's preeminence in the Persian literary pantheon, Iranian readers and critics are nearly unanimous in thinking of him as the poet's poet in the Persian language and as the literary artist who best represents aesthetic and cultural ideals past and present.

This characterization of the Iranian view as "nearly unanimous" leaves room for the most outspoken dissenter, the Azarbâyjâni social reformer Ahmad Kasravi (1890-1946), whose rejection of Hâfez is as culturally telling as is the general praise for the poet. For Kasravi, who was at first a Shi'i cleric, then an official in the Ministry of Justice, then a teacher and historian, and finally a self-styled leader of a reform movement, was an Iranian intellectual who attempted to eliminate paradox, ambivalence, contradictions, and the balancing of polar opposites from his cultural personality in a single-minded drive to improve Iran. But the rejection of such dualism led Kasravi, whose movement never attracted significant support, to reject lyric poetry in general and to argue quixotically for impracticable changes in language and society.(39)

On the other hand, Ruhollâh Khomayni (1902-1989) had an almost lifelong interest in Hâfez's poetry. In the mid-1930s, he wrote Hâfez-inspired ghazals and spent almost as much time reading the latter's *Divân* as he spent reading the Koran. In 1979, under the pen named "Hendi" appeared a slim volume of traditionalist verse attributed to Khomayni. Its thirty-five ghazals showed the unmistakable influence of the fourteenth-century poet from Shirâz.(40) Why Khomayni found Hâfez so appealing and inspiring will become apparent in the later treatment in this chapter of Sufistic elements in Hâfez's verse.

In any case, Hâfez is the culminating phenomenon in the brilliant lyric verse tradition that began in Greater Khorâsân with Rudaki (d. 940/1) and others some five centuries earlier. Hâfez's poems exhibit the final harmony of the separate strains of descriptive, amatory, didactic, homiletic, mystical, and panegyric expression which developed severally and then partially merged in earlier periods of Persian literature. In his poetry, these strains blend to form, as 'Ali Dashti puts it, a distinctive melody, sometimes Khayyâmic in tone or stance, sometimes like Sa'di (c.1215-c.1290) in lyricism, and like the Sufi Jalâloddin Rumi (1207-1273) in intensity of feeling.(41)

The Khayyâmic stance has received its due in the previous chapter, while the intensity of Sufi feeling associated with Rumi receives attention in due course in this chapter. But Hâfez's debt to earlier poets, chief among them Sa'di, in terms of the craft of lyric verse here deserves brief consideration as a preliminary to the business of this chapter, which is the discernment of cultural elements in the Persian aesthetic as illustrated by Hâfez's ghazals.

For many Iranian readers, Sa'di is the most typical of Persian poets of the first rank and the most respected stylist ever. A peripatetic court poet and born surviver, whose cleverness and understanding of human nature served

66

him in good stead during and after the cataclysm of successive waves of Mongol invasions and in the context of service in various courts of capricious rulers, Sa'di is famous for three works.(42) First and foremost is the *Rose Garden* (1258), a prose-verse compendium of tales and world-wise advice, the style of which even such contemporary authors as Âl-e Ahmad acknowledge as influential and inspirational in Persian prose today. Then there is Sa'di's *Flower Garden* (1257), a verse composition of some 4,000 *Shâhnâmeh*-like couplets and the most famous moralistic piece of premodern Persian literature. More relevant to the subject at hand is Sa'di's third major work, his *Divân*, which reveals him as the verse stylist *par excellence* of classical Persian poetry. No Persian lyric poet after Sa'di could afford not to be intimately acquainted with his ghazals, including Hâfez, whose own ghazals exhibit numerous echoes of his Shirâzi predecessor.

Among Sa'di's ghazals, the most famous is the following, a poem often referred to as "The Caravan Ghazal," which epitomizes the courtly, love ghazal as of the second half of the thirteenth century.

[1]O camel-driver, go slowly because my soul's peace is departing
and that heart which I had is with my heart's thief departing.
[2]I have remained separated from her, helpless and afflicted
            because of her,
as if far from her a sting were going into my bones.
[3]I thought with magic and charms to conceal my inner wound.
But it will not stay hidden as blood spills over my threshold.
[4]O camel-driver, stop the camel-litter, do not hasten away
            with the caravan,
for in love of that flowing cypress, my soul seems to be departing.
[5]She departs, moving proudly, and I taste the poison of loneliness.
Seek traces of me no longer as all signs are from my heart departing.
[6]My proud beloved passed by and left me a sickly life.
I am like a fiery censer as from my head smoke is departing.
[7]Despite all her injustice and that baseless covenant of hers,
I hold her memory in my heart or it goes onto my tongue:
[8]Come again and sit before my eyes, o lovely heart-stealer,
for my disturbed state and screams go from earth to the heavens.
[9]At night I neither sleep until dawn nor heed anyone's advice,
and I am not going this way on purpose,
            for from my hands the reins are departing.
[10]I said I'd cry until the camel, donkey-like, gets stuck in the mud;
this I cannot do either because with the caravan my heart is departing.
[11]Patience from union with my beloved, turning away
            from my beloved,
although beyond my power, my work goes far beyond that.
[12]Of the soul's departure from the body they say all kinds of things.
I, with my own eyes, have seen my soul departing.

[13]"Sa'di, o faithless one, this groaning is unbecoming."
But I cannot endure torment, my situation is going beyond groaning.

As a typical ghazal, Sa'di's "Caravan" poem exhibits thirteen end-stopped couplets and the poet's own *nom de plume* at the end of the poem. The subject of the poem is, typically, love, with the lover-speaker revealing a conventional lover's plight vis-à-vis separation from an aloof, perhaps cruel, beloved. Despite some specificity in the setting of a caravan's departure, the ghazal is likewise typical in its representation of the beloved and the lover's emotions in stylized, idealized terms. Also obvious in the translation is a certain shapelessness to the ghazal, a lack of inevitability in the order of its constituent couplets some of which might be deleted without serious impairment to the structure of theme or imagery. In short, whatever intensity and verbal magic imbues the original ghazal, one of the best known poems in the Persian language, few traces of poetic integrity and other effects grace the translation.

This implies that formal, aural features of such Persian ghazals may be more significant in aesthetic terms than thematic and other features of content. A few basic features highlighted in the following transliterated text of Sa'di's poem verify this implication and provide a basis for several specific observations about the Persian aesthetic.

[1]ay sârbân âhesteh row k-ârâm-e **jânam miravad**
v-ân del keh bâ khod dâshtam bâ delsetânam **miravad**
[2]man mândeh'am mahjur **az-u** bichâreh-o ranjur **az-u**
gu'i keh nishi **dur az-u** dar ostokhânam **miravad**
[3]goftam beh nayrang-o fosun penhân konam rish-e da**run**
penhân nemimânad keh **khun** bar âstânam **miravad**
[4]mahmel bedâr ay sârbân tondi makon bâ kârvân
k-az 'eshq-e ân sarv-e ravân gu'i ravânam **miravad**
[5]u miravad dâman **keshân** man zahr-e tanhâ'i **cheshân**
digar mapors az man **neshân** k-az del **neshânam miravad**
[6]bogzasht yâr-e sarkesham bogzâsht 'aysh-e nâkhesham
chon majmari porâtesham k-az sar **dokhânam miravad**
[7]bâ ân hameh bi**dâd-e u** v-in 'ahd-e bibony**âd-e u**
dar sineh dâram **yâd-e u** yâ bar zab**ânam miravad**
[8]bâz ây-o bar chashmânam ne**shin** ay delsetân-e nâzanin
k-âshub-o faryâd az za**min** bar âsm**ânam miravad**
[9]shab tâ sahar mi naghnavam v-andarz-e kas mi nashnavam
v-in râh na qâsed miravam k-az kaff 'en**ânam miravad**
[10]goftam begeryam tâ ebel chon khar foru mânad beh **gel**
v-in niz natvânam keh **del** bâ karvânam **miravad**
[11]sabr ze vesâl-e **yâr-e man** bar gashtan az didâr-e man
garcheh nabâshad **kâr-e man** ham kâr az ânam **miravad**
[12]dar raftan-e jân az badan guyand har now'i sokhan

man khod be-chashm-e khishtan didam keh **jânam miravad**
[13]sa'di faghân az dast-e **mâ** lâyeq nabud ay bivafâ
tâqat nemiyâram jafâ kâr az **faghânam miravad**.(43)

The transliterated text shows that the original composition consists of an opening closed couplet followed by twelve open couplets, the whole poem exhibiting a monorhyme pattern of aa, ba, ca da, etc. The end rhyme throughout the poem consists of the word *miravad* [he/she/it goes, is going] preceded by the pronominal suffix ...*am*[my] attached to words which feature the masculine rhyme syllable *[x]ân*. In other words, the poem exhibits a five-syllable end rhyme which establishes the grammatical pattern of the poem's statements as well. In this case, that a verb concludes each couplet reinforces the fact that all of the couplets are end-stopped: although couplets are linked by means of the monorhyme, each couplet is syntactically independent of preceding and succeeding couplets.

What is remarkable about this pervasive monorhyme scheme is its naturalness. Persian verbs generally appear at the end of clauses, and *miravad* [he/she/it goes, is going] is an everyday word. There are no exotic words in the poem, no startling images either. The poem seems almost artless in construction, a factor in its special appeal because beneath an almost nonchalant surface of what appears a simple pattern is a great deal of craft. For example, readers will note in the transliteration other highlighted syllables not part of the end rhyme, in all but the first, and only closed, couplet. These syllables divide each couplet into four parts, three that rhyme together and the fourth which is part of the overall end rhyme. Here, too, nothing about the rhyme is at all forced, nor is the word order unusual. Without further discussion of instances of alliteration, assonance, puns, and the like, and the metrical pattern's appropriateness to the scene and rhythm of a caravan's departure, readers can appreciate that Sa'di's artful structuring of aural features in the "Caravan Ghazal" point to a hallmark of Persian lyric poetry which is almost always intended to be recited and heard rather than to be read silently. This needs bearing in mind in any evaluation of poems by otherwise such different poets as Akhavân-e Sâles, Farrokhzâd, Ferdowsi, Khâqâni, Khayyâm, Nâderpur, Nimâ Yushij, Qatrân, and Shâmlu, presented in translation throughout this study.

Back to Hâfez, on the subject of the life of this leading figure in Persian poetry, no more is known than about the lives of such famous predecessors as Ferdowsi and Khayyâm. In fact, to observe that Hâfez was born in Shirâz around the year 1320, was a professional poet formally associated with several successive rulers' courts there, had an intimate knowledge of the Koran and Persian literature, composed some five hundred ghazal poems and a handful of poems in other traditional verse forms, was famous in his own lifetime, and died around 1390, practically exhausts the indisputable biographical facts.(44)

No matter, of paramount significance about Hâfez are the facts that his poems have survived and that Iranians have always considered him the apogee of Persian lyric expression. As such and because, in comparison with other great traditions of lyric verse, traditional Persian lyric poetry is distinctive in terms of how it achieves poetic effects, Hâfez's ghazals become a natural focus of attention in any attempt to characterize the nature of Persian lyric poetry.

It may strike some readers as strange that they have never heard of a poet so famous and revered in his own culture as is Hâfez. Part of the explanation for general Western ignorance of Hâfez is that his poetic voice has had no Edward FitzGerald, as Khayyâm's epigrammatic quatrains did, nor a Matthew Arnold, as did Ferdowsi's epic episode of *Rostam and Sohrâb*.(45) Of course, lyric poetry, especially when it is very culture-specific in form and imagery, resists translation more than other literary species. Thus, Hâfez has remained almost mute in the English-speaking world, except for the signal success of Sir William Jones (1746-1794) in an eighteenth-century version of the most famous Hâfezian ghazal of all in the West, a poem generally referred to as the "Turk of Shiraz." Called "A Persian Song," Sir William's poem reads:

> Sweet maid, if thou would'st charm my sight
> and bid these arms thy neck infold;
> that rosy cheek, that lily hand,
> Would give thy poet more delight
> Than all Bocara's vaunted gold
> Than all the gems of Samarcand.
>
> Boy, let yon liquid ruby flow,
> And bid thy pensive heart be glad,
> Whate'er the frowning zealots say:
> Tell them, their Eden cannot show
> A stream so clear as Rocnabad,
> A bower so sweet as Mosellay.
>
> O! when these fair perfidious maids,
> Whose eyes our secret haunts infest,
> Their dear destructive charms display;
> Each glance my tender breast invades,
> And robs my wounded soul of rest,
> As Tartars seize their destin'd prey.
>
> In Vain with love our bosoms glow:
> Can all our tears, can all our sighs,
> New lustre to those charms impart?
> Can cheeks, where living roses blow,
> Where nature spreads her richest dyes,

Require the borrow'd gloss of art?

Speak not of fate: ah! change the theme,
And talk of odours, talk of wine,
Talk of the flowers that round us bloom:
'Tis all a cloud, 'tis all a dream;
To love and joy thy thoughts confine,
Nor hope to pierce the sacred gloom.

Beauty has such resistless power,
Than even the chaste Egyptian dame
Sigh'd for the blooming Hebrew boy:
For her how fatal was the hour,
When to the banks of Nilus came
A youth so lovely and so coy!

But ah! sweet maid, my counsel hear
(Youth should attend when those advise
Whom long experience renders sage):
While music charms the ravish'd ear;
While sparkling cups delight our eyes,
Be gay; and scorn the frowns of age.

What cruel answer have I heard!
And yet, by heaven, I love thee still:
Can aught be cruel from thy lip?
Yet say, how fell that bitter word
From lips which streams of sweetness fill,
Which nought but drops of honey sip?

Go boldly forth, my simple lay,
Whose accents flow with artless ease,
Like orient pearls at random strung:
Thy notes are sweet, the damsels say;
But O! far sweeter, if they please
The nymph for whom these notes are sung.(46)

For its English audience, "A Persian Song" exuded exotic allusiveness in references to the proverbially wealthy Central Asian cities of Samarqand and Bokhârâ, Shirâz's Roknâbâd River and Mosallâ garden, Turkic armies that had invaded the Iranian region in successive waves of Ghaznavids, Saljuqs and others from the tenth century onward, the famous Koranic story of the infatuation of Potiphar's wife Zolaykhâ with Joseph, and the likening of the whole poem to "orient pearls." Of course, such allusions would have been conventional and commonplace in the original Persian for Hâfez's fourteenth-century audience. In both cases, however, such imagery seems intended not to impart the impression of an individual speaker's representation of a personal or private experience, but rather to provide texture for a generalized experience. Hâfez accomplishes this through the use of highly conventional diction, images, subjects, rhetorical devices, and aural features of the ghazal verse form, as described above in the discussion of Sa'di's "Caravan Ghazal." In "A Persian Song," except for the exotic Persian local color, Sir William is operating in a similarly classicist tradition. In other words, he makes no attempt to communicate a novel experience in a novel way; rather, he voices conventional romantic and almost courtly love themes and a secondary, equally conventional, *carpe diem* theme with an almost Khayyâmic implication that death is likely the end to everything, in a style equally conventional. That he succeeds is the result of his skill at manipulating familiar, rather than experimenting with new, chords.

This is a significant feature in the Persian aesthetic: its enduring classicism, exhibited through the adherence to convention in terms of subject and manner of treatment and through the emphasis on generalized, typical, almost impersonal experiences as opposed to romantic or modernist lyric statements that emphasize individuality, reality, subjectivity, and uniqueness.(47)

In cultural terms, such aesthetic classicism implies conservatism and resistance to innovation. This has certainly been the case in the evolution of modernist Persian poetry in the twentieth century, as most readers and a majority of poets and critics have been unwilling to accept poetic works which exhibit a lack of traditional forms and styles. Interestingly, even such thoroughgoing modernists as Farrokhzâd, Sepehri, and Akhavân-e Sâles maintain traditional quantitative metrical feet in their poems, while even Nimâ Yushij, the "father" of modernist Persian poetry, composed as many traditionalist as modernist poems during his forty-year career.

However, despite the very clear Hâfezian echoes in "A Persian Song," much about Sir William's poem is English and not Persian, so much in fact that it seems less a translation than an English poem which a Hâfezian ghazal inspired. Therefore, to discern further characteristics of the Persian muse therein, one must turn to the Persian original, here presented in its most popular Persian variant followed by a literal translation.

اگر آن ترک شیرازی به دست آرد دل ما را / به خال هندویش بخشم سمرقند و بخارا را

بده ساقی می باقی که در جنت نخواهی یافت / کنار آب رکن آباد و گلگشت مصلا را

فغان کاین لولیان شوخ شیرین کار شهرآشوب / چنان بردند صبر از دل که ترکان خوان یغما را

72

بآب و رنگ و خال و خط چه حاجت روی زیبا را   زعشق ناتمام ما جمال یار مستغنی است

که عشق از پرده عصمت برون آرد زلیخا را   من از آن حسن روزافزون که یوسف داشت دانستم

جواب تلخ می‌زیبد لب لعل شکرخا را   اگر دشنام فرمایی و گر نفرین دعا گویم

جوانان سعادتمند پند پیر دانا را   نصیحت گوش کن جانا که از جان دوست‌تر دارند

که کس نگشود و نگشاید به حکمت این معما را   حدیث از مطرب و می گو و راز دهر کمتر جو

غزل گفتی و در سفتی بیا و خوش بخوان حافظ

که بر نظم تو افشاند فلک عقد ثریا را

[1]If that Turk of Shirâz should accept my heart,
for her Indian mole I will give up Samarqand and Bokhârâ.
[2]Cupbearer, pour the remaining wine since you will not find
in paradise the banks of the Roknâbâd and the Mosallâ garden.
[3]Alas that these vivacious, beguiling, city-disrupting gypsies
have plundered patience from the heart
             just as the Turks take the public banquet.
[4]The beloved's beauty is beyond needing my imperfect love;
what need has the beautiful face of color, beauty marks, and eyeliner?
[5]I have known Joseph's daily-increasing beauty which enabled love
to bring Zolaykhâ from behind the curtain of modesty.
[6]If you malign or curse me, I am nonetheless your suppliant;
the bitter answer suits the ruby, sugar-chewing lip.
[7]Heed advice, o beloved, since fortunate youths
love the advice of the wise elder more than life:
[8]Talk about the minstrel and wine and search less
             for the secret of the world,
a puzzle which no one will ever solve with philosophy.
[9]You have uttered a ghazal and pierced the pearl, o Hâfez;
come recite it pleasingly that upon your verse
             the heavens scatter the necklace of Pleiades.(48)

    In this ghazal's opening couplet, Hâfez presents the reader with a striking hyperbole. Perhaps recognizing the impossibility of verbalizing in concrete terms either perfect beauty or the effect of what he may feel is perfect beauty, the poetic speaker asserts that should the object of his affection accept or reciprocate his love, he would be ready to proffer the distant, proverbially wealthy and exotic cities of Samarqand and Bokhârâ in exchange for the beauty mark on the beloved's face.

The second couplet abruptly shifts subject, tone, and address, as the speaker turns to the cupbearer and asks for wine, intimating that the request stems from the realization that paradise, whatever bliss it may offer, will be incapable of matching the exquisiteness of the existential moment beside the Roknâbâd River in Shirâz's Mosallâ garden.

In the third couplet, the speaker generalizes about the devastating appeal of the class of beloveds, here called "gypsies," of which it seems assumed the "Turk of Shirâz" is a prime example. The allure of such beloveds is described with the image of Turkish plunderers, a simile as striking as the preceding hyperbole and paradox. In fact, the reader's impression after three couplets may be that of bombardment with "poetic" extravagance in terms of the power of the conceits and images.

In couplet 4, the speaker considers the "Turk of Shirâz" as epitomizing the perfection of beauty and attraction described in couplet 3, and depicts the beloved as not needing the love of the likes of him. In all three couplets dealing with love to this point, the speaker seems to be speaking to himself, his mood and stance vis-à-vis the beloved the sort of traditional, perhaps courtly love mode observed in Sir William Jones' "A Persian Song."

Couplet 5 fits into the general context of love and the lover's total enthrallment in couplets 1, 3, and 4. Through the allusion to the story of Joseph and Zolaykhâ, a symbolic narrative very popular with poets working in the tradition of Sufi imagery and thought, Hâfez may inspire the reader to interpret the images of the beloved as an implicit description of an emotion and relationship beyond terrestrial, romantic love and as a reference to a beloved only metaphorically possessed of corporeal existence.

The sixth couplet reiterates the beloved's embodiment of the quality of self-sufficiency, here demonstrated through scornful aloofness, with the image of the beloved's rebuffs further developing the courtly love stance.

In the seventh couplet, the speaker suddenly exhorts the beloved, previously portrayed as perfect, aloof, reproachful, and self-sufficient, to bear in mind that youths blessed with good fortune hold dear the advice of the wise elder and cherish it, in fact, more than their own lives, hearts, or beloveds. This couplet seems to give voice to a distinct, third theme:-- couplets 1, 3, 4, 5, and 6, treated love; couplet 2 was *carpe diem*; but the explicit motivation is here different--take advantage of wine and song, and search less for the secret of things, since no one can fathom ultimate questions through ratiocination or philosophical inquiry. In view of couplet 7, which asserts the value of the elder's advice, couplet 8 is most likely the substance of that advice.

In the ninth and final couplet, the speaker steps aside and addresses himself, lauding his own poetic effort as he does in many ghazals, hyperbolizing on it as grandly as he did on the subject of the beloved's beauty in the opening couplet.

Readers of the "Turk of Shirâz" ghazal who sense the multiplicity of theme which this cursory explication has emphasized will recall the earlier observation about Sa'di's "Caravan Ghazal" to the affect that its couplets exhibited a lack of inevitability in their arrangement. It so happens that from an Iranian point of view, unity of theme and imagery is not crucial to reader appreciation and enjoyment of traditional poems. Iranian critics, for example, rarely analyze whole ghazals; they concentrate upon individual verses and couplets as particularly appealing, artful and memorable. Iranian lovers of poetry quote couplets out of their ghazal context when a literary quotation is appropriate in conversation or writing. Iranian readers are infrequently interested in determining the thematic unity of a whole ghazal; they prefer to find in a particular ghazal especially apt expression of familiar images and themes. In short, for many Iranian readers, a ghazal is good if all of its individual couplets are striking and uplifting, and if it exhibits no problems in its overall patterns of rhyme and meter. Of course, these same readers rarely make a distinction between the terms "poetry" and "verse." The word for poetry in Persian is *she'r*, which also denotes a whole verse composition, a quotable line or couplet from a poem, or the lyrics to a song. The term for verse, as opposed to prose [*nasr*], is *nazm*, a denotation of which is "the stringing of pearls," a metaphor traditional Persian poets and scholars often used to describe the essence of poetic structure. In his rendition of "The Turk of Shirâz" ghazal, Sir William Jones has Hâfez describe his ghazal as "like orient pearls at random strung," while Hâfez himself puns with the metaphor in paralleling his ghazal with the Pleiades constellation.

Such a conception of lyric poetry implies, besides already discussed classicist tendencies, the prizing of values associated with ornament and embellishment, a culture-specific aesthetic of decoration and a mental cast not primarily partial to organic unity. According to Ehsan Yarshater, "The Persian literary mind is of a meandering and centrifugal turn. It has a strong predilection for embellishment and arabesque. It does not take easily to a controlled and balanced construction that leads from divers premises to a climax and resolution."(49) He adds:

> the best of Persian lyrics are highly embellished. Here, the ornaments are not applied or added to a poetical creation. In good Persian poetry ornaments are not of an "appliqué" type, but are an integral part of the texture. In such poetry, it is impossible to separate ornament from expression and imagery. The ornaments are so aptly used and so subtly imbedded in the poem's texture that often one does not consciously notice them. A prime example of this art is exhibited in the lyrics of Hâfez.(50)

As for the nature of such embellishment, Yarshater asserts:

ornamentation is effected on at least three planes. [1] The musical plane: This has to do with the orchestration of the sounds in a broad sense, and includes embellishing devices such as alliteration, homonymy (jenâs), isokolon (tarsi'), and internal rhyming. [2] The semantic plane: This has basically to do with playing on the associative meaning of words and their connotations, and includes amphibology, antithesis, congruence and various types of allusion. It is through such semantic elaborations that a line achieves a contrapuntal design, in which the different strands of thought combine in a fascinating tapestry of ornamentation. [3] The metaphorical plane: By this I mean the embellishing similes, metaphors, tropes and hyperboles which serve to enhance the basic imagery or expression of the poem.(51)

The upshot is that: "If Persian poetry . . . is robbed of its ornamental aspect, it often loses not only its attraction but also its character. Decoration . . . may be considered the most emphatic tendency of Persian art in general."(52)

In pre-modern Iranian art from the Achaemenids (559-330 BCE) to the Qâjârs (1796-1925), both the media of artistic expression and their vocabulary stress the decorative, the formal, the ceremonial, and the ritual. The most widespread and best known Iranian art form is the Persian pile carpet whose varied patterns during the four centuries from the early Safavid period (1501-1736) to the present seem expressive above all of the beauty of pattern as decoration. Within Iran for nearly 1,000 years, one of the most important visual arts has been calligraphy, a primarily decorative art and a literal embellishment of the written word. Divâns of Hâfez, for example, are still published primarily through lithography of handwritten texts, like that above of "The Turk of Shirâz," penned with careful adherence to traditional calligraphic principles. The mainly religious architectural decoration in Islamic Iran, from the early Saljuq period (1055-1157) to the Qâjârs, strikes many observers as decorative more than anything else, with its glazed tile façades, scalloped archways, arcades, domes, minarets, courtyard pools, and the like. The visual imagery on such architectural surfaces is above all decorative: symmetrically arranged floral motifs, patterns of rectiliniar shapes, arabesque systems, combinations of bright colors, and little narrative or figural didactic content.

In Persian speech, special importance is given to style, allusiveness, word play, punning, and other sorts of embellishment. Public speaking and essay writing are often reckoned appealing and persuasive more on account of features of style and presentation than as a result of the argument's evidence or flow. In Iranian hospitality, proper greetings, leavetakings, modes of address, seating arrangements, and conventional ritual accompanying almost all social events count for as much if not more than the "content" of the occasion. Iranian official public life has always been famous for its ceremonial, decorative character. The layout and bas reliefs at Persepolis, the organization of structures at the Royal Square in Esfahân, and Mohammad Rezâ Shâh Pahlavi's orchestration of his coronation in 1967 and the observance of the anniversary of 2,500 years of monarchy in 1971 are examples of this. Two thousand years ago, the Roman poet Horace began a statement of preference for the simple bucolic life in one of his odes by declaring "Persicos odi . . . apparatus" [I hate Persian pomp]!

Such stereotypical, Persian Iranian inclinations to pomp, ceremony, and decoration relate to the performance aspect of Hâfez's ghazals, in particular, and the bulk of traditional Persian poetry, in general. Hâfez's ghazals seem intended to be heard, as noted earlier, rather than read, and in originally specific situations. As described by one scholar:

> The actual setting for the practice of professional poetry was the kind of convivial gathering which has at all times been the common form of entertainment in Middle Eastern society. They are designated by terms like *bazm*, which is usually rendered into English by the word "banquet," and *majles*, a word that can be applied to almost any kind of gathering. The Islamic Middle Ages derived their models for these occasions in particular from memories of the splendour and extravagance of the pre-Islamic court of Iran.(53)

The pomp, formality, and ceremony characteristic of Persian Iranian public life parallels impersonality and formal performance in Persian poetry. In the case of Hâfez, his ghazals do not represent particular, identifiable moments in the actual, emotional or imaginative life of an individual speaker.

The poet effects deliberate distance between the man Hâfez and the poetic speaker whose *nom de plume* "Hâfez" appears near the end of most of his ghazals. The reader does not get introduced to a wife, mother, brother, father, son, friends, specifically rendered locales, or many other concrete, specific features often expected in lyric statement. War, political changes of fortune, misery of the population at large, and other significant events which marked life in fourteenth-century Shirâz are notably lacking as elements of the texture of Hâfez's ghazals. As for the beloved, the most frequently described object and represented object of address in Hâfezian and other Persian ghazals, only conventional attributes and details are presented. The poet makes no attempt to give an impression of a specific or actual beloved. The poetic beloved remains an abstract, idealized figure whom only the reader can flesh out with imagined details. Even the sex of the beloved bespeaks the conventionality, decorativeness, abstractness, and distance from the everyday world that characterize the traditional Persian aesthetic.

In classical Persian lyric verse, as described by Yarshater in *The Cambridge History of Iran,*

77

as a rule, the beloved is not a woman, but a young man. In the early centuries of Islam, the raids into Central Asia produced many young slaves. Slaves were also bought or received as gifts. They were often made to serve as pages at court or in the households of the affluent, or as soldiers and body-guards. Young men, slaves or not, also served wine at banquets and receptions, and the more gifted among them could play music and maintain a cultivated conversation. It was love toward young pages, soldiers, or novices in trades and professions which was the subject of lyrical introductions to panegyrics from the beginning of Persian poetry, and of the ghazal.(54)

In other words, the feminine pronouns used above in the translation of Sa'di's "Caravan Ghazal" should be masculine (Persian personal pronouns do not generally reflect gender). As for Hâfez's "Turk of Shirâz" ghazal, the image of the Turkish beloved is thus explained: he is compared to one of those slaves or pages originally from Central Asia. In short, the beloved in such classical Persian ghazals is almost a theatrical persona whose individual personality is undepicted and whose function is to incite feelings and actions associated with love. The conventional depiction of beloveds masks real love situations.

Even the character "Hâfez" in his ghazals is impossible to describe except as a mask. This speaker-character does not talk with the reader in the terms in which any fourteenth-century intellectual of Shirâz might have mulled over the actualities of day-to-day life. Rather he assumes a certain stylized stance, almost as an actor, and speaks in a uniformly stylized way. The "Turk of Shirâz" ghazal is interesting in this regard, because at the end of the poem the speaker indulges in self-praise and speaks of the ghazal not as an intimate lyric statement but as a performance.

Perhaps the most important contextual difference between traditional Persian and much Western poetry is that the former not only does not hide its artifice or, in other words, ask the reader to suspend disbelief as the act of hearing/reading begins, but it even flaunts the artifice. Hâfez presents his ghazals to an audience of the elite of his day, in fact the royal court, as carefully crafted compositions intended to please that audience through their appreciation of his superior craft. Hâfez does not introduce novel topoi, images, meters, or figures of speech; he draws on his culture's literary past with which he expects his audience to be familiar; and he tries to out-perform his predecessors. Hâfez's art allows for no private symbolism, disregard for conventions and rules, or forays into unprecedented arenas of thought or imagination. His educated audience has definite expectations, which he fulfills to a degree that is beyond their expectations.

This impersonality of the traditional Persian lyric poet, the conventional formality of subject and treatment of lyric expression, the rigid system of prosody, and the stance of the poetic speaker as a performer and his poem as performance are features of a heritage that has survived in Iran among many educated poetry lovers to this day. For them modernist Persian verse, for example some poems by Akhavân-e Sâles and later poems by Forugh Farrokhzâd, are not poems because they lack conventional features of traditional verse, violate conventional boundaries of appropriate subject matter and conventional diction, and are personal, individuated statements.

At the same time, broadly read and less tradition-bound Iranian literary people seem to agree that much of what is revered as great poetry in the classical period from Rudaki (d. 940/1) to Jâmi (d. 1492) is merely correct, serious, artful, and sophisticated verse. Some, including Farrokhzâd--contrary to the popular view in Iran that traditional Persian verse is the single most significant contribution of Iranian culture to world civilization--go so far as to argue that Hâfez may be the only traditional Persian lyric poet to deserve consideration as a poet of the first rank.(55) The issue is beyond the purview of this essay except as an indication that it has been easy for Iranians to assume that *she'r* [poetry] and *nazm* [verse] were synonymous because traditional Persian poetry emphasized adherence to conventional principles of a comprehensive system of verse. In the words of Nimâ Yushij (1895-1960), the "father" of modernist Persian poetry, Iran has always had many *nâzems* [versifiers], but very few *shâ'ers* [poets].(56)

Hâfez's distinctive and self-conscious sense of his craftsmanship is part of what has endeared him to audiences for six centuries: he knows his talent and is not averse either to displaying it as a virtuoso or to drawing attention to it as in the closing couplet of the "Turk of Shirâz." Many Iranians seem not to expect or appreciate (false) humility from their artists, especially from those who practice the most revered art of all in Iran: poetry. But Hâfez's candid pride would not have been willingly appreciated through the centuries did he not epitomize for many readers a further cherished quality in persons in the public eye: the presumed courage to be non-conformist or anti-establishment, which is one aspect of didacticism that seems an enduring feature of Persian aesthetics.

As observed in the previous chapter, the myth that holds that Khayyâm dared to challenge the orthodoxy of his day with his individualistic, heretical quatrains accounts for his status as a giant in Persian literature despite his lack of actual participation as a professional in the literary arena. In Sa'di's case, despite his awesome verbal skills and craft, approval is sometimes only begrudgingly given, owing to Sa'di's life story of clever accommodation to patrons and circumstances of the moment. On the other hand, the Esma'ili propagandist Nâser Khosrow (d. 1088) holds a special place in the hearts of some contemporary readers because of his presumed refusal to succumb to the temptations of the orthodox establishment of his day.(57) The cultural bottom line, in other words, is that many educated Iranians whose historical fate has been the inevitable dedication of their services and talents to the authorities of the moment take special pleasure and pride in those of their number who somehow (seem to) avoid so doing.

Hâfez even today strikes many readers as having been such a one, at least intellectually.

Numerous Hâfezian ghazals, not to mention scores of individual couplets in many other ghazals, persuade readers of the poet's freespiritedness. An example is the following ghazal, here entitled "A Call to Libertinism."

[1]What is clandestine wine and pleasure? A foundationless activity.
I have joined the ranks of the libertines; whatever will be will be.
[2]Loosen the knot from the heart
        and do not call the heavens to mind,
because the thought of no geometrician can unravel such a knot.
[3]Do not marvel at the world's revolution,
for fortune's wheel knows thousands of such tales.
[4]Grasp the cup with deference,
        composed as it is of Jamshid's skull, and Bahman's, and Qobâd's.
[5]Who knows where Kâvus and Kay went
or how Jamshid's throne went with the wind?
[6]Because of longing for Shirin's sweet lip
I see tulips still blooming from blood in Farhâd's eyes.
[7]Perhaps the tulip knew of the world's fecklessness:
from birth to death it did not put down its cup of red wine.
[8]Come, that we might lose ourselves in wine.
In these ruins, perhaps, we will find a treasure.
[9]The Mosallâ breeze and the waters of Roknâbâd
dissuade me from excursions and trips.
[10]Like Hâfez, do not grasp the goblet except with the harp's wail;
the joyous heart has been tied
        to the stringed silky instrument of pleasure.(58)

In "A Call to Libertinism," the criticism of hypocrisy, the assertion of the fruitlessness of rational inquiry, the observation of the cruelty of fate, the recognition of the transience of things, and taking solace in forbidden wine communicate the poet's daring, almost blasphemous, disregard for the values of the political and religious establishment of his day. Hâfez's stance in this poem can be summarized in a single word in the opening couplet: *rendân* in Persian, which appears as "libertines" in the translation. Hâfez's continuing popularity, especially among non-establishment intellectuals, has much to do with the perception of him as a *rend*, a term for a reckless individual unconcerned with or unconstrained by prevailing mores, a privately moral person who holds his exterior up for reproach (either because of a lack of concern for what others think or because of deliberate courting of disfavor).(59)

Several dimensions of these denotations of *rend* are obvious clues to Hâfez's appeal as a cultural personality. First is the significance of behaving without regard to one's reputation in a culture in which propriety, formality, and approved style count for so much. In other words, persons who cannot afford to be reckless in their own behavior may prize such qualities in the vicarious experiences of such mythologized historical figures as Khayyâm and Hâfez. Second, insofar as political concerns have long been a major reason for circumspectness in public in Iran, behavior that exhibits disregard for public opinion strikes some latently anti-establishment people as heroically anti-establishment. Hâfez's personae have convinced many Iranian readers that he courageously resisted the political orthodoxy of his day. Third is the sheer romantic appeal of individualist behavior for people who cannot achieve great public individuality in a patriarchal culture in which the only true individuals have generally been the monarch and his representatives. A fourth attraction of the *rend* personality is its implicit ambiguity, the possibility that a religious spirit, perhaps a gnostic intent, is behind it all. From early Achaemenid days, as pragmatic and worldly as Iranians have been in many spheres of endeavor, they have always seemed likewise inclined to metaphysicality in the sphere of religion or in appreciation of spiritual meaning beyond the mundane. The reader senses the possibility of such ambivalence in the "Turk of Shirâz." It exists here in the "Call to Libertinism" at least in the very denotation of *rend*.

A further, extremely salient feature of Hâfez's ghazals as well as of Persian aesthetics in general is the related phenomenon of ambivalence [*ihâm*], to illustrate which Hâfez's famous "Visitation" and "Cup of Jamshid" ghazals serve particularly well. The "Visitation" ghazal reads:

[1]Perspiring and tresses in disarray, smiling and intoxicated,
shirt wide open and singing a ghazal, a wine-pitcher in hand,
[2]narcissus eyes bellicose and lips mouthing "alas,"
midnight he came to my bedside and sat down.
[3]He brought his head to my ear and in a sad voice said:
"O my mad love, are you asleep?
[4]A gnostic given such a nocturnal glass is an infidel to love
if he is not a wine-worshipper."
[5]Be gone, o ascetic, and do not scorn drinkers of the dregs;
for this only was given us from the very beginning.
[6]What He poured into our cup we drank,
be it celestial wine or that of intoxication.
[7]The wine cup's smile and the beloved's curled tresses,
o how many repentances such as Hâfez's have they broken!(60)

The opening two couplets of "Visitation" present the reader with a very tangible and concrete picture of the beloved. Its depiction of alluring wantonness borders on the extravagant: the open shirt, singing a song, wine in hand, hair in disarray--altogether a bewitching and very physically present image and portrait. This tangible scene continues to the end of the fourth couplet. Then in couplet 5, the words "ascetic," "gift," and "beginning (of time)" combine with "infidel" in couplet 4 and the vigil scene in couplet 3 to create the sense that the love emotion is religious or that love is a religion. In the sixth couplet, the word "He" refers to God, the creator, and wine, a creation of God, is accepted as a gift for whatever it is, mere physical intoxicant or heavenly inspirant. Then, in the final couplet, the word "repentance" appears as Hâfez announces that wine and the beauty of the beloved destroy the resolution to repent.

The net effect of such religious imagery is to convince the reader of the ghazal's special seriousness and to heighten the sense of the dedication and perseverance, as in a religious commitment, that the lover must possess. But the imagery may do more.

For there is something in the impact of the poem which a reader can not quite put his or her finger on. The image of the beloved seems to relate only to secular love, yet . . . . The image of wine may relate to pleasurable intoxication, yet the "wine of heaven" . . . . The warning to the ascetics may relate merely to the question of judging others by appearances, yet . . . love and wine are treated as one in terms of their worship and effects--their primary effect is loss of self, a lover is "mad," i.e., has lost self. Perhaps "love" need not be taken allegorically here, because love naturally operates on several levels. But wine has no such extension of self. It is treated here-- possibly wine of heaven--as if it were part of allegorical meaning. As to what it can symbolize, if "cup" can metaphorically represent "heart," then wine is what the heart contains, the intoxicating, warm, flowing juice of loss of self, of giving, of being part of ultimate reality. The point need not be pressed, but the ambivalence is decidedly there.

The embodiment of ambivalence seems an essential aspect of Hâfez's cast of mind, suggestively represented in both the "Turk of Shirâz" and the "Visitation" ghazals. Some Iranian critics argue that ambivalence is the key to Hâfez's special poetic effects. Through it, Hâfez forces readers to think of both physical and metaphysical, this-worldly and other-worldly dimensions of the beloved and representations of levels of love experiences and emotions. In this regard, Hâfez's is a culminating poetic imagination in a lyric tradition in which the subjects of address initially were ma'shuq [the beloved], ma'bud [the worshipped], and mamduh [the praised], i.e. respectively a romantic beloved, Allâh, and a royal figure or other patron. By Hâfez's day, epithets, imagery, and states originally associated with only one of these three objects of poetic address had merged in multilayered, ambivalent contexts, with Hâfez the master at maintaining the tension, mystery, and significance of the merging of ma'shuq [beloved] and ma'bud [adored] figures, and sometimes ma'shuq and mamduh [praised].

Hâfez's very famous "Cup of Jamshid" poem serves as a perfect example of this tendency. Actually, this ghazal seems at the other end of the spectrum in comparison with "A Call to Libertinism" because its theme operates primarily, if not exclusively, on a metaphysical level.

82

One important allusion in "Cup of Jamshid" is to Jamshid himself, the legendary Iranian king already described in chapter 1 as the first Iranian king to possess for a long time the (halo of) divine approval called *farr*. The poem also presents the image of the Magian elder or Zoroastrian priest assumed to be a fire-worshipper and possessor of esoteric knowledge. Then comes a reference to "that friend," the gnostic Mansur Hallâj (d. 922), as the classic mystic-martyr. Christ is also cited as a revered Moslem prophet, a figure of the perfect man, and a miracle-worker.

The ghazal describes specifically the "cup of Jamshid" [*jâm-e jam*], an image with a history in Persian poetry back to the Ghaznavid period. For example, the following quatrain, which some Iranian editors attribute to Khayyâm, provides a conventional meaning for the image:

> In search of Jamshid's cup I crossed the world,
> I never rested days nor slept at night.
> I heard the secret from a master, so
> I knew the world-revealing cup was I.

Hardly a statement Hedâyat's or FitzGerald's Khayyâm would utter and in fact a poem composed probably by Ruzbehân Baqli of Shirâz,(61) this quatrain embodies gnostic or Sufi meaning.

Sufism has been defined as "that aspect of Islamic belief and practice in which Moslems seek to find the truth of divine love and knowledge through the personal experience of God."(62) Some scholars believe that the very devastation of the Mongol invasions stimulated Sufism in the thirteenth century as a consolation for the hardships of this world. Sufism had existed by this time for hundreds of years, having grown out of reactions to the worldliness of the Omayyad caliphate (661-749) on the part of devout ascetics who emphasized the Koran's stern warnings about Judgment Day. Piety and the forsaking of worldly things were hallmarks of these early Sufis. Their name presumably derives from the Arabic word *suf* [wool] in reference to coarse woollen garments some of them wore to demonstrate their rejection of creature comforts. There then developed a classical mysticism of love in which the mystic or Sufi endeavors out of love for God to lose him- or herself in love and God.

Sufism was a phenomenon that inspired and drew inspiration from every corner of the Islamic world. But some scholars argue that different Moslem peoples made distinctive contributions to it. One such view is that "when Sufism gripped the mind and soul of Iran, and the abounding poetic imagination of the Persians discovered this new theatre to display itself, Islamic mysticism developed aesthetically in a manner soaring high above the ranges of speculation."(63)

As a major mode in Persian poetry from Abu Sa'id Ebn-e Abi-l-Khayr (d. 1048) to Jâmi (d. 1492), Sufism represented a specific attitude and answer to life's dilemmas and travails. It is at one extreme of a Persian cultural spectrum of attitudes toward the material world and life in it. For example, Persepolis represents Iranian acceptance of this world, confidence in being able to manage life with Ahurâmazdâ's help, and optimism toward the future. The Khayyâmic view as well involves acceptance of this world but in a spirit of resignation without optimism or confidence, because the future offers nothing but the darkness of non-existence. A third, contrasting attitude is represented in Ferdowsi's world, which is planned and guided by Allâh who had reasons that Iranians must accept for allowing their civilization to succumb to the Moslem Arabs. In the *Shâhnâmeh*, Ferdowsi also communicates an ultimate optimism that relates to one's reward in the next world, whereas in this world even all-powerful monarchs and Rostam die, and before him his son Sohrâb. As for Sufism in Persian literature, it begins in the same religious faith that permeates the *Shâhnâmeh* and proceeds to a rejection of the inherent worth of this world, seeing it merely as a reflection of another.

However, those Sufis who did not pay lip service to religious laws and institutions posed, as did individualistic Khayyâmic resignation, a threat to government and religious institutions. And qualities of individualism, rejection of the blandishments of this world, and unswerving principles were and remain part of Iranian cultural life as desiderata or wishful thinking. The facts of everyday Iranian life may have caused Sufism to be dead in today's Iran as a viable or relevant life style. But the respect many educated Iranians have for such great Sufis as Faridoddin 'Attâr (d.c. 1220) and the already cited Jalâloddin Rumi (1207-1273), simply called *mowlânâ* [our master] in Persian, imply that Sufi values are highly prized in the contemporary world where the life of the spirit is viewed as too often subordinated to the life of acquisition and where ideals of equality and brotherhood are often obscured in political and social hierarchies.

The most revered of the Persian Sufis is Rumi. Born in Balkh, located in today's Afghanistan, Rumi fled westward with his family in the face of the first Mongol wave and settled in Konya in the region of Rum in today's Turkey, whence his name. He is the eponymous founder of the Mevlevi order of Sufis, famous as the whirling dervishes, and the author of the famous *Masnavi-ye Ma'navi* [Spiritual Couplets] poem of 26,000 closed couplets which presents in lyrical, narrative, and didactic modes a verse compendium of the Sufi's quest and life. He also composed hundreds of ghazal poems, collected in the *Divân of Shams-e Tabrizi*, named after the Sufi guide whom Rumi followed and loved. One of these poems, called "one of the most splendid and sublime productions of his genius" by Rumi's most famous editor, follows:

> [1]What is to be done, O Moslems? I do not recognise myself.
> I am neither Christian nor Jew, Zoroastrian nor Moslem.
> [2]I am not of the East, the West, the land, or the sea;
> I'm not of Nature's mint, nor of the circling heavens.

[3]I'm not of earth, water, air, fire;
I'm not of the empyrean, nor of the dust,
            nor of existence, nor of entity.
[4]I'm not from India, China, Bulgaria, or Turkestan;
I am neither from Mesopotamia nor from Iran.
[5]I'm not of this world or the next, nor of Paradise or Hell;
I am not of Adam and Eve, nor of Eden and Paradise.
[6]My place is the Placeless, my trace is the Traceless;
It is neither body nor soul: I belong to the soul of the Beloved.
[7]I have put duality away and have seen the two worlds as one;
I seek only one, I know, see, and call only one.
[8]He is the first and the last, the outward and the inward;
I know none other than "O lord" and "O lord, lord."
[9]Intoxicated with Love's cup, the two worlds
            have passed out of my ken;
I have no business save carouse and revelry.
[10]If once in my life I spend a moment without you,
from that time and from that hour I will repent of my life.
[11]If once in this world I win a moment with you,
I will trample on both worlds and dance in triumph forever.
[12]O Shams of Tabriz, I am so intoxicated in this world that
I have no tale to tell except of drunken revelry .(64)

The image of Shams of Tabriz in Rumi's poem highlights another aspect
of Sufism that seems of continuing cultural significance: the role of the
shaykh or Sufi *pir* [elder] or *morshed* [guide]. In the "Turk of Shirâz," when
the speaker admonishes the beloved to heed "the advice of the wise elder,"
Hâfez is operating in the context of this guru relationship. The same holds
true in the "Cup of Jamshid" with the speaker's revelation that he visited
"the Magian elder" to find an answer for his problem. Rumi's love for his
mentor and for his own followers may humanize the patriarchal relationship.
But the fact of an authoritarian guide initiating a younger novice or follower
remains. Although a variety of mystical paths and approaches existed in
medieval Iran, brotherhoods and orders that proliferated from the twelfth
century onward and that exist at least in name in Iran today were organized
around the figure of the knowing leader, the order's founder or his
successors, whose teachings and guidance served to direct aspiring mystics
on their quest for God. The same unquestioning obedience was due the *pir* or
morshed that was due the king in the secular world or one's father in the
family world. In other words, Iranian Sufism seems another manifestation of
the Iranian patriarchal order which is discussed in the context of Ferdowsi's
Shâhnâmeh in chapter 1 and which the next three chapters present as a basic
cultural force with which twentieth-century Iranian authors have contended
in their writing and lives.

As for Hâfez's "Cup of Jamshid" ghazal, which exhibits Sufi imagery, content, and a knowing guide, it reads:

[1]For years my heart sought Jamshid's cup from me,
from a stranger it sought what it itself had.
[2]A jewel beyond the shell of being and space
it sought from the lost ones at the sea's edge.
[3]I took my problem to the Magian elder last night
because he solved enigmas with visionary grace.
[4]I saw him vibrant and smiling, a cup in hand;
and in that mirror he was viewing myriads.
[5]I said: "When did the Sage give the world-seeing cup to you?"
He said: "On the day he made this blue dome."
[6]He said: "That friend for whom the head of the gallows rose,
his crime was that he revealed secrets.
[7]If the Holy Spirit's grace again gives aid,
others also will do what Christ used to do."
[8]"Beloveds' chain-like tresses are for what?" I asked.
Hâfez, he said, was complaining because of a frenzied heart.(65)

In this ghazal, the cup or goblet of Jamshid is described as something the speaker's "heart" has sought from him, something which the "heart" itself had, a jewel (the Persian word *gowhar* also denotes "essence" and "pearl") beyond time and place, which the "heart" sought from the people at the edge of the sea who do not know where they are, something the whereabouts of which the speaker hopes and expects the Magian elder to apprise him, and finally something the whereabouts of which the Magian elder has apparently revealed to the speaker in the final couplet. In couplet 4, the Magian elder is described as having a cup or goblet in his hand, a cup described as a "mirror" and then as a "world-seeing cup" which the Magian elder asserts was given him by God at the beginning of the world.

The cup of Jamshid and the world-seeing cup in the hand of the Magian elder are one and the same in medieval Persian literature. The meaning ascribed to it by Shabestari (d. c. 1320) is the sense, according to a standard Persian dictionary, intended by Hâfez in the "Cup of Jamshid" ghazal. Shabestari declares that *jâm-e jam* is a symbol for "the knowing (wise) soul (self, person)" and asserts that "when man perfects his *nafs* [soul, self, person], he becomes inclusive of all creation . . . when he becomes *'âref* [gnostic, knowing, mystic], he is the *jâm-e jam*."(66)

The cup of Jamshid, therefore, is a quality of knowing oneself; and, as the famous Prophetic Tradition beloved by Sufis goes: "He who knows his soul (self, person) knows his lord," it is a quality of merging with the rest of creation. It is the quality of being one with the Lord. This explains the Magian elder's assertion that he received the cup at the beginning of the

world--it is a capacity all human beings are given from the beginning of time. It explains, as well, the allusions in the sixth and seventh couplets.

In couplet 6, reference is made to that "friend" Hallâj whose blasphemies, in terms of Moslem orthodoxy, resulted in his execution by hanging. He had committed a crime, the crime of "revealing secrets," that is, of revealing the self-knowledge which possession of *jâm-e jam* gives one. Hallâj is credited with uttering the blasphemous *anâ'l-haqq* [I am the truth, i.e., God], a logical visionary conclusion for one who has come to know self and thus has lost concerns of self-interest and merges with creation and its creator.

In the seventh couplet, the Magian elder declares that with an infusion of grace, others can accomplish the miraculous feats of Christ. The speaker's problem is thus not so much knowing what the *jâm-e jam* is--after all he intimates in the second couplet that he knows metaphorically what it is by declaring that it resides in the heart. The speaker's concern is rather how one attains possession and recognition of possession of *jâm-e jam*.

The image of the Magian elder looms large both in Hâfez's search for *jâm-e jam* and in the resolution of the poem. Concerning the latter, because the poem structurally must have a determinate ending, either the Magian elder apprises Hâfez of the answer he seeks or he communicates to Hâfez that the search is fruitless, and the goal impossible to attain. But the poet reveals that the Magian elder was a man who solved puzzles and who himself possessed *jâm-e jam*. So necessarily a person who reaches the stage attained and exemplified by the Magian elder will recognize his possession of *jâm-e jam* and, at the same time, in his wisdom be able to inspire others in their search.

The image of the Magian elder is likewise conventional in classical poetry. He is a leader of the Zoroastrians, a priest of the religion of the gods of light and darkness, of presumed fire-worship, and monastic retreats far from cities and mundane concerns. His is a religion in which wine, the intoxicant and inspirant, is not unlawful. Hâfez uses the image of the Magian elder in many poems, in one ghazal saying: "The door of meaning opened on that day/ when I began residing at the threshold of the Magian elder."(67) So, as a figure of otherworldly mystery performing rites and worship strange to the Moslem, the Magian elder symbolizes wisdom, the wisdom of experience and esoteric knowledge. His actions in the ghazal reveal that he is surely a qualified guide and source of inspiration for the speaker; and it is in his words that the answer to the speaker's quest must be found.

The speaker asks two questions. First, when did God give you this world-seeing cup? The answer cites the day of creation, with the Magian elder citing Hallâj and Christ in revealing the dangers of *jâm-e jam* (Hallâj's fate) and its powers (Christ-like actions and miracles). The second question is: What are the chain-like tresses of the beloveds for? The answer: Hâfez spoke from a frenzied heart. The solution to Hâfez's problem must lie in this exchange.

The beloveds are called "idols," objects of religious worship and unquestioning belief, in whose service the worshipper must forget self and commit himself to their bidding and to sacrifice, even of self. These beloveds have tresses like chains, chains to capture and to restrain: to capture the heart of the lover and to bind the lover to him/herself, to restrain the lover from . . . What is this all about, asks Hâfez.

The verse initially seems out of context with the previous seven couplets. Of course, the subject of the poem is the heart, the seat of affection and love. But the poem has proceeded otherwise to this point. It is as if the speaker suddenly bursts out with this question from the force of emotion he has been feeling throughout. Indeed, the Magian elder replies that the speaker Hâfez is asking this question, is complaining so to speak, because of a heart in the frenzy of love, captured by the chains of the irresistible tresses of the beloveds perfect enough to worship--after all, only a lover would see those tresses as chains. And in the single word "frenzied" lies the Magian's final answer to Hâfez. By virtue of the frenzy of his heart, because of which he has relinquished his freedom and has become a captive of the beloved, Hâfez has lost his self, his self-interest, his personality as distinct from the beloved's, and is possessed of *jâm-e jam*: Hâfez is a lover, love bringing self-knowledge and loss of self therein.

This higher plane of the order of ideal love is another dimension both of Hâfez's great appeal and the traditional Persian aesthetic. From Persepolis to near the end of the Qâjâr era, Persian art characteristically depicted an ideal world far from the trials and tribulations of the real world of invasions, epidemics, earthquakes, and oppressive rulers. It does not matter that Hâfez's Shirâz was very down to earth and not easy to live in or that few Iranians could afford to live lives of love or survive on thoughts of love. Iranians have needed both art that transcended their realities and artists, like Hâfez, who maintain the fiction of the ideal.

As for Hâfez, he maintains his poet's mask admirably, never letting down his defenses, and leaves posterity with a unique corpus of poems attesting to the indomitability of the human spirit and unflagging confidence in human capacity to realize goals of the heart and spirit. Hâfez assiduously tends and nurtures his poetic garden vision, arranging it as a formal, verbal paradise of exuberance and possible joys, and never allows his personal experiences to find their mundane and meaningless way as experienced into his garden. Whatever defeats, sorrows, apprehensions of the insignificance of it all, and the like which Hâfez suffered in his personal and professional life, however much his world may have often seemed a desert or sown environment, Hâfez had the admirable fortitude to refuse to remove the mask of his *nom de plume* in public.

This fortitude is an especially appealing dimension of Hâfez's already noted individualism, or Iranian assumption of such. After Hâfez, for over four centuries, no other literary figure had this sort of appeal for Iranian readers. Then came the modernist trend in Persian literature, inspired in large measure by literary developments in the West where the poetic speaker had long since become an individual person. The chief figures among the first generation modernists were Nimâ Yushij (1895-1960) in lyric poetry and Sâdeq Hedâyat (1903-1951) in prose fiction. The latter is the quintessentially individualistic contemporary Iranian writer *par excellence* and Iran's most famous author after Hâfez. Hedâyat and his masterpiece are the subject of the next chapter.

But a culturally significant question remains before leaping from Hâfezian ghazals of the fourteenth century to Hedâyat's prose fiction of the mid-twentieth century. The question is: How relevant to twentieth-century Persian poetry and Iranian aesthetics and culture are such elucidated classical elements as thematic dualism and allegory, the preeminence of aural features in poetry, classicism, the aesthetics of decoration or ornamentation, the unity of the performer, the flaunting of artifice and craft, impersonality and idealism, moral superiority of the poet, religious seriousness and sadness, gnostic tendencies, and didacticism. A detailed answer would require comparative analysis of classical, post-classical traditional, traditionalist, and modernist poems for essentially non-cultural reasons. Short of that, describing literary developments from Hâfez to the twentieth-century would likewise involve a lengthy discussion without primary emphasis on cultural issues. At the same time, many Iranian readers themselves ignore the intervening centuries and pick up their poetry reading with the twentieth-century, there taking sides in a continuing debate between traditionalists and modernists. The thoroughgoing modernist and *engagé* poet Ahmad Shâmlu (b. 1925) represents some of the issues of the debate in a 1954 poem on the nature of modernist Persian poetry. Called "Poetry Which Is Life," the poem reads, in part:

> Poetry was not from life formerly.
> In the arid sky of his mind,
> the poet mused only about wine and beloved.
> He daydreamed day and night,
> [5]snared in foolish images of the beloved's hair,
> or, a wine cup in one hand and the other on the beloved's tresses,
> clamored drunkenly on God's good earth.
>
> Since the poet's subject was this alone,
> his impact also could be nothing more:
> [10]he could not use his poem as a drill.
> Or with the aid of poetry,
> in battle he could not shove aside
> a demon out of the people's way.
>
> In other words, the poet's existence had no impact.
> [15]It made no difference whether he lived or not.

89

One could not use a poem as a gallows.

On the other hand, I myself on one occasion
fought alongside Shen Chou of Korea with my poetry.
Once, also, a few years ago I hanged the poet Hamidi
[20]on the gallows of my verse.

The subject of poetry today is another matter altogether . . .
Today, poetry is the people's weapon
because poets themselves are branches in the forest of the masses,
not greenhouse jasmine or hyacinths.
[25]Today's poet is no stranger to the pains of the masses;
today's poet smiles with the people's lips
and grafts onto his or her own bones their pains and hopes. . .

The pattern of today's poet's poem, I said, is life!
It is from life that a poet
[30]paints one pattern over another
with water and colors of poetry.
The poet writes poetry, that is to say,
touches the wounds of the old city,
that is, tells the night a story of pleasant morning.
[35]The poet writes poems, that is to say,
screams the pains of his homeland, that is,
revives weary spirits with song.
The poet writes poetry, that is to say,
fills cold and empty hearts with joyous excitement,
[40]that is to say, opens up sleeping eyes to rising morning.

The poet writes poetry, that is to say,
explains human achievements of the day,
that is to say, writes victory proclamations of the age . . .
Dry debate about the meaning of special words
[45]has nothing to do with poetry either . . . if poetry is life,
in the depth of the darkest phrases
we shall feel the sunny warmth of love and hope.
This one recited the song of life in blood,
and that one the din of life in a mould of silence.
[50]But . . . although its rhyme of life
is nothing but the long drawn-out blow of death,
in both poems the meaning of each death is life!(68)

4

THE MODERNIST IRANIAN WRITER'S
ALMOST INEVITABLE NIGHTMARE

> Why do you marvel that in the world's meadows the
> owl follows the nightingale and lamentation song?
> Khâqâni

> In life there are sores which . . . consume the soul in
> solitude like leprosy.   The Narrator, *The Blind Owl*

Sâdeq Hedâyat's *The Blind Owl*, printed in a limited mimeograph edition
in Bombay in 1937 and published in Tehrân in late 1941, is the most
controversial piece of Persian prose fiction in history and the only Iranian
novel to achieve any appreciable audience in translation. Roger Lescot's
1953 French translation called *La Chouette aveugle* received notice in
French literary circles, while D.P. Costello's 1957 English version called
The Blind Owl: A Novel from Persia has remained in print since 1969 as a
Grove Press Evergreen Black Cat Edition. Costello's translation in the 1969
edition is the text cited throughout this chapter, in which the discussion
presupposes reader familiarity with the novel.(69)
    Not that reading *The Blind Owl* will have immediately prompted insights
into Iranian culture. On the contrary, this landmark work in modernist
Persian literature by the most famous Iranian writer since Hafez strikes most
readers as an enigmatic narrative mélange in reading after reading. After only
a few pages into the novel, they realize that they are dealing with neither
generalized, classicist experience à la Sa'di nor realistic, modernist
experience à la Jalâl Al-e Ahmad, but rather symbolic, surrealist experience,
which per se makes *The Blind Owl* initially and at least temporarily
difficult.
    But the most significant contributing factor to the enigmatic character of
The Blind Owl is its narrative point of view: the story is told in the first
person by a character who relates events and describes states in such terms as
to cause readers to question his reliability and credibility as a narrator. For
this reason, a key to a relatively full appreciation of *The Blind Owl* lies in

the determination of who the protagonist/narrator is and from what perspective he speaks. For once having established both his identity as an individual or type and his specific point of view, readers can perhaps begin to unravel the narrative's mysteries, including those cancerous sores whose description begins the novel. Concomitant with such unraveling will come discernment of what about the novel strikes such familiar cultural chords for many of its Iranian readers, beginning with a latter-day Khayyâmic skepticism and the dark side to Hâfez's tenacious representation of ideals in the face of reality. In *The Blind Owl*, that reality includes both the weight of historical and cultural traditions, of which the national defeat immortalized by Ferdowsi in the *Shâhnâmeh* is the largest part.

As to who the narrator of *The Blind Owl* really is, sociological, literary comparatist and psychological approaches provide clues. Âl-e Ahmad's much cited essay called "The Hedâyat of *The Blind Owl*," written shortly after Hedâyat's April 1951 suicide in Paris, offers several salient suggestions. Labelling Hedâyat "a writer of the dictatorial period," that is to say, of Rezâ Pahlavi's rule over Iran from 1921 to 1941, Al-e Ahmad states:

> During his life he [Hedâyat] witnessed only political chaos and suffocating dictatorship. The reality which held sway over Iran during the forty-some years of his life was marked by triviality, deceit, poverty, misery, anarchy and . . . tyranny . . ., a central government which . . . administered nothing but arrests and seizures, nothing but strangulating death. Whenever I read in *The Blind Owl*: "Just then the voices of a band of drunken policemen rose from the street. As they marched by they were joking obscenely among themselves . . . In terror I shrank back from the window" (p. 91), I'm reminded of the fear and terror that for twenty years descended upon the nation like a nightmare in a dark night of dictatorship, particularly if we keep in mind that this terrifying coming and going of the drunken patrolmen is . . . the refrain of the book.

Al-e Ahmad proceeds to assert: "Apart from its value as art, *The Blind Owl* is a social document, an indictment of the government of the day." He elaborates:

> The silence which ruled in those days lay in depression and seclusion, itself the result of censorship by the government, and can be read more in *The Blind Owl* than in a handful of official papers and the silence of writers. Seclusion and solitude, fear of the drunken patrolmen, mistrust of the deceitful realities and speciousness presented instead of reality, nostalgic denial of existing realities, and contentment with dreams and nightmares are all characteristics of people living under the rule of spies and secret police. When a person

is afraid to talk to his friends, his wife, his colleagues, or somebody else, at least "he can talk to his shadow well."(70)

Perhaps the ultimate sociological reading of *The Blind Owl* is that which postulates that the figures of the old men laughing throughout the novel represent Rezâ Shâh Pahlavi himself, vis-à-vis whom such sensitive, nonpatriarchal Iranians as the narrator were immobilized, unable to fulfill their desires or even to express their feelings.(71) This sort of reading establishes a parallel between Rostam and Sohrâb, on the one hand, and the old man and the narrator of *The Blind Owl*, on the other. In other words, Iranian father figures do not allow their sons to grow up in non-conventional molds. They must either await their turn and learn to become patriarchs, or their fathers will snuff out their lives one way or another, just as Rezâ Pahlavi snuffed out the lives of those Iranian "sons" who did not do his bidding. Much of the empathy Iranian readers feel for the narrator of *The Blind Owl*, while they may neither fathom any connections between him and themselves nor be able to verbalize their sense of the novel's thematic impact, may derive from this shared feeling of powerlessness vis-à-vis the patriarchal system. In this context, in clinging to his sensitivity, childhood, and dreams of an ideal, the narrator of *The Blind Owl* becomes a heroic, modern antihero.

Literary comparatist investigation of possible literary inspiration and foreign influences has drawn attention to Hedâyat's extensive use of European literary material in *The Blind Owl* in the form of imagery and the like inspired by Edgar Allen Poe, Rainer Maria Rilke, and others. Such literary debts and allusiveness should persuade readers that images which Hedâyat's protagonist employs are not the products of a wildly unusual or "abnormal" mind, but rather the workings of a fertile and "normal" creative imagination inspired by and in tune with contemporary, literary intellectual currents and creativity. At the same time, after all possible literary analogues and influences receive their due, experts recognize that *The Blind Owl* is essentially Iranian in terms of characterization, plot, and theme.(72)

Psychological readings have found Freudian and Jungian views in *The Blind Owl*.(73) The critic Homayoun Katouzian sees *The Blind Owl* as the chief example of a discrete group of Hedâyat fictions, among them "Buried Alive," "Three Drops of Blood," and "The Man Who Killed His Passionate Self," which he terms

> psycho-fictional stories . . . in which the basic question or theme is ontological rather than sociological. In these stories the main characters ask questions which know no cultural boundaries and seek solutions to problems which are not specific to any given sociohistorical framework; they look for a raison d'être, or at least an excuse for living which can not simply be achieved by the removal of specific socio-economic constraints or a change in social atmosphere.

In *The Blind Owl*, according to Katouzian,

> The father, the uncle, the father-in-law and the odds-and-ends seller are all but a single entity, the narrator's "other," materialistic, erotic, soulless and physical "self" warring with his pure, perfect soul which it finally defeats: he succumbs to the needs of his "other self," impersonates it, imitates it, and becomes it.(74)

But the implications of this sort of reading of *The Blind Owl* seem as culture-specific as universal. In other words, the protagonist in the novel wages an inner struggle very common in Iranian culture where the pure life of the spirit is prized, but where the demands of everyday life compel thinking Iranians to be practical, materialistic, and acquisitive, and where, for example, Sufism is much admired but cannot serve as a basis for real living. Or, in terms of this reading, grown up Sohrâbs will be horrified to recognize that they are inevitable Rostams, that becoming patriarchal comes with the cultural territory.

In any case, such sociological, literary comparatist and psychological scrutiny of *The Blind Owl* as alluded to here at the very least implies the relevance of the novel in a Persianist appreciation of Iranian culture. The insights into culture that such scrutiny provides are considered in the following analysis of the book, which focusses specifically on the narrator's identity in terms of his societal functions or occupations, either as he sees them or as they are in fact.

In these terms, the narrator is an Iranian artist confronting nightmarish dilemmas in his life, the possibilities and limitations of his art, and his view of life beyond his art. Actually, he is an Iranian artist in two senses. During the first part of the story (Costello's translation, pp. 1-43), he identifies himself as a painter of pen-case covers. But perhaps he has never really been a painter, because he does not mention this occupation during the whole of the second major section of the story (pp. 46-128) and refers therein to pen-cases only in a single passage where he says: "My life appeared to me just as strange, as unnatural, as inexplicable as the picture on the pen-case I am using this moment as I write" (p. 104). However, it is at least certain that the narrator is another sort of artist, a writer who plans to write his story for his shadow on the wall as a means of getting to know himself better and who asserts that he has begun to write as the second major section of the story commences (pp. 45-46). As he says: "I hoped by this means to expel the demon which had long been lacerating my vitals, to vent onto paper the horrors of my mind" (p. 45).

What is immediately relevant about the fact that the narrator of *The Blind Owl* is an artist is that an artist figure as narrator or speaker is a significant device in Persian literature. In traditional poetry, as illustrated earlier in the analysis of several of Hâfez's most famous poems, the ghazal verse form conventionally includes a nom de plume by means of which the poet-speaker generally refers to himself at the end of the poem, presenting himself as a representative of his audience or of human beings in general as he faces the issues raised in the ghazal.

The Iranian artist as narrator or spokesperson is important in modernist Persian literature as well. For example, Al-e Ahmad presents his own personality as a writer in two extremely telling volumes called *Lost in the Crowd* (1966) and *A Stone on a Grave* (1981), which are discussed in the next chapter. The prominent short story writer and novelist Sâdeq Chubak has a 1945 poem called "The Sigh of Mankind," which is the writer's own quasi-autobiographical testimony to the waste land of the Rezâ Pahlavi years. In it the speaker-writer implores his audience not to mourn or bury him. He has not died, merely fainted--other circumstances, a different environment, may revive him.(75) Of course, the chief narrator in Chubak's masterful novel called *The Patient Stone* is the would-be writer Ahmad Aqâ. Around this young, destitute teacher in search of something to write about, a gripping story of tragedy after tragedy unfolds, from which only he emerges unscathed, perhaps eventually to write the story he has experienced involving concerns about Iran's past, present, and future that seem quintessentially Iranian. Forugh Farrokhzâd presents herself the poet as a person in many of her poems from 1953 through 1966. In her famous "Another Birth" (1963), quoted in translation in Chapter 6, she presents the directly opposite view to Hedâyat's in representing the Iranian artist as speaker. While recognizing the ordinariness and tragedies of life, the poet-speaker of "Another Birth" raises her voice in a song of vitality and hope. Nothing could be more different from the speaker of *The Blind Owl* who voices not only Khayyâmic fatalism, but a perhaps total despair that Khayyâm's attempts at a *carpe diem* stance mute.

With the realization, therefore, that an Iranian artist is speaking, the action of *The Blind Owl* seems appropriately reviewed in cultural terms. Of course, from the outset, the fact that the narrator is an artist may itself have cultural ramifications. In Iranian culture, at least beyond the religious community, as described earlier in conjunction with Hâfez, the literary artist is perceived as a cut above other people. He--rarely have "shes" been artists in Iran--is more sensitive, suffers more, is less corruptible and more deserving of trust. Most importantly, he understands and sees more. In the words of the scholar Farhang Jahanpour:

> . . . in Iran poets and writers are regarded as prophets, and creative writing has the sanctity and authority of holy writ. One does not read a book to challenge it, but to be led and enlightened by it. Therefore, Iranian poets and writers . . . have a social status and responsibility far greater than that of their Western counterparts. The "committed" or *engagé* writer is the eye, the ear, and the conscience of the society

95

and, for better or for worse, exerts a profound influence upon the minds of the reading public.(76)

The Blind Owl begins with the assertion that spirit-consuming, cancerous sores or wounds or pains exist in life which cannot be described to people because their reaction to such descriptions by virtue of personal beliefs and conventional attitudes is mocking laughter. Humankind has not yet found a medicine for these cancers. Only the temporary forgetfulness induced by wine and opium offer any balm. But their effects once dissipated ironically increase the intensity of the pain of these sores, which the narrator asserts are actually unnatural, supernatural events.

The opening sentence of *The Blind Owl*, quoted at the beginning of this chapter, has achieved the status of a modern enigmatic proverb. It appears on the screen at the end of the popular motion picture *Dâsh Akol* (1972), which is based on Hedâyat's story by the same name, as if to explain the tragedy of Dâsh Akol's secret love for Marjân.(77) In general, the line seems a truism to those literary Iranians who are often ready to assert that life is an unhappy business at the end of which individual human beings must face their fate alone.

From the novel's very opening statement, the reader accepts the possibility of a Hedâyatesque world wholly devoid of realizable ideals and optimism. One's experience with fiction might prompt the expectation that a naturalistic or surrealistic drama is about to unfold, those styles, so to speak, often appropriate for the expression of a view of life as a painful, hellish experience and people as a sordid, evil lot. At the same time, the reader looks forward to finding out what these mysterious sores or pains are.

A personal narrator, an "I," then appears and introduces his intention to describe one such extraordinary event which, he asserts, has poisoned and scarred his existence from the beginning to the end of time. He declares that he will try to write down what he remembers merely for the purpose of believing the unbelievable himself. That others believe what he writes is of no importance to him, there being such an abyss, he says, between them and himself anyway. He merely wants to introduce himself to his shadow on the wall, bent and appearing to devour everything he writes. Perhaps he and his shadow can come to know each other better. Ever since he severed all connections with others he has wanted to know himself. All others seem merely shadows to deceive and mock him anyway.

At this point, the title of the story begins to work upon the reader's imagination insofar as the neckless shadow on the wall could well seem an owl shape. In fact, toward the end of the novel the narrator himself observes: "My shadow on the wall had become exactly like an owl and, leaning forward, read intently every thing I wrote" (p. 123). It is night time, which is when shadows are cast on the walls, the time when the predatory, sinister, reclusive owl is active. This shadow on the wall, a reflection of the narrator, seems ready to devour the narrator's every word. The owl is the narrator, as

96

the narrator's shadow is himself. The action promises to this point to be, therefore, "self-analysis" and "writing as therapy."(78) At the same time, the reader surely begins to wonder about the curious epithet of "blind" combined with "owl" in the book's title. Because in popular lore the owl has a special gift of vision at night, a blind owl must therefore be a helpless creature with no special quality that would make him different from or better than other creatures. Assuming, as Iranian critics do, that the narrator is the title character, the reader now wonders with what sort of blindness he is afflicted. Because the only piece of the book not presented as part of the narrator's own account is the title, the phrase *The Blind Owl* becomes even more important as a direct statement to the reader by the author without the subjective, personal, intermedial voice of the narrator. It is Hedâyat's only direct communication with the reader of his fiction.

The narrator reveals that in this "rotten" world just once a ray of sunlight seemed to shine, a fleeting ray, a shooting star, which manifested itself in the form of a woman or angel. For an instant in that manifestation the grandeur and splendor of all his misfortunes were revealed. But he was unable to hold onto this inevitably passing ray.

He lost contact with her two months and four days earlier, but her sorceress's eyes and destructive rays were unforgettable. After that moment of revelation of her whose name he never mentions, he completely cut himself off from humankind and lives within the four walls of his room, a truly owlish habitat, a room that later seems both womb and tomb as well.

The narrator reveals that, aside from drinking wine and smoking opium, he spends his days painting an unvarying scene on pen-case covers in his room in a house outside of the city far from other dwellings. Painting pen-case covers, he says, is his way of killing time. But even he is struck by the bizarreness of the scene he always paints: a stooped, old man, like an Indian fakir, is crouching under a cypress tree and biting his left forefinger in surprise; opposite the old man is a girl, separated from him by a stream of water; the girl is leaning toward the old man offering him a morning glory. It is a scene that seems both strange and natural to the narrator. But what happened to him caused him to stop painting altogether.

Two months and four days earlier, on the thirteenth and final day of the annual Iranian New Year's celebration, everyone had left the city in accordance with custom.

As described earlier (see pages 61-62, above) the Iranian New Year, called *Nowruz* [new day] in Persian, is the most traditional and joyous event in the Iranian calendar. It begins on the vernal equinox, March 21st usually, the very first day of spring. New Year's customs include anticipatory spring housecleaning, the purchase or sewing of new clothing, presentation of gifts by older to younger family members, and of bonuses and special *'aydi* [holiday gratuities] to employees and workers, a ritual New Year's fish and rice dinner, visits to the homes of friends and relatives, and much more. It is an extremely sociable time which officially begins on the last Tuesday evening before the New Year with a traditional gathering at which people jump over a small fire while ritually calling for the fire to draw the winter's yellow sallowness from them and to inspire them with its red of life. The official end to *Nowruz* celebrations comes on the 13th of Farvardin, to which the narrator of *The Blind Owl* alludes here. On that day, because staying at home is assumed to bring bad luck, everyone leaves home for a picnic or other outing. The old year's atmosphere thus leaves the home, and fresh new air will be brought back.

In contrast, the narrator shuts his window so as not to be disturbed by people. But near dusk, the door to his room suddenly opens, and an old man enters (p. 7) who resembles the man depicted on the narrator's pen-case covers and what the narrator always assumed his father looked like. He introduces himself as the narrator's uncle. The narrator perceives a resemblance between himself and his visitor.

The reader begins to wonder here exactly what the narrator looks like, whether he is old or young, and what his name is. Perhaps the lack of a name and self-depiction of appearance reinforces a gradual reader reaction that the narrator is supposed to represent more than one man or even one sort of man.

The narrator suddenly decides to get something to offer to his visitor, even though he knows nothing is in the house. He comes across a flask of old wine that had apparently been bottled on the occasion of his birth. But while reaching up to the shelf to get the flask, he sees a scene outside from a small window or aperture near the ceiling (p. 8).

It is the scene he had always painted. There she is, on one side of the stream opposite the old man under a cypress tree. She seems to be offering the old man a flower. He is gnawing at his left forefinger. Her grace and motions are those possessed only by dancers in Indian temples. Her slanted Turkoman eyes emit a supernatural and intoxicating light. She seems the sort of vision that comes to one in an opium dream. The old man under the cypress tree laughs a hideous laugh.

Head in hands, the narrator sits in reverie for minutes, hours, who knows how long. In the meantime, his uncle has left. The narrator further contemplates the scene, like something in the limbo world between corporeality and spirituality. When he finally summons the courage to look again outside the window, he discovers that the window is no longer there. Nor outside of his house is there the slightest trace of the scene. It had never existed.

The reader realizes at this point that the window and the scene have been figments of the narrator's imagination, images he has drawn to his consciousness in his recounting of his life. The reader then suspects that the man who came through the door was himself another imagined event and wonders again about the physical appearance of the narrator who has admitted a resemblance between himself and his uncle. Perhaps the uncle is an image for part of the narrator's own personality. The story has taken on

98

the coloring of a surrealistic tableau: there is an air of déjà vu about everything, of the naturalness of the unnatural, of the expectedness of the unexpected.

Everything, the room, the old man, the uncle, the shadow, the girl, they may all be in the narrator's mind. As part of his mind, they are part of him, they are he or at least what he has been able to this point to discover in his attempt to describe his cancer and know himself. The reader wonders what real, external events and experiences have prompted these mental events and whether or not another world of physically real people exists in which the narrator has lived that has brought him to this mental state.

The narrator proceeds to reveal his habit of taking an evening walk. On this particular rainy and foggy night two months and four days earlier, he felt his dark thoughts being cleansed in the rain. On this occasion happened that which he declares should not have happened. More than ever before, the narrator was having a vision of the beautiful woman, a terrifying and blurred vision, a motionless and lifeless vision such as one might find on pen-case covers.

It must have been well past midnight when in the thickness of the mist the narrator could hardly see in front of himself. Then he saw a woman dressed in black seated on the platform in front of his house. It was she. He would have known her even if they had not met before. It was like being in a deep sleep. He opened the door and stepped aside for her to enter. This she does, and listlessly and without a word lies down on his bed. The narrator wonders whether she is ill or lost. She had arrived like a sleep walker. The narrator experiences at this moment an unspeakable admixture of pleasure and pain. It has the quality of the deepest sort of sleep. At this moment all of the painful events of his life are reflected in her black, slanted, Turkoman eyes. His heart stops. He is afraid to breathe. Perhaps like a cloud or smoke, she might disappear. Her weary eyes, as if having seen death, slowly close. In her sleep, she is chewing the fingernail of her left forefinger.

Thinking she is perhaps hungry or thirsty, the narrator, although knowing there is nothing in the house, looks for something to give her. He finds the bottle of wine and slowly pours some into her mouth through her closed teeth. Her body was warm. But then the narrator senses that her hair is cold and realizes that she is dead. No pulse, no breath. Hoping to warm her lifeless body, he undresses and lies beside her on the bed. They are intertwined like a mandrake plant. He accepts the fact that she has surrendered her body and soul to him on his bed in his room. She had submitted to him with closed eyes, this ethereal creature who, he says, had haunted him all his life and had in fact poisoned his existence.

Because the reader has already come to expect events to be mental, there is no reason for this event to be other than another product of the narrator's imagination. The narrator has achieved fruition with the spiritual, ethereal creature he had sought for his whole life. He has taken her life and soul into himself. The wine, it is seen, which the uncle had not stayed to imbibe, is the gift of death, the "darker drink" of which FitzGerald's Khayyám speaks. Wine bottled on the occasion of one's birth is the acknowledgment of the one fact that becomes certain at the moment of birth: death. The narrator's imagined beloved has accepted death at the hands of the narrator in the room of his imagination, on the bed of his desires, now her bed. But the narrator does not think he has killed her, nor does he display awareness that his wine may be poisonous.

The narrator then says he needs to do two things: first, to capture those eyes on paper; second, to dispose of the corpse. He spends the night unsuccessfully trying to draw the eyes. Toward dawn, the corpse's cheeks miraculously redden, and her eyes open and look at him for the first time. He is able to draw them. He puts the paper into his till. He himself begins to doubt the reality of the whole experience.

The narrator decides to cut the body up into pieces. He does this grizzly chore and puts the pieces into a suitcase. He lifts up the suitcase. It is incredibly heavy. He realizes that he will not be able to carry it by himself.

Outside it is once again raining--the only ray of sunshine in the narrator's mental world was the ray of sunlight that had manifested itself in the form of the ethereal girl. The narrator runs into an old man seated under a cypress tree who laughs a blood-curdling laugh and informs the narrator that he has a hearse carriage for taking corpses to Shâh 'Abdol'azim. In addition, he makes coffins that are always the right size, and he knows the narrator's address. The narrator climbs aboard the carriage, holds the suitcase atop himself, and off they go. The weight of the suitcase is incredible. But it is a familiar weight pressing on him.

They pass through mountains and fields and across rivers. They pass by houses shaped like cones, prisms, and cubes without windows, eventually reaching a desolate area near Shâh 'Abdol'azim.

Shâh 'Abdol'azim is a popular Shi'i shrine located in the town of Rayy, which was a famous city from pre-Islamic times known in the West as Rhages. The Shi'i shrine there is named after the son of a Zaydi imam who died in 868. The allusion to this shrine is one of a number of details that define the geographical and temporal setting of *The Blind Owl*.(79)

The narrator proceeds to offer a couple of old coins to the driver for his services. They are two *qerâns* and one *'abbâsi*. The latter coins are named after Safavid Shâh 'Abbâs the Great (ruled 1587-1629) and ceased being used in the early years of the twentieth century. *Qerâns* were instituted by Qâjâr monarch Fath 'Ali Shâh (ruled 1797-1834); and the term, although not the coin, remains in currency. The use of *qerân* and *'abbâsi* coins implies that the temporal setting of the action is from the late nineteenth through early twentieth centuries, that is up to Hedâyat's writing of the novel in the 1930s.

When offered these coins by the narrator, the old hearse driver laughs. He then says that he knows how to dig graves. He proceeds to dig a grave and in the process unearths a ceramic vessel. The narrator again reaches for coins

100

with which to pay him. The latter laughs and reminds the narrator that he has unearthed the pitcher, implying that that is recompense enough. The detail of such a Rayy pitcher serves to make the geographical and temporal setting more definite. The sort of pottery referred to would probably be medieval, Saljuq for example. It would have value and be considered very old in the late nineteenth or early twentieth century.

The grave digger proceeds to bury the body and cover the grave in such fashion that no one could guess that there was even a grave there. The narrator becomes aware of his own soiled, ripped and bloodied clothes to which worms are clinging. His efforts to rub the blood out merely spread it all over him.

It is a drizzling dusk. When it becomes dark, the narrator loses the tracks of the hearse carriage and wanders about in lonely darkness, the same darkness her eyes caused. There is total silence. The solitude is dizzyingly pleasurable. Extreme weariness overcomes him. Suddenly he hears a grizzly cough and sees an old man with a small, kerchiefed bundle under his arm seated beside him. The old man asks if he wants a ride to the city and offers him his ceramic vessel. The narrator tries to pay the old man with a couple of coins, at which the old man laughs. They take off in the hearse, in which the narrator reclines with the piece of pottery on his chest. It is as heavy as the weight of a dead person. They pass by homes of geometric shapes. The narrator, overcome with the odor of death, feels that he has always been in a casket and that he has always been led about by a hunched over, old man.

On reaching his home, the narrator rushes inside and gets his money to offer something to the driver. But the latter had gone, just like his uncle earlier. He opens up the kerchief and looks at the pitcher. On it is her face with her eyes. He takes out his drawing of the night before and compares the two. They are identical. Maybe the artist's soul had entered his soul. He wants to escape from himself. Once again he sees all the misfortunes of his life. He has never felt so accursed and unfortunate; but at the same time he experiences the joy of knowing that long ago, perhaps thousands of years ago, another kindred spirit has existed, the bones of whose people may be in the lilies of today. Among those people was one ill-fated artist like himself. Placing the two pictures in front of himself, the narrator begins to smoke opium, stares at the pictures and falls into opiatic ecstasy. The weight seems to disappear from his chest. Weightlessness, the apparitions of forms, ethereal caresses, the sound of his blood coursing in his veins, and ecstasy descend upon him.

He grows weary and desires forgetful sleep, to disappear into nothingness (p. 42). He begins to dream and then to move backward in time to his childhood, to smallness, until he is attached to a thin hook hanging at the bottom of a deep, dark well. He gets free of the hook and moves into the distance, into an eternal night where there is a precipice. For a moment he experiences pure forgetfulness. Then he comes to and finds himself in a

small room and special circumstances that seem both strange and natural for him (p. 44).

The new world into which the narrator "awakens" is by his own report completely familiar, even more comfortable than his former/earlier life and surroundings, as if it were a reflection or echo of his real life. It was an old world into which he had been born, like his basic, original environment.

The weather was still twilight (p. 44). He was awake, a tallow burning in the room. He senses that his body is hot and that his clothes have blood stuck to them, his hands too. But despite his fever and dizziness, a special excitement arose in him stronger than the thought of cleaning the spots of blood, stronger than the fear that the constable would come and arrest him. For some time he had been expecting to fall into the hands of the constable. But he had made a decision to gulp the flask of poisonous wine before his arrest. It was the need to write which had become a sort of necessary duty. He wanted to extirpate the demon tormenting his internal being. Finally after some doubt, he brings the tallow forward and starts writing.

He writes that although silence is always best, it is out of his hands now because what should not have happened has happened. A drunken lot of policemen may be on their way right now. He is not concerned about saving his own skin. And there is no denying what has happened. Even if he can clean the spots of blood, before he falls into their hands he plans to drink a glass from the flask of inherited wine on the shelf above.

Now, he says, he wants to squeeze his whole life like a cluster of grapes and drip the extract or wine of it, drop by drop, into the dry throat of the shadow like holy water from the religious shrine at Karbalâ. He wants to transfer to others the cancerous pains that have tormented him (p. 47), echoing the very first sentence of the novel. Nothing is left in life for him. He wants merely to write to communicate thoughts to the ill-omened shadow which reads and devours whatever he writes.

He reveals that yesterday he appeared to be a broken and ill youth, but today he looks like a bent old man with white hair, fistular eyes, and a harelip. He is afraid to look around, for everywhere he sees his double. In order to explain his life to this shadow, he has to tell a story. He says he does not even know where he is: Nishâpur, Balkh, or Banares. He has no certainty about anything and doubts the law of gravity and physical reality.

Now that he looked into the mirror he recognized himself. No, the "me" of the past is dead and decomposed. But no barrier exists between the past "me" and the present "me." Life is a tale, a fairy tale. Time has no importance or meaning for the narrator, he says. Something about yesterday could seem older and less significant than something which happened a thousand years ago.

At this point, in assuming that the narrator has somehow physically or metaphysically awakened to the real world or reached a state of different or greater consciousness than that of the first part of the story, the reader may hypothesize that the second part of the story, about to unfold (pp. 46-128),

will reveal the external events or experiences that triggered the earlier internal or imagined sequence of events (pp. 4-43). Consequently, the reader can expect to confront images, characters, and actions that were transmuted into the images, characters and actions that peopled the narrator's mind in the first part of the story.

At the same time, now that the narrator declares that he has physically begun writing his story for his shadow, the reader must feel that if the shadow is a reflection on the wall of the narrator, insofar as the shadow and the reader share the action of devouring the written words, the shadow and the reader are one and the same in that sense. But if that is so, then the reader is likewise identified with the narrator:

$$\text{reader} \quad = \quad \text{shadow} \quad = \quad \text{narrator}$$

$$\text{reading} \qquad\qquad\qquad\qquad \text{reflection}$$

This may mean that the author as distinguished from the narrator/protagonist assumes that the narrator and Iranian readers have something in common and expects the latter either to be sympathetic toward the protagonist or to experience horrified recognition. Put in other words, Hedâyat is implying that somehow those cancerous sores initially characterized as a fact of life exist in every Iranian (as well as in non-Iranians, perhaps). Thus readers have all the more reason not to lose themselves uncritically in the surrealistic and mysteriously symbolic sequence of events. It is a life-and-death matter to comprehend exactly what has happened and who the narrator is. For when the narrator comes to know himself, Iranian readers will presumably have come to know aspects of their own selves and situations as well. Of course, if the novel's title accurately reflects the character or situation of the protagonist, perhaps he will never learn to see. If that is the case, then the owl shadow shapes of the readers who can read, i.e., who can see, have the whole responsibility to perceive who the protagonist is and what the cancerous sores plaguing him are.

Actually things are more complicated than that. Toward the end of the novel, the narrator/protagonist says: "My shadow on the wall had become exactly like an owl" (p. 123). It is possible that the narrator/protagonist is not the owl of the book's title himself; but rather the shadow is, as the narrator explicitly observes, mistakenly thinking that the owl-shadow can see. In other words, the narrator never compares himself to an owl. At the same time, it is possible that the author Hedâyat is implying that just as the owl-shadow literally looking over the narrator's shoulder cannot see or read what he has written, perhaps readers of the novel, owl-like in their reading, may themselves not be able to see what the story is all about. On the other hand, no internal reason presents itself for one to assume that owl-like readers outside the novel need be blind.(80)

As the narrator says, in order to explain his life to his stooping shadow, he is obliged to tell a story. He asserts that, of course, life itself is a fiction, a mere story, and that he even doubts the existence of tangible, solid things and clear, manifest truths.

He reveals that he lives in a room built of sun-dried bricks that stand upon the ruins of thousands of ancient houses. It, he says, is like a tomb. And since he has been confined to his bed, people have been paying little attention to him. The room's two windows face the world of "the rabble," one toward the courtyard and the other onto the street, where a butcher's shop is located and where an old man selling odds and ends sits by his wares. These, the narrator says, are his links to the outside world.

As for his private world, there are his nurse and his wife, who was also nursed by Nanny and whose mother raised the narrator. The narrator never saw his parents. The account of them he believes is one that Nanny has told him, according to whom the narrator's father and uncle were identical twins who went to India as merchants of Rayy wares. There his father fell in love with a lingam temple dancer named Bugâm Dâsi who became pregnant; and the narrator was born. But his uncle returning to Banares after a trip also fell in love with Bugâm Dâsi and had sexual relations with her since she could not tell him apart from his brother. When Bugâm Dâsi learned what had happened she declared that she would never have anything further to do with either brother unless they submitted to a "trial by cobra."

The brothers were shut up in a dark room with the serpent. One died; and the other, apparently the narrator's uncle, emerged as a white-haired old man. Subsequently because the narrator became just an extra mouth to feed, his parents left him with his paternal aunt on a trip to Rayy. His mother also left a wine bottle full of red wine and cobra venom, the same venom that killed either his father or his uncle in the trial by cobra. The narrator wonders if his mother, the only character in *The Blind Owl* with a proper name, is still alive.

Thereafter, his aunt became a mother to the narrator. He loved her deeply and even married her daughter because she looked like her mother. It was at the bedside of his dead aunt, he says, that her daughter made advances to him which were interrupted by her father, who forced them to marry to save the girl's reputation. Subsequently as his wife, his cousin would never let him near her, although he asserts that she had lovers right and left. He then tried to befriend her lovers to learn from them how to seduce his wife. In his desire for her, the narrator wasted away. The doctor was called and prescribed a special diet and fumigation of his room. His condition grew worse. He had a terrible cough, and dreams and fantasies.

The narrator reveals that once his condition improved somewhat, he decided to go away, to somewhere where people could never find him again. He then proceeds to relate the events of four consecutive days interspersing the narrative with his reflections.

The first day is the day of the narrator's departure. He leaves the city, approaches the Suren River, and finds a peaceful spot where he sees a little girl in a black dress biting her fingernail as she walks past. He recalls that his aunt, his wife, and he had come here once on the 13th day of the new year. Continuing his reverie, the narrator finds himself back in the city at sunset in front of his father-in-law's house where he sees his little brother-in-law. He sets the boy on his lap and kisses him on his half-opened mouth, imagining that his sister's lips must taste the same. At that moment, his father-in-law passes by laughing convulsively. Utterly embarrassed, the narrator goes home and shuts himself in his room. Taking to his bed, he falls asleep and begins to dream that the old odds-and-ends man has been hanged on a gallows in Mohammadiyeh Square. The narrator awakens after dreaming that his mother-in-law was dragging him forward to be hanged as well.

A new day dawns, and Nanny brings him breakfast and sits with him for a while. At midday, she returns with his dinner. But he upsets the soup bowl and begins to scream, causing the whole family to come to his room. He notices that his pregnant wife has not yet given birth. The doctor arrives and prescribes opium for him. That evening the narrator gets up and looks out the window. He hears a group of drunken policemen singing, and cringes in terror, although he realizes they are not coming for him because they do not know . . .

In the darkness a motionless shadow shape gazes steadily at the narrator, reminding him of the butcher. The narrator looks at himself in the mirror and becomes fearful of his own reflection. He returns to bed, closes his eyes, and senses an indistinct world beginning to take shape around him that is more real than the real world. He falls asleep and dreams of wandering free through an unknown town full of dead people, a butcher's shop and an old man like the odds-and-ends man. Arriving at his father-in-law's house, his brother-in-law's head topples off at the narrator's touch. Screaming, he awakens.

It is morning again, of the third day. Nanny brings breakfast, and from the window the butcher and the odds-and-ends man are visible. The narrator returns to his room and makes a frightful resolution. He takes his bone-handled knife. Now that death is coming to get him, he is going to take "the bitch" with him. At that moment a funeral procession passes by his window: ordinary people are undergoing temporarily what the narrator in his coffin-room undergoes all of the time. He really hopes to pass into oblivion and nonbeing. He thinks about death. His life appears to him just as strange, as unnatural, as inexplicable as the picture on that pen-case he is using this moment as he writes. It is a picture of the surprised old man, the girl in the black dress with a morning glory, the stream between them. He is seated beside his opium brazier. He relates that Nanny told him that she saw the odds-and-ends man coming out of his wife's room. That same evening, the crisis approaches. His wife enters the room. Her mere visit brings him incredible joy. She leaves the room after a brief exchange. Time passes, minutes, hours, centuries, he does not know. Pain causes him exquisite pleasure. His wife returns. He falls at her feet, sobbing and coughing, kissing her legs. Time passes. When he comes to, she is gone.

His nurse brings him his supper, but runs away terrified. She returns as he is coughing up blood. He falls asleep and is later that night awakened by the song of the policemen. He suddenly remembers the wine that will make all "the nightmares of life" fade. He decides to give his wife, the bitch, some too so that they might die together in a single convulsion. This is how strong his love for her is.

He comes to a frightful decision. He gets out of bed, rolls up his sleeves and takes out the bone-handled knife, and puts on a cloak and scarf, assuming a guise that is a cross between the butcher and the odds-and-ends man. He visits his wife's room. A sneeze and cough interrupt him. Otherwise he would have cut the bitch to pieces. He tosses the knife onto the roof and goes back to his room.

The next morning, the fourth, Nanny brings breakfast to him. On the breakfast tray is a knife she had bought from the old odds-and-ends man.

That night, the narrator is feverish with death murmuring its song in his ear. He hears the policemen's song again. He dresses as on the previous night, takes the knife and goes toward the "bitch's" room. Love and hatred become one. He undresses but keeps the knife! They embrace. She encircles him like a cobra around its prey. She bites through his lip. Their bodies are soldered into one. He thinks she has gone mad and jerks his hand involuntarily. The knife plunges into her. She releases him. She is dead, her eye in his hand. He is drenched in blood. He looks in the mirror and is exactly like the odds-and-ends man.

The agitation seems to awaken him. He rubs his eyes and realizes that he is back in his own room. It is almost dawn. He looks for the vase he had been contemplating and comparing to his drawing of the ethereal girl (in the first part of the novel) as he smoked opium late at night and was transported to the state "between sleep and coma" (which was his during the second part of the novel). But the vase is gone. An old man is running away with something like it under his arm. The narrator looks at himself. His clothes are torn and bloodstained. Blister flies are circling about him. Tiny, white maggots are wriggling on his coat. He feels the weight of a dead body on his chest. In the context of the references to his "own room" (p. 129), the crowing rooster, the maggots, blister flies, and the vase, the narrator's description of the charcoal ashes in the brazier indicates that the longer second part of the novel has taken place in his opium-induced state through the course of one evening. This means that the novel ends with the narrator back in a conscious state where he was the previous evening contemplating the vase.

Of course, the reader wonders if the narrator, now awake, will now recognize the torn clothes and congealed blood for what they have been shown to be during his subconscious revelation of his wife's stabbing. In one view, the narrator is "unable to rise beyond a certain level of self awareness . . . The epilogue leaves no doubt that he has relapsed into fantasy, for after having become the odds-and-ends man he wakes up 'as if from a long, deep sleep' (p. 129), and the narration connects, without a break, to where the fantasy of Part One left off."(81)

In other words, at the end of the novel the narrator, awake in his real world, about which he formerly could only fantasize, may not have achieved his goal of self-knowledge, because he never was able to write his words down--only in his dream of his life (pp. 44-128) did he put imaginary pen to imaginary paper, as opposed to his explicit intention in the first part of the novel (pp. 2-3) to write the truth which he seems unable to confess to himself when awake (pp. 1-43 and 129-130). It is unlikely, then, that he will be able when awake to face or remember what he was able to verbalize only when asleep. In fine, the extent to which his attempt at self-knowledge has succeeded may be defined by the weight he senses on his chest.

At the book's end, the reader may feel little hope of finding the real or external world of time and place from which derives the consciously evoked, yet internal, world of the first major section of the book and those explicit dream or reflective sections of the second two-thirds of the book. Furthermore, if what the narrator has presented as truth in the novel's first section has proved to be a product of his imagination, whether deliberate prevarication or not, then the reader may not be able to trust the narrator's dream recounting events in the second major section as a true reflection of what has actually happened to him. An initial impulse at this point, along with an acknowledgement of the richness of the novel's texture and atmosphere created by the evocative flow of the narrator's recounting of things, may be to accept the judgment of some Iranian critics that readers should desist from attempting to read the book analytically and critically.(82)

Because practical literary criticism did not develop as a traditional dimension of literary art in Iran, contemporary critics who are analytical in their attitudes are uniformly inspired by familiarity with Western literary critical theories and practice. In contrast, traditional readers of literary works in Iran are persons, perhaps well acquainted with prior accomplishments in a genre or species, who, as described in the previous chapter on Hafez, are prepared to be transported by a piece of literature at hand provided that it add to or embellish the received tradition in a particular medium. In these terms, Hedâyat's novel is problematic. First, it is a work which seems almost private in imagery and symbolism. Second, the narrator's personality is variously interpreted with a range of opinion that is testimony to subjectivity of Iranian reader responses to imaginative literature, not unlike the earlier observed variety of opinion about the world view embodied in Khayyâmic quatrains, which different readers have characterized as agnostic, hedonist, orthodox Sunni, and Sufi.

Such constant diversity of opinion in these regards in Iran seems at the very least to point to a strong tradition of creative reading without a concomitant critical tradition. That tendency aside, the critical reader must seek to discern a minimal, unspeculative thematic core in *The Blind Owl* and attempt as part of this alternative reaction to the novel to dispose of problematic aspects of the narrative one by one, leaving only the question of the narrator's reliability, which may have its own answer.

For example, the mysterious or ambiguous details of the setting may be the author's deliberate removal of narrative time and place from a real world environment in order to broaden the focus of the narrative themes and to make them applicable somehow to people of various times and places by limiting the setting to no one specific time and place. That none of the characters except for Bugâm Dâsi has a name may contribute to the same end. On the other hand, cultural factors may account for the ambiguity or mystery of the novel's setting: the narrator's perception of time and place may be a reasonable stance for a particular sort of Iranian confronting an actual Iran.

In any case, it is certain that the action takes place in and near the cities of Tehrân and Rayy, the latter a place of great antiquity and historical importance and now an urban center just south of Tehrân. As described earlier in passing, the temporal setting as well has precise limits: any time from the latter part of the nineteenth century through the first decades of the twentieth century, that is up to the 1930s, the actual time when Hedâyat wrote the novel; in the second major section, the narrator offers anachronistic details which place him in his imagination in pre-Mongol Iran.

Now, the reader's realization of the facts of the geographical and temporal setting--Rayy (the quintessential city of all ages), a medieval-to-contemporary life span for in the narrator's imagination, the narrator's namelessness and facelessness, the incremental repetition of images of scenes breeding in the reader a sense of familiarity, and the connection between the narrator and reader through the owl-shadow image--all lead to the sense that *The Blind Owl* must embody themes relevant to readers of different times and places and that its action somehow typifies more general Iranian experience than the individual narrator's.

Then there is the observation to the effect that the fact that a story takes place on the site of a buried city, according to Freud, is particularly appropriate to stories about repressed desire.(83) The same questions raise themselves again about what is being repressed, about what it is that the narrator can not or at least does not directly say, about who he really is, and about those cancerous sores.

Several possibilities become evident in reflection at this point on the title of this chapter: "A Modernist Iranian Writer's Almost Inevitable Nightmare." The second major section of *The Blind Owl* may literally be a nightmare. The whole book strikes the reader as the proverbial bad dream.

But any sense of Hedâyat's attempt at a representation of cultural themes seems contradicted by the personality of the narrator who may not seem to represent more than himself and may seem to be a unique or atypical and perhaps deranged individual for whom sympathy, much less identification, is difficult. For the themes to seem to have relevance to many readers, the narrator must seem in basic ways to embody Iranian characteristics. There has to be something of the Iranian reader or Iranian culture recognizable in the narrator and much of the narrator in the Iranian reader. Something about his life has to have the qualities which the reader imputes to life. In other words, the events of *The Blind Owl* must be linked to the lives of Iranian readers.

During the course of the action, the narrator changes, in his own words, from a sickly youth to a white-haired old man, a man resembling other men in the novel. In this sense, regardless of how real the other characters in the novel are, the narrator eventually sees himself as similar to other people. Because he has actually been like other people since the beginning, his recognition of the fact rather than any dramatic change in his character constitutes the resolution of the novel. One could call it a Khayyâmic recognition: FitzGerald's character in *The Rubaíyát of Omar Khayyám* does not change through the 101 stanzas of that poem, but merely is able finally to recognize and resign himself to the truth that he had guessed almost from the outset.

More of Khayyâm imbues the narrator of *The Blind Owl* than this, however.(84) Therein may lie basic cultural connections between Iranian readers and the narrator of the novel, because many readers feel akin to Khayyâm, the character in FitzGerald's poem, as they seem not to feel with respect to the narrator of *The Blind Owl*. First, these two characters have similar views about the world. They believe that physical creation, in particular that of humankind, was an accident and that humankind is subject to the dictates of fate, making individual effort pointless. In their view, humans are of no more importance than flies. Molecules are merely transmitted from one being to another. Wine and opium are the sole medicine, although they bring forgetfulness rather than a cure. Death, the final, irrevocable, annihilating fact, is the only certainty. In this last named Khayyâmic parallel, the reader and the narrator may differ only in that the latter as a thoroughgoing secular Iranian intellectual has allowed the fact of human mortality to become a near obsession for him, whereas most readers have religious or cultural contexts to which they cling so that the vision of certain future death and endless nothingness does not become a present nightmare. The narrator of *The Blind Owl*, therefore, is that sort of modern man, like FitzGerald's Khayyâm, who is on his own, an individual dissatisfied with the answers of faith and reason or religion and science, who recognizes that at birth the bird of time begins its fluttering, that the bottle of wine commemorating birth is really a symbol of future death, and that, insofar as physicality and sexuality intimate mortality, any attempt to see the world as a garden or Eden or paradise is doomed to failure. The world for this narrator is his room, not unlike the womb from which he came or the grave to which he will be eventually consigned. Thus, the narrator and the reader both share the sore or pain of life itself, which is the clock of aging and death that begins ticking at birth. Individual reactions to this realization may differ. But the realization can bring the narrator and the reader together in their common fate.

It may be particularly natural for the Iranian literary artist characterized by the narrator of *The Blind Owl* to react obsessively to mortality and, despite his protestations to the contrary, to time and history as well. The Iranian writer is likely to be especially conscious of and familiar with the lengthy, continuous history of Iran. The Iranian countryside is covered with monuments to this history, really monuments to human mortality and the transience of human achievement: archeological mounds, abandoned caravanserais, vestiges of citadel walls, crumbling mud brick structures merging again with the ground from which their components were taken. The great monuments in which some life still inheres from Susa and Persepolis to Tus and old Nishâpur are testimony as much to great dying as to great glory. The Iranian writer perhaps feels that Iranian glory is dead. The present thus becomes an unsatisfactory epilogue, and the future hardly worth struggling for. The sensitive artist can hardly help becoming past-oriented. Consequently, he or she has to shoulder the burden of the past: it is as heavy as a corpse. The present becomes full of the torment which Akhavan-e Sales communicates in "The Ending of the *Shâhnâmeh*" and "I Saw Susa" (see pp. 16-19, above).

For both the narrator of *The Blind Owl* and the speaker in "The Ending of the *Shâhnâmeh*," a complicating fact in their artistic sensitivity to Iranian history is their view of Islam as an alien force. Akhavân-e Sâles calls it "false lights" after the true light of Achaemenid and Sasanian days. In *The Blind Owl*, the narrator has no faith in Allâh and Islam: the old Koran reader has yellowed, decayed teeth which have rotted after years of Koran recitations; and the horses leading the hearse carriage in the misty darkness seem not to have hooves, as if their feet were chopped off like the limbs of thieves in accordance with Islam's "barbaric" law. For that matter, Rayy's greatest glory was pre-Islamic.

Ordinary Iranians who have religious faith and anticipate the Hidden Emâm's tomorrow or perhaps even Ruhollâh Khomayni's vision of things to come on earth can hardly appreciate the artist's vision, whether historically framed by Akhavân-e Sâles in his own persona or surrealistically framed by Hedâyat in the persona of the narrator of *The Blind Owl*, who knows that "ordinary" people will laugh at him and his cancer-like torments.

In his obsession with mortality, the narrator finds only one consolation, the Khayyâmic recognition that others have had the same feelings in the past. As for the present, the narrator would like to have at least the satisfaction of feeling significant in being different from other people. If life is an affliction because it is temporary and the fear of death gnaws at one, and if Iranian life obliges one to feel the death in 2,500 years of history, one could at least be special in being individualistic, in not being like the rabble. This means trying to be spiritual rather than physical, because physicality and sexuality themselves merely heighten the fear of individual death and the burden of historical dying. So the narrator clings to vision of the ethereal girl, the memory of his wife in her youth, and the image of the spiritual side of his mother and aunt. He would like to see himself as a sickly youth and not as the white-haired old men who are his uncle, the butcher, his father-in-law, and the odds-and-ends man. That sickly youth could be the young, sensitive, prototypical Iranian artist for whom, even if the past weighs heavily upon him, has future creativity before him. In Iranian terms, one is recognizable as an artist because of differences from other people. However, Hedâyat's self-revelation may be that Iranians may today not have even the consolation of having special individual artists different from ordinary Iranians as a distinctive feature of their culture.

The Blind Owl represents, in fine, the failure of one sort of Iranian psyche and cultural personality to achieve harmony with himself and the world beyond him in the contemporary age. It is literally the failure of its protagonist, but also Hedâyat's confession of his own failure. Hedâyat personally strove to escape the ramifications of the seventh-century Arab Moslem invasion through telescoping of his cultural past, leapfrogging to pre-Islamic Iranian days, and through Promethean defiance and vilification of Islam as an alien cultural force. Hedâyat failed in his personal and public life to overcome what he detested, or to survive within its context. His inclination to slink to the shadows and to refuse to participate in the society of his fathers played havoc with his psyche. In addition, his final answer was exile from Iran, first through a voyage to Paris, and then through suicide, a remedy which invariably kills the patient. One can accept Al-e Ahmad's view that Hedâyat's suicide was a courageous statement of refusal to live in a degraded Iran.(85) Yet one is hard put to discern effects of Hedâyat's action on anyone other than himself or on Iranian society and culture. His was an onanistic gesture in life as well as in *The Blind Owl*, where the main character is unable or unwilling to participate in "intercourse" as other people are because that might cause personal floodgates to open and force the character to be, and to understand that he is, like everyone else.

But, as argued above with respect to the narrator of *The Blind Owl*, Hedâyat's individual cultural personality may be less unusual than is commonly supposed. Of course, his was literally as unique as his famous character's. But he seems also a manifestation of a perspective very much a perennial part of the Iranian cultural scene. This assertion gains plausibility when one compares Hedâyat with the most prominent Iranian writer of fiction two generations later, Gholâmhosayn Sâ'edi (1935/6-1985).

His age's leading dramatist as well as a prolific short story writer, essayist, ethnographer, and editor of literary magazines, Sâ'edi seems at first the opposite of Hedâyat. He was a man of modest Tabriz origins who spoke Persian with traces of an Azarbâyjâni accent. He was a physician by training, with a specialization in psychiatry. He was perceived by some acquaintances as extremely gregarious and unreservedly *engagé* in his literary activities. Characters similiar to their author rarely appear in Sâ'edi's stories. He seems more a camera than Hedâyat, who seems a sort of a projector whose personality imbues not only the title character in *The Blind Owl*, but numerous other characters as well, such as the protagonists in "Buried Alive" and "Three Drops of Blood."

But in other respects, among them several intriguing coincidences, the personalities of Hedâyat and Sâ'edi exhibit similarities.

The leading prose writers of their ages--Al-e Ahmad was the leading figure in the generation between them--, both Hedâyat and Sâ'edi died in Paris not long before their fiftieth birthdays. Both had escaped from what they felt were intolerable conditions in Iran. Yet they both knew they would not survive in exile. Hedâyat went to Paris to die, and committed suicide by turning on the gas in the kitchen stove. Some of Sâ'edi's friends think his death was self-inflicted too. In their view, his disregard for his own health, despite the fact that he was a physician, together with his excessive smoking and consumption of alcoholic beverages, his refusal to engage in physical exercise, and his inclination to brood on unpleasant facts, were symptoms of deliberate, gradual self-destruction. Such speculation aside, it seems clear that Sâ'edi died in exile mostly of exile. And Hedâyat's sense of exile or alienation led him to the same place, death in Paris. Both Hedâyat and Sâ'edi are buried there in Section 85 of Père Lachaise Cemetery. Before his final trip to that spot, Sâ'edi's most public activity during his exile in Paris was an April 1984 improvisatory theatre performance and talk at Hedâyat's gravesite on the thirty-third anniversary of Hedâyat's death. Sâ'edi felt a special affinity to Hedâyat.(86)

Both Sâ'edi and Hedâyat did much of their living through their writing. Their almost constant thoughts of death and suicide throughout their lives contrasted with their energetic efforts at permanence through creative activity. They seem quintessential examples of Iranian tension between self-destruction and creativity. Only in their writings, in addition, were they able to be wholly open. In his personal life, Hedâyat was withdrawn and shy, able to communicate easily only with a few close friends, who invariably comment on his great sense of humor in private. Also a witty man, Sâ'edi seemed gregarious to some, but was really very shy, shunned large groups of people and relaxed only with intimates. In Paris, Sâ'edi's Gallieni apartment was as much a prison as the narrator's room in *The Blind Owl*. But Sâ'edi disliked leaving it and cringed from travelling around the city. During his years in Paris, he made no effort to learn French, deliberating cutting himself off from the society about him.(87)

112

Neither Sâ'edi nor Hedâyat had children. In the next chapter, the potential cultural significance of this for an Iranian man, Al-e Ahmad being the case study, is hinted at. Hedâyat never married and was allegedly uncomfortable in social situations in which he might be paired with a woman. Sâ'edi had woman acquaintances; but friends say he was unwilling to enter into serious relationships with them. He finally married after going into exile, but even then did not immediately introduce his wife to visitors and seemed embarrassed at having married so late, as if others might think him "a dirty, old man" for so doing.

The burden that oppressed Hedâyat was cultural history itself, whereas Sâ'edi was haunted by the cultural burden of the oppression of the masses which was the legacy of that history. Consequently, Hedâyat buried himself in the study and dreams of the past, while Sâ'edi inundated himself in the present. Both he and Hedâyat are the sorts of personalities Nimâ Yushij could have had in mind in his famous poem usually given the title "Ahoy There, People," which the poet recited at the First Congress of Iranian Writers held in Tehrân in the summer of 1946. The poem reads:

Ahoy, you over there,
sitting on the shore, happy and laughing,
someone is dying in the water.
Someone is struggling frantically
[5]in this turbulent, heavy, dark, familiar sea.
When you are drunk
with thoughts of getting your hands on your enemy,
when you vainly think
you have given a hand to a weak person to produce better,
[10]when you tighten your belts, when,
when shall I tell you
that someone in the water
is sacrificing his life in vain?
Ahoy, you over there
[15]seated comfortably on the shore,
bread on your tablecloths, clothes on your bodies,
someone is calling you from the water.
He beats heavy waves with weary hands,
his mouth agape, eyes wide with terror,
[20]he has seen your shadows from afar,
has swallowed water in the dark blue deep,
each moment his impatience grows,
he raises above the water
a foot, at times,
[25]at times, his head . . .
Ahoy, you over there,
he still has his eyes on this old world from afar,

113

he is shouting and hopes for help.
Ahoy, you over there
[30]calmly watching from the shore,
the wave beats on the silent shore, spreads
like a drunk fallen unconscious,
retreats roaring, and this call comes from afar again:
    'Ahoy, you over there'. . .
And the sound of the wind
[35]more heart-rending by the moment,
and his voice weaker in the sound of the wind;
from waters near and far
again echoes this call: 'Ahoy, you over there'. . .(88)

No one apparently heeded the cries of either Hedâyat or Sâ'edi, and for the reasons the metaphors in Nimâ's poem describe. Furthermore, many of the people who lionized these two writers merely took advantage of their essentially translucent, politically naive souls, the Tudeh (Communist) Party in the case of Hedâyat, and the Mojâhedin Organization in the case of Sâ'edi.

As alienated, tortured, conscience-stricken, sincere, sometimes helpless men, and as writers of great creativity, Hedâyat and Sâ'edi were cursed in another respect as well. They could not honestly believe in the popular, leftist notion that the common people represented the salvation for a corrupt and decadent Iranian culture. For Hedâyat, the ordinary people were a despicable, animalistic rabble. For Sâ'edi, they were no better or worse than middle class and upper class Iranians, just with less education, money, and power. A number of literary confrères criticized Sâ'edi for what they construed as his pessimism in this regard. But they were mistaken; and therein lies a great difference between Hedâyat and Sâ'edi. The latter actually believed in a new day for Iran, whereas Hedâyat despaired of any sort of renaissance.

Sâ'edi's very brief story called "The Umbrella" clearly implies this underlying optimism. It is the tale of an official of the Census Bureau who as usual one day leaves his office for home at six p.m. The sky is threatening rain. And Mr. Hasani has errands to do. But he has his umbrella. He visits the grocer, the shoemaker, the haberdasher, and the cobbler. By this time the rain begins. He has misplaced his umbrella. He backtracks, but the shopkeepers can't help him. He trudges toward home in the rain. Then, as Sâ'edi tells it:

> When he arrived in front of the house, he no longer had the strength to stand. He kicked at the door a couple of times and leaned against the wall to recover his breath. Then he pounded angrily with the doorknocker. A moment later came the sound of hurried footsteps. "Who is it?"

114

"Open up!"

His wife, carrying a lamp in her hand, opened the door a little way and, recognizing Mr. Hasani, stepped back a few paces.

"Oh my, what's happened to you? How did you get into this state? What on earth have you been playing at?"

"Aren't the lights working?"

"The power's been cut off since noon. What happened? Did you fall?"

Mr. Hasani went in and, still clutching the packages in his arms, leaned against the wall and said: "I couldn't get a bus, I couldn't get a taxi, none of them would take me. Someone took my umbrella, stole it; I've been struggling through the rain, wading through the mud; I'm soaking wet, tired out, washed up." And his eyes filled with tears.

Without a word, Mr. Hasani's wife came forward and, holding up the lamp, took the packages one by one from under her husband's astonished gaze. Hanging on Mr. Hasani's arm was the umbrella.(89)

Sâ'edi's Mr. Hasani is not helpless or hopeless, as many Hedâyat characters are, but merely incompetent. His individual problem, reaching home without getting wet, has a solution, i.e., the utilization of his umbrella, which he mistakenly thinks he has lost. If the story were a social allegory, Sâ'edi's message would be quite clear: individual Iranians have at their disposal the means by which to resolve their individual problems, if only they exercise the perspicacity to recognize the availability of such means.

In his stage play called *The Clubwielders of Varazil* (1965), Sâ'edi creates an allegory on this very issue, focussing on Iranian society as a whole.(90) Set in an Iranian village whose peasant farmers have been plagued by visitations of wild boars, the play opens with one villager calling the others at night to the square in front of the village mosque. To the right and left are two buildings, now vacant, which belong to the owners of the village. To the right of the mosque, between it and one of the buildings, is a desolate area from which a villager called Moharram emerges. Moharram has recently suffered the loss of his land through the depradations of the boars. He now resides in the ruins next to the mosque. His personal tragedy has soured him on the others who, he says, now look at him as if he were inferior to them. The other village males arrive on the scene: the village chief who is the oldest of the group, the local mullah, the barefoot town fool who pays more attention to snaring flies than to the serious business at hand, a second villager (Ne'mat) whose farm land has been devastated by boars, and Asadollâh, who seems the most worldly-wise of the group. All of them are carrying clubs or staffs.

They discuss how to deal with their problem, which threatens to destroy their economic well-being. Perhaps they should pack up and leave for another village before winter sets in. They decide to make use of the drums kept in the mosque, to beat them loudly at night to frighten the boars away.

115

But they are horrified to discover that the drums have mysteriously disappeared.

In their helplessness, Asadollâh suggests that he seek the help of a man called "Monsieur" in a nearby village. While Asadollâh is on that mission, the drums are found in the ruins where Moharram lives, and the villagers decide to try them. Ne'mat refuses to cooperate.

Asadollâh returns, not knowing that his farm land also has now been destroyed. He tells the villagers that Monsieur himself will arrive on the morrow with a pair of hunters to see to the elimination of the boars and that all he wants in recompense is the right to cart away the carcasses.

The villagers prepare the village owner's house for the hunters. Moharram chides the mulla for helping such "infidels" as their prospective guests. The mulla had earlier questioned the wisdom of bringing "foreigners" into the village. The cheerful Monsieur talks with a hint of foreignness, perhaps an American accent, in his Persian.

The hunters rid the village of boars within a week or two, but are consuming almost all of the local food in the process. As Moharram puts it to Monsieur, who gets a good chuckle out of it, the hunters are no less voracious than the boars. Even after their work is done, they decide to rest in the village for a spell, perhaps not to leave at all. Consequently, the villagers summon Monsieur again. He says that he cannot force the hunters to leave, but that he has a solution. He could bring two other hunters even more experienced than the first pair, to kill the first two. The villagers have no choice, they think, but to agree to this plan. The second pair of hunters would want only room and board for their troubles.

The new hunters arrive, spend a night, and the next morning call out across the square to the still sleeping hunters 1 and 2. The villagers join in, and tell hunters 3 and 4 to fire a couple of shots to awaken hunters 1 and 2. Finally the latter appear in the doorway and window of their residence, rifles in hand. Hunters 3 and 4 aim their weapons at hunters 1 and 2. The villagers cheer them on. Hunters 3 and 4 seem momentarily to have second thoughts about their mission, then retrain their sights on hunters 1 and 2. The villagers renew their clamor. But, suddenly seeing that both pairs of hunters have trained their sights on them, the villagers run for their lives, dropping their clubs and staffs in the process.

In *The Clubwielders of Varazil,* Sâ'edi offers a warning to his Iranian audience not to resort unthinkingly to foreign resources for solutions to domestic problems when Iranians have "clubs" of their own which may be efficacious in dealing with "boars." His warning was not heeded by the Pahlavi regime and Iranian society of the Pahlavi era, nor--if one deems Shi'i Islam an originally and essentially non-Iranian force--during the first years of the Islamic Republic of Iran.

In another play called *Short 'A,' Long 'A'* (1968), Sâ'edi depicts the malaise of Weststruckness which many feel plagued Pahlavi Iran and argues that Iran's only real weapon in dealing with contemporary external dangers to its cultural vitality is a sense of social responsibility and cooperation.(91) Set in a contemporary, middle class, Tehrân neighborhood, this two-act play depicts urban Iranian cynicism, the lack of social responsibility, and, at an allegorical level, the insidious influx of Western values into Iranian lives, robbing them of their own culture.

Even when Sâ'edi cannot suggest a solution to perceived social ills, he at least argues that life goes on, and some of it promising. Hedâyat, on the other hand, finds consolation only in shared tribulations, the future never more promising than the present. Sâ'edi's most famous work, his 1970 screenplay called *The Cow*, reveals both affinities with Hedâyat and the ultimate differences in cultural outlooks of these two giants of contemporary Persian literature.

The Cow, which was based on a 1964 short story,(92) was transformed by Dâryush Mehrju'i into Iran's most popular motion picture ever among secular-minded, literary intellectuals. Set in the contemporary period, *The Cow* tells the story of a middle-aged villager who derives his sense of identity and significance among his peers by virtue of owning the only cow in the village. When the cow dies mysteriously, its distraught owner refuses to believe the news and begins behaving like a cow himself. The screenplay ends when the owner of the cow dies in a fall suffered when being led cow-like by friends to a hospital in a nearby city for treatment of his illness.(93) *The Cow* is a sad story of an individual's tenuous hold on personal significance and life in the face of unknown forces and fate, to which the suspiciousness of the behavior of foreigners, in this case residents of a nearby village, contributes a significant dimension. But parallel to the unfolding tragedy of the owner of the cow is woven the simple romance of two young villagers whose promising wedding takes place just as the death of the owner of the cow becomes imminent.

In this fashion, Sâ'edi voices hope in his writings along with his Iranian nightmare. Hedâyat, on the other hand, sees only the latter whether awake or asleep, whether speaking through his characters' personae or through his own actions in life. Of course, in this last regard, Sâ'edi seemed in Paris to be of the same mind.

But Sâ'edi is essential political, while Hedâyat is personal. Therefore, Sâ'edi does not appear as a personal force or character in his fictions; whereas Hedâyat's shadow lurks in almost every story. Hedâyat is "the blind owl" in some senses, as Kayomars Derambakhsh implies in his 1974 television motion picture of *The Blind Owl*. The first half of the movie faithfully depicts the actions in the first part of the book. But once the camera shifts to the longer second section, Derambakhsh proceeds to treat Hedâyat the person. The camera presents still shots from photographs of the writer, recreates his life in Tehrân and Paris, and closes with the Paris apartment in which Hedâyat commited suicide, and his gravesite at Père La Chaise cemetery. In effect, Derambakhsh abandons *The Blind Owl* as fiction, as a novel, and asserts identity between Hedâyat and his title character.(94) This is not the place for a discussion of parallels between Hedâyat and his most famous character (95). But the possibility that Hedâyat used his narrative as a vehicle for presenting himself, albeit heavily masked, and for raising the most serious issues which individuals face as individuals highlights one clear characteristic of later modernist Persian literature, the centrality of the individual literary artist and that artist's representation of issues, conflicts, and themes in individual and personal ways. In the next two chapters, the treatment of the careers of Jalâl Âl-e Ahmad and Forugh Farrokhzâd emphasizes this feature of contemporary Persian literary culture as much as anything else.

5

CULTURAL DILEMMAS
OF AN IRANIAN LITERARY INTELLECTUAL

> Intellectuals are the aggregate of persons in any society who
> employ in their communication and expression, with
> relatively higher frequency than most other members of their
> society, symbols of general scope and abstract reference,
> concerning man, society, nature, and the cosmos. Intellectual
> action arose out of religious preoccupations . . .: a tradition
> of awesome respect and of serious striving for contact with
> the sacred underlies the vital intellectual traditions and the
> actions which carry them forward . . . the function of modern
> intellectuals in supplying the doctrines . . . of revolutionary
> ideological movements is to be considered one of their most
> important accomplishments.   Edward Shils, 1968(96)

At the time of his sudden death at forty-six years of age in September
1969, Jalâl Âl-e Ahmad was the best known literary intellectual in Iran.
During that decade, younger Iranians in the last years of high school and at
colleges and universities throughout the country thought of him as a bold
spokesman, as someone who dared to question Pahlavi government policy
to the limits official censors allowed and who served as their conscience
with his direct, forceful, and unrelenting critiques of Iranian society. Iranian
writers and critics generally acknowledge Âl-e Ahmad as the central literary
figure of the day. Some argue that Al-e Ahmad's is the best prose in Persian
since Sa'di's *Golestân* (1258).

Among other prominent intellectuals, Al-e Ahmad had numerous friends
and followers. He had a close relationship with his neighbor Nimâ Yushij
(1895-1960), the leading first-generation modernist Persian poet. Prominent
short story writer and moviemaker Ebrâhim Golestân (b. 1922) was a
longtime acquaintance whom Al-e Ahmad named as an executor of his
estate. In the late 1940s, Al-e Ahmad lived at poet Nâder Nâderpur's house
for two years, and they were close friends then. One prominent Al-e Ahmad
follower was Samad Behrangi (1939-1968), a Persian teacher, educational
and social reformer, Turkish folklorist and short story writer from

Azarbâyjân who himself became a hero for many Iranian college students after his mysterious death by drowning in the Aras River. A second follower was Rezâ Barâheni (b. 1935), the most vocal literary critic of the 1960s and a controversial social critic later incarcerated in 1973 by the Pahlavi regime and again in 1981 by the Khomayni regime. Al-e Ahmad's most famous follower and closest associate during the 1960s was Gholâmhosayn Sâ'edi (see pages 111-117, above) who was the leading dramatist and a prolific short story writer during the 1960s, also incarcerated by the Pahlavi authorities on several occasions, the last being for eighteen months up to June 1975.

In short, Al-e Ahmad was the leading spokesman for the non-establishment Iranian intelligentsia from the mid-1950s until his death. No other individual was able to assume that spokesperson's role during the last decade of Pahlavi rule, although social reformer 'Ali Shari'ati (1933-1977) attracted a broad-based following with his socialist cum Islamic revival intellectualism. In the same decade, younger Iranians opposed to the Pahlavi monarchy seemed to revere Al-e Ahmad as a prescient martyr to the cause of intellectual freedom and social revolution. Furthermore, they often invoked his name in 1978 in behalf of the overthrow of the Pahlavi monarchy, a cause many allege he would have wholeheartedly supported. In the early 1980s, the Islamic Republic of Iran approved the naming in Al-e Ahmad's honor of a section of a new north Tehrân boulevard and a high school in the Tajrish neighborhood where he lived from 1953 until his death. Also in the 1980s, some anti-Islamic Republic intellectuals went so far as to blame Al-e Ahmad for predisposing his followers to accept the theocratic regime which such secular-minded intellectuals find so abhorrent.

The above details imply that no serious inquiry into post-World War II Iranian literary life can be undertaken without attention to Jalâl Al-e Ahmad. One important dimension of such inquiry is the subject of cultural conflicts and dilemmas which thinking Iranians have faced at least since the Constitutional Movement (1905-1911) brought the issues of political nationalism, modern secular versus traditional religious values, individual rights of citizens, and the influence of the West in Iranian life to the center of the Iranian social and political arena. Because in his personality and views Al-e Ahmad clearly embodied such conflicts and dilemmas, their description is undertaken here through focus on him as a case study.

For the purpose of this chapter, Sâ'edi or the poet Ahmad Shâmlu (b. 1925) or a number of other Iranian writers might serve as well. But Al-e Ahmad has been chosen because of his preeminence and for four other reasons. First, his writings (excepting diaries, notebooks, and marginalia) have been published in relatively authoritative and uncensored editions subsequent to the fall of the Pahlavi regime. Second, Al-e Ahmad's stories and essays offer revealing autobiographical details in abundance on specific cultural issues. Al-e Ahmad's willingness to present autobiographical material in various contexts is unusual among Iranian literary intellectuals

120

who generally are "self-censors," resulting in an extreme paucity of autobiographical writing in Iran.(97) Third, unlike some other Iranian writers whose contributions have been exclusively in the realms of art and the world of ideas, Al-e Ahmad also played an active role in and reflected on the great events of his day: World War II, the Tudeh Party of Iran, the politics of the Mosaddeq era, the emergence of the SAVAK police organization in the late 1950s, Mohammad Reza Pahlavi's modernization programs of the 1960s, and the Westernization of urban Iran in the same period. Fourth, unlike some other literary Iranians who reacted to Pahlavi Iran by withdrawal from the scene through emigration or psychological resignation to the powers that be, Al-e Ahmad presumably recognized that he could neither thrive outside of Iran nor ignore the problems and contradictions he observed within the country. In these regards, he serves better than, for example, novelist and short story writer Sâdeq Chubak (b. 1916), the poet Mehdi Akhavân-e Sâles (b. 1928) or the painter and poet Sohrâb Sepehri (1928-1980), even though those individuals are surely Al-e Ahmad's peers as literary artists. The point is that their involvement in the issues and events of the post-World War II era was just less sustained or significant. In short, Jalâl Al-e Ahmad is a particularly appropriate subject for a Persianist inquiry both into how secular-minded, literary Iranians deal with the complexities of Iranian life and into what possibly enduring cultural features their struggles may reveal.

The story of Al-e Ahmad as an Iranian intellectual began in the summer of 1943.(98) At that time, as a twenty-year old Tehrân high school graduate, he travelled outside of Iran for the first time, visiting the shrine to Shi'i Emâm Hosayn (d. 680) at Karbalâ in Iraq. That fall Al-e Ahmad entered the undergraduate Persian literature program at the Teachers' Training College in Tehrân. The following year he joined the Tudeh Party of Iran. Also during the War years Al-e Ahmad became familiar with the writings of social reformer Ahmad Kasravi, whom a member of a Shi'i religious group asassinated in 1946, and journalist and social critic Mohammad Mas'ud, whom a member of the Tudeh Party assassinated in 1947.

Al-e Ahmad's first published story, called "Pilgrimage," was inspired by his 1943 trip, and appeared in a spring 1945 issue of *Sokhan*, the best known Iranian literary journal from the World War II years into the 1970s. Subsequent issues of *Sokhan* featured several other Al-e Ahmad stories. Then in February 1946, his first book was published, a collection of twelve stories including "Pilgrimage" and called *The Exchange of Visits*. The collection reveals Al-e Ahmad as especially sensitive to Shi'i Moslem religious customs, laws and superstitions which seemed to him to contribute to the perpetuation of ignorance among the general population and to Iran's helplessness in the face of the Allied Occupation that took place in August 1941 and resulted in the deposition and exile of Rezâ Shâh Pahlavi in favor of his son Mohammad Rezâ.

121

Al-e Ahmad finished his undergraduate program at the Teachers' Training College later in 1946 and began his teaching career in 1947 at twenty-four years of age. Teaching Persian language and literature at the secondary and college levels were to remain Al-e Ahmad's primary source of income throughout his adult life. He participated in a Ph.D. program in Persian literature at The University of Tehrân in the late 1940s, but never submitted his dissertation, which was on the subject of Persian versions of *A Thousand and One Nights* narratives.

By 1946, Jalâl had a reputation as a writer of promise. He participated and received mention in the First Congress of Iranian Writers held at the Iran-USSR Cultural Society in Tehrân in the summer of 1946. This reputation led to his becoming an editor of the Tudeh Party's monthly *Mardom*, in which capacity he collaborated on fourteen issues. He also spent six months as an editor of the Tudeh Party's publishing house Sho'leh'var. In the latter part of the summer of 1947, after the defeat of the Communists in Azarbâyjân, Al-e Ahmad published a second collection of short stories called *Our Suffering*. If *The Exchange of Visits* shows Al-e Ahmad as typical of post-World War II writers in emphasizing the value of social commitment in their literary art, the stories in *Our Suffering*, which Al-e Ahmad later characterized as stories portraying the defeat of leftist movements in Iran with a socialist realist point of view, present an Iranian writer typically subordinating artistic concerns to predetermined messages. Years later, Al-e Ahmad agreed that these stories were seriously flawed for this reason.

In January 1948, a *sécession* took place within the Tudeh Party, when a small group of intellectuals, later asserting their objections to the fact that party leadership was following Moscow's directives, formally broke from the Party. The most prominent among them was Khalil Maleki (d. 1969), who subsequently established the Third Force Party (i.e., a force other than America and Russia). Al-e Ahmad, who joined Maleki in leaving the Tudeh Party, dedicated a third collection of short stories called *Seh'târ* (1948) to him at a time when Maleki was being vilified in the Tudeh press and on Moscow radio. Al-e Ahmad viewed this period and the Tudeh reaction to the defections as a time of enforced silence. From this period dates a series of translations from French of works by Camus, Dostoyevski, Gide, and Sartre to which Al-e Ahmad was attracted because they seemed relevant to Iranian problems or Western concerns with similar problems.

Then, with the oil nationalization issue, the formation of the National Front Movement in which Maleki's Third Force Party was a constituent organization, and the election of Mohammad Mosaddeq to Parliament and his designation as Prime Minister in April 1951, Al-e Ahmad had again involved himself directly in politics.

In 1950, Al-e Ahmad married Simin Dâneshvar (b. 1921), then a teacher of art history at the University of Tehrân where she remained employed until the mid-1970s. Also a translator and writer of fiction, Daneshvar authored a 1969 novel called *The Mourners of Siyâvash* which became the bestselling

Iranian novel ever by the late 1970s. Al-e Ahmad came to trust Dâneshvar's critical judgment and showed her almost everything he subsequently wrote before submission to publishers. In addition, because Al-e Ahmad's anti-establishment views through the 1950s and 1960s often brought official reaction in the form of temporary suspension from his teaching assignment of the moment, the Al-e Ahmads needed Dâneshvar's university income.

Al-e Ahmad's fourth collection of short stories called *The Unwanted Woman* appeared in 1952, featuring a preface by *Sokhan* editor-in-chief Parviz Nâtel Khânlari who had spoken of Al-e Ahmad's promise as a writer at the First Congress of Iranian Writers in 1946. An expanded edition of *The Unwanted Woman* published in 1964 lacked Khânlari's preface because Al-e Ahmad disapproved of Khânlari's assumption of government posts from the mid-1950s onward, a typical reaction of many writers and other intellectuals to those among themselves who chose to work in the upper echelons of the Pahlavi regime.

With the fall of Mosaddeq and his nationalist government in mid-August 1953 and the return of Pahlavi monarchical control, Al-e Ahmad's days of direct political activity ended. Subsequently, he considered writing as a sort of political activity and his pen as a political weapon.

In early 1955, Al-e Ahmad published his first piece of longer fiction, a once-upon-a-time allegory called *Tale of the Beehives* on economic exploitation in general and on the then timely subject of Iranian oil in particular.

Also during the early post-Mosaddeq period, Al-e Ahmad began to travel a great deal throughout Iran. Other writers shortly followed suit in what seems to have been a Marxist-inspired impulse to get to know the people before trying to influence them to political awareness. In Iran's case, this meant non-urban peoples, over fifty percent of the population living in more than 65,000 villages. The upshot of Al-e Ahmad's excursions was the publication of a series of ethnographic articles and monographs on various Iranian locales, among them Yazd, Khorâsân, two villages near Qazvin, Khârg Island, and the Caspian littoral region of his ancestors called Owrâzân. Then in the early 1960s he assumed editorship of a monograph series published by the Institute of Social Studies and Research at the Faculty of Letters of the University of Tehrân and supervised five of their publications. Among them was *Ilkhchi* (1964), a volume which his close friend and follower Sâ'edi authored on the subject of a village in his native province of Azarbâyjân.

In 1958, Al-e Ahmad published a second piece of longer fiction called *The School Principal*, a first-person account of most of a school year experienced by a new principal in an elementary school in a newer Tehrân neighborhood. As an indictment, however mild, of the Iranian educational system and as a novel concerning middle class life, *The School Principal* was almost unprecedented. Readers saw in it details of their own experience rather than

123

authors' more typical excursions into lower class or village life. With *The School Principal*, Al-e Ahmad began his most influential years as a writer.

In fiction, Al-e Ahmad published a second allegory in 1961 called *By the Pen*, which was never allowed distribution during the Pahlavi era. It is the story of a religious-political revolution which overthrows a corrupt monarchy, but is eventually replaced by the return of that monarchy. In the story, which has a pseudo-historical, once-upon-a-time setting, Al-e Ahmad had at least two thematic intents. First, the story is designed to depict the effects historically consequent upon the official linking of the Twelver Shi'i religious establishment and the Iranian monarchical state with the advent of the Safavid Dynasty (1501-1736). The consequence of this, according to Al-e Ahmad, was the creation of a society no longer willing to suffer for principles and ideals, but preferring to pay lip service to past heroes and martyrs instead. Secondly, the novel portrays the course of the defeat of leftist movements in post-World War II Iran, specifically the inclination on the part of the Tudeh Party to put on a show of martyrdom rather than to organize practical resistance against Western influence.

In the fall of 1962, Al-e Ahmad clandestinely published a polemic essay called *Weststruckness* which ran through numerous underground printings in subsequent years and became his most popular piece of nonfiction. Actually, the first chapter of *Weststruckness* had appeared in a journal called *Kayhân-e Mâh* which began publishing in the spring of 1962 and was banned after two issues because, according to Al-e Ahmad, it included the section from *Weststruckness*.

Weststruckness is a forceful, angry polemic secondarily attacking the hollowness and decadence of contemporary Western civilization and primarily warning Iranians not to succumb to the disease of adopting Western evils. Al-e Ahmad argues that although Iran and the West have been in conflict for millennia, only in recent centuries has it been an uneven, unequal contest with the dominant West forcing upon Iran treaties, products, educational ideas, and alien cultural values. The essay struck a chord in many Iranian readers who surreptitiously passed around copies of the book, the possession of which in the late 1960s reportedly could lead to incarceration. From the vantage point of post-Pahlavi Iran, the special significance of *Weststruckness* lay in Al-e Ahmad's recognition of two facts he argues secular-minded urban Iranians were ignoring: first, the role of traditional Shi'i Islamic values as the basic mind set of the vast majority of the Iranian population; and second, Islam's potential as a social and political force in Iran's future.

From the early 1960s onward, Al-e Ahmad made a number of important trips abroad. Actually his first visit to Europe had been with his wife to Rome in the summer of 1957, but for Al-e Ahmad it was just sightseeing. In the summer of 1962 he travelled again to Europe, this time sponsored by the Iranian Ministry of Education to study European school textbooks. Then in the spring of 1964, he made the Moslem religious pilgrimage to Mecca, the record of which he published in early 1966 with the title *Lost in the Crowd*. In the summer of 1964 Al-e Ahmad accepted an invitation to attend the International Congress of Anthropologists in Moscow. Upon his return to Tehrân, Al-e Ahmad presented an oral report to the Iran-USSR Cultural Society which was printed later that year in *Payâm-e Novin*, the Society's journal. A fourth important trip was his visit to Harvard University during the summer of 1965 to participate in an international writers' conference, in which his wife Simin and Sâdeq Chubak had participated in earlier summers. Al-e Ahmad prepared a report of this trip as well, which he published a year later in *Jahân-e Now* magazine. In 1967 he published an essay called "Israel: Agent of Imperialism," a report of a two-week trip to that country in the winter of 1963. All of Al-e Ahmad's travel reports as well as their nationalist, leftist, somewhat anti-American tone were typical of non-establishment Iranian writers of the day.

Another activity of Al-e Ahmad from the early 1960s onward was his assistance of younger writers and college students. Typical of a number of prominent literary figures of the day, Al-e Ahmad attracted and nurtured a following among younger intellectuals some of whom thought of themselves as in the Al-e Ahmad camp as it were. As for his interest in students outside the classroom, Al-e Ahmad regularly lectured at colleges throughout Iran. In one speech which Al-e Ahmad gave to Abâdân college students in 1961, he notes general characteristics of contemporary Persian literature, chief among them factionalism, pessimism, humanism, the influence of translations of Western literary works on contemporary Persian literature, and the status of Persian literature as an avocation rather than as a profession owing to the limited number of readers and the inability of writers to support themselves through writing. In the spring of 1964, Al-e Ahmad participated in a question-and-answer session with university students in Tabriz. He there asserted an Iranian tendency to make cultural heroes out of literary figures after their death, but not to hold writers in much respect while they are alive.

In January 1968 at the Faculty of Fine Arts of the University of Tehrân, Al-e Ahmad gave a memorial speech on Nimâ Yushij, stressing the poet's individualism and perseverance as a pioneer. Later in 1968, Al-e Ahmad visited the University of Mashhad where he addressed enthusiastic groups of students. The activist poet Ne'mat Mirzâzâdeh, who organized that visit, recalls Al-e Ahmad's tirelessness in sitting and talking for hours with students whose own professors generally would not become involved in such informal rap sessions.

The content and flavor of Al-e Ahmad's interaction with students are communicated in his lengthiest collection of essays, a volume called *Hasty Assessment* (1965), whose publication by a Tabriz press Sâ'edi had encouraged. Its eighteen articles also included a number of linguistic and literary critical pieces, as had earlier essay collections *Seven Articles* (1956) and *Three More Articles* (1958). *Hasty Assessment* reveals Al-e Ahmad as a significant literary critic whose first important literary essay was called "The Hedâyat of *The Blind Owl*," published shortly after the author's April 1951 suicide in Paris. In it, Al-e Ahmad suggests that Hedâyat's masterpiece represents its author's views on the oppressive atmosphere in Rezâ Shâh Pahlavi's era. It was the first of a series of insightful critical testimonials. Two others were: "The Old Man Was Our Eyes" on Nimâ Yushij, published shortly after the poet's death in January 1960; and "Samad and the Folktale," which appeared in a special Fall 1968 memorial issue of *Arash* magazine and was a tribute to Behrangi. In the mid-1960s, Al-e Ahmad tried unsuccessfully to persuade the Ministry of Education to publish Behrangi's elementary Persian textbook designed for speakers of Azarbâyjâni Turkish. Altogether, Al-e Ahmad published some twenty literary critical essays from the early 1950s onward.

In 1966, Al-e Ahmad was closely associated with *Jahân-e Now* magazine, that year being edited by Barâheni. Only four issues of the Al-e Ahmad circle were published. In two of them appeared essays entitled respectively "What and Who Is an Intellectual?" and "Is an Intellectual Native or Foreign?" They later became chapters in Al-e Ahmad's posthumously published work called *On the Services and Treasonable Activities of Intellectuals* (1978), in which he sketches the history and evaluates the contribution of *rowshanfekr* [intellectual] Iranians to their society. One of the book's most interesting chapters, called "Recent Examples of *Rowshanfekri* [intellectualism]," discusses the career of, and Al-e Ahmad's association with, Khalil Maleki, who had been one of the subsequently famous "fifty-three persons" sentenced to prison in 1937 in accordance with terms of a 1933 anti-communist law and who also became a leading socialist and nationalist theoretician in the 1940s. Maleki was the first signatory to the *sécession* declaration in early 1948 from the Tudeh Party, the founder of The Third Force Party, editor of *'Elm va Zendegi* magazine from 1950 until it was banned in 1960, and, according to Al-e Ahmad, the best possible example of intellectual commitment to social and political progress. Al-e Ahmad's specific stimulus for focussing on Maleki in this chapter was the early 1966 trial of the latter and several socialist associates accused by the Pahlavi government of seditious activity. Maleki, who had been previously convicted and sentenced to prison several times in post-Mosaddeq Iran, was sentenced this time to three more years in prison. As upsetting as that was for Al-e Ahmad who saw this 1966 trial as the Pahlavi government's definitive condemnation of socialism and political freedom, what he found more disconcerting about the trial was the reaction of those Iranian intellectuals who either had been followers of Maleki in the 1940s and 1950s or at least owed him debts as their intellectual mentor. At some trial sessions, Al-e Ahmad was the only court visitor except for the defendant's family members. He wonders why no one else was there to offer at least moral support. The open letters he wrote to *Khândanihâ* magazine asking these and other questions were naturally not published. Al-e Ahmad's disenchantment at this point with Iranian intellectuals who he assumes had been co-opted by the government or were afraid to appear interested in or supportive of Maleki was typical of those writers in the later Pahlavi era who felt that they were firm in their refusal to submit to government inducements or threats.

However, a more serious problem confronted Al-e Ahmad and other non-establishment writers at this point: a new official censorship system. In 1966, a Pahlavi government directive informed publishers that copies of books in press had thereafter to be approved by a Writing Bureau at the Ministry of Arts and Culture before distribution. To register their disapproval of this form of censorship, Al-e Ahmad, Sâ'edi, Barâheni, and several other writers met in December 1966 with Prime Minister Amir 'Abbâs Hovaydâ, who then established a committee to investigate the issue of censorship with a representative of the writers participating. Regardless, the new censorship system remained in force, which encouraged the writers to think of possible group action.

In late 1967, Al-e Ahmad spearheaded a drive by anti-establishment writers to boycott a literature symposium planned by the government. Subsequent to their success in having the symposium postponed and as a means to combat government censorship, they decided to form an organization of writers. In April 1968, the group produced a declaration signed by Al-e Ahmad, Dâneshvar, Shâmlu, Nâderpur, Sâ'edi, Barâheni, and some forty-six others. In this fashion, the Writers' Association of Iran came into being for the express purpose of guaranteeing writers' rights against government censorship. But because these writers had no real leverage with the government in the form of either broad-based readership or services of theirs the government might need, the organization did not prove very influential or effective except as a moral rallying force for its members. Furthermore, it ceased to function for all intents and purposes when Al-e Ahmad died in September 1969. (Almost eight years later, in the spring of 1977, the organization reemerged and sponsored the famous *Ten Nights* of readings at Tehrân's Goethe Institute that autumn. Then, after the fall of the Pahlavi regime, it functioned for a year or more, during which time six issues of its journal called *Nâmeh-ye Kânun-e Nevisandegân-e Irân* appeared. The first featured a fifty-page memorial section on Al-e Ahmad. In 1981, the Islamic Republic of Iran suppressed the organization and its publications. In June of that year, organization member Sa'id Soltânpur, a political activist and minor poet and dramatist, was executed by the government for "warring against Allâh." Subsequently, an Organization of Writers of Iran in Exile was established in Paris, but without the participation of any leading Iranian literary figures except for Sâ'edi.)

In early 1968 Al-e Ahmad published his fourth and lengthiest novel called *The Cursing of the Land*. Like *The School Principal*, it is a story with an essentially autobiographical protagonist and plot. The action deals with the Pahlavi land redistribution program of the 1960s, the cornerstone of a wide-ranging reform officially termed "The White Revolution," and recounts a year in the life of a school teacher in a village where the new Pahlavi agricultural system fails and the villagers lose their traditional roots and sense of identity as well. The novel was unavailable in bookstores until the last days of the Pahlavi monarchy in 1978, although two chapters had appeared earlier in *Andisheh va Honar* and *Arash* magazines. The expression in *The Cursing of the Land* of a sense of loss of roots taking place during the later Pahlavi era became a commonplace among non-establishment writers.

Equally significant is a comparison of the outcomes of Al-e Ahmad's four novels, which seem to indicate an increasing sense of pessimism typical of post-Mosaddeq intellectuals. In other words, the protagonists become progressively or ultimately passive as modern individuals vis-à-vis political force and oppression. In *Tale of the Beehives* (1955), the bees decide to return to their ancestral home. In *The School Principal* (1958), the title character renounces corrupt society and prefers to preserve innocence by retreating to his individuality. In *By the Pen* (1961), 'Abdozzaki goes to India to escape the returned monarchy, and Asadollâh goes to the desert to live a solitary dervish life. The cynical teacher protagonist in *The Cursing of the Land* (1968) also takes leave of the village once it is in disarray. Anti-establishment intellectuals in general became progressively pessimistic about social progress in Iran during the post-Mosaddeq 1950s and 1960s.

Shortly before his own death at Asâlem, a Caspian littoral village on the road between Enzeli and Astârâ where he and his wife had a summer cottage, Al-e Ahmad returned to Tehrân to attend the funeral of Maleki, his political leader and ally of twenty years earlier. It was his last relatively public appearance.

On the day of his death, according to Dâneshvar, Al-e Ahmad complained in the morning of severe pain in his neck. Regardless, he busied himself with repairing the chimney in their cottage. He was planning a trip to Tehrân the following week and then to come back to Asâlem with Sâ'edi-- the two of them were going to spend some time studying Tâti-speakers in the area. Al-e Ahmad did not have to worry about returning to Tehrân for the beginning of the academic year because he knew he was to be suspended once again from teaching duties, this time from the Nârmak Technical School, as a result of his writings and speeches. He took a shower at noontime. After lunch, he took a nap, complaining in mid-afternoon of feeling very cold. Then he went to a friend's house for a half hour or so, stayed outside talking, and returned home pale and complaining of pain from his legs to his chest and from one wrist and arm to the other. He decided to go to bed. Simin went for the doctor. When she returned, Al-e Ahmad was dead.

The local doctor and the Al-e Ahmad's family physician determined the cause of death as a heart attack. Simin herself accepted this diagnosis at the time and wrote about it in a 1981 essay called "Jalâl's Sunset."(99) But

128

Jalâl's younger brother Shams, who had rushed to Asâlem from Tehrân when told of Jalâl's death and who proceeded to investigate its circumstances, became convinced that the Pahlavi government had assassinated his brother.(100) Other anti-establishment writers shared this view. For example, Barâheni tried to draw attention in the English-speaking world to alleged Pahlavi government crimes through citation of Al-e Ahmad's death as an example. He dedicated a 1976 collection of his verse in English "to Jalâl Al-e Ahmad, friend, killed." Then, in his *The Crowned Cannibals: Writings on Repression in Iran* (1976, 1977), Barâheni asserts: "During the Shah's reign . . . dozens of writers have been liquidated: . . . Jalâl Al-e Ahmad, one of the most formidable writers of oppositionalist literature in Iran, was mysteriously killed on the coast of the Caspian Sea."(101)

Even Dâneshvar in a 1983 interview wavers from her original view, responding as follows to a question about her husband's death: "They tormented Jalâl so much he eventually died of frustration. Harassment by SAVAK and constant suspensions from his teaching caused his premature death. However, as to whether or not they actually killed him, I don't know, I'm not certain. If they did, it was so expertly done that I was unaware."(102)

The popular attitude about Al-e Ahmad's death (for which no compelling evidence exists) is the same attitude which anti-establishment Iranians have held with respect to the deaths of Behrangi, Shari'ati, and popular wrestling champion Gholâmrezâ Takhti (1930-1968), among others.(103) In short, the extent of fear and cynicism many Iranians felt about the Pahlavi government and its security arm SAVAK was such that almost any death of an opposition figure in circumstances other than extreme old age was assumed to be an assassination.

Back in Tehrân, several thousand people accompanied Al-e Ahmad's casket from his family's home to the cemetery. Friend and associate Eslâm Kâzemiyeh recalls how upset the mourners were, mostly people who thought they were truly Al-e Ahmad's friends because he often had that effect on people he met: he listened to whatever was told him, was genuinely curious about others' personal situations and problems, and recalled such facts about people the next time he saw them. On behalf of the Writers' Association of Iran, Nâderpur presented the eulogy at graveside. The Iranian print media were full of expressions of grief and remembrances. On the evening of the seventh day after his death, Sâ'edi and Barâheni spoke at services at Firuzâbâdi Mosque.(104)

For the traditional fortieth day of mourning, Dâneshvar, Shams Al-e Ahmad, Sâ'edi, Kâzemiyeh, Manuchehr Hezârkhâni, and several others traveled to Mashhad, where Ne'mat Mirzâzâdeh had made arrangements for memorial services at both Hâj Mollâ Hosayn Mosque and the Faculty of Letters at The University of Mashhad. Mirzâzâdeh recalls not telling the mourning party or anyone else of the location of the first service until shortly before it was to begin out of fear that SAVAK might decide to have it cancelled. Shari'ati was reportedly the only professor willing to participate in the service at the University.(105)

But once the Mashhad services were over, the government refused to give permission for further memorial tributes.(106) And much less writing on Al-e Ahmad appeared subsequently, until the late 1970s, than might have been expected, except for remembrances on the anniversary of his death. From 1977, when censorship began to relax, through the early years of the Islamic Republic of Iran, Al-e Ahmad received renewed attention, including a 750-page memorial volume published in September 1985.(107)

Of all the eulogies, articles and other remembrances, perhaps the most artful was the 1969 elegy called "Anthem for the Bright Man Who Went into the Shadows" by Shâmlu, presented here in a translation by the expatriate poet Esmâ'il Kho'i (b. 1938):

> Contentment-like, he was thin,
> slim and tall, like a difficult message in one word.
> And with eyes of question and honey;
> and with a face scorched by truth and wind.
> [5]A man with the whirling of water:
> a laconic man who was his own résumé.
> Beetles stare at your corpse with suspicion.
>
> Before being turned to ashes by the wrath of the thunderbolt,
> he had forced the steer of the tempest to kneel before his might.
> [10]To test the faiths of old
> he had worn out his teeth on the locks of ancient gates.
> On the most out-of-the-way paths he struggled,
> an unexpected passerby
> whose voice every thicket and bridge recognized.
> [15]Roads remain wakeful with the memory of your steps;
> for you were going to welcome the day:
> although the dawn emitted you
> before the cocks heralded morning.
>
> A bird bloomed in its wings,
> [20]a woman in her breasts, a garden in its trees,
> a bloom in your angry look, in your haste.
> We bloom in your brook,
> in defending your smile that is certitude and faith.
> The sea envies you for the drop you have drunk from the well.(108)

A forceful pronouncement by one of Iran's most persistently secular, modernist, and anti-establishment intellectuals, Shâmlu's poem seems an imprimatur for the preceding sketch of Al-e Ahmad's career as that of a tireless, conscientious, individualistic critic, whose concerns were the exact issues that one would in retrospect expect an Iranian writer to have addressed during the post-World War II era, among them: Westernization and modernization, the superficiality, inefficiency, and corruption of the Pahlavi regime, Iranian identity and national integrity in a modern world, the role of religion in contemporary Iranian life, and the social responsibilities of writers and other intellectuals.

However, a contrasting side to Al-e Ahmad emerges in the characterization of personal dimensions to his life as recorded in autobiographical material in his published works and corroborated by the recollections of acquaintances. This other Al-e Ahmad is full of conflict, contradictions and dilemmas which seem to be the common lot, to one degree or another, of many secular-minded Iranian intellectuals of his and subsequent generations. Not that Al-e Ahmad was especially typical of Iranian intellectuals in general or that other intellectuals of his and subsequent generations necessarily agreed with many of his views. Nonetheless, the conflicts particular to his life and his reactions to them are typical and singularly revealing of conflicts in Iranian culture today.

Jalâl Al-e Ahmad was born into a religious family from the village of Owrâzân in the Caspian province of Gilân. The Al-e Ahmad family was closely related to prominent Shi'i cleric Ayatollâh Hâjj Sayyed Mahmud Tâleqâni (1910-1979), an opposition figure imprisoned several times during the Pahlavi Era. Al-e Ahmad's father, his older brother, two brothers-in-law, and a nephew were all Shi'i clerics. The family referred to themselves as sayyeds, that is they claimed to be direct descendants of the Moslem prophet Mohammad. Incidentally, "Jalâl," the first name Al-e Ahmad used throughout his adult years, was really a shortened form of Jalâloddin, which means "splendor of religion." His full name, which he never used, was Sayyed Jalâloddin Sâdât Al-e Ahmad.

Jalâl was born after one brother and seven sisters, only four of the latter living through mature years. His younger brother Shams, actually "Shamsoddin" [sun of religion], also a writer, has been primarily responsible for making Al-e Ahmad's writings available from 1978 onward, which he has been able to do because of close ties for several years with the Islamic Republic of Iran.

By Al-e Ahmad's own account, his early childhood years were spent in the relatively luxurious environment of an important cleric's home. But when the Ministry of Justice during the reign of Rezâ Shâh Pahlavi began regulating and bureaucratizing registry operations, Jalâl's father refused to participate. He thereafter functioned unofficially as a neighborhood religious elder responsible for leading the community noon prayer at the local mosque, preaching sermons, and attending to other neighborhood religious needs.

Al-e Ahmad's father was a stern, demanding patriarch who treated his wife and children as his inferiors and cursed and swore at them when irritated. The whole family, which did its best not to displease him, seems to have thought of this minor religious figure as a great man. In turn, he seems to have had a sense of self-importance. None of his children was apparently ever able to talk frankly with their father whose first wife gave birth to thirteen children altogether. He also married a second wife who died before his first wife died. In addition, he had at least one *sigheh* [temporary wife] as described here.(109)

When Al-e Ahmad was thirteen years of age and in the sixth grade, an incident occurred at home that created a lasting impression on him. One day the mailman delivered a printed invitation to "Mr. and Mrs. Al-e Ahmad" to attend a party commemorating the first anniversary of Rezâ Shâh Pahlavi's 1936 banning of the *châdor* veil traditionally worn by Iranian women. Al-e Ahmad's father becomes angry at receiving such an invitation and tells his son to inform the people at the mosque he would not be coming that day because he was not feeling well, and also to tell his uncle to stop by the house. When Jalâl's mother interrupts to suggest that he be allowed to eat some lunch before going on the errand, the father replies: "You loudmouth. Are you interfering in my affairs again? Now I've got to take you to a reception, bareheaded and barebottomed."

After returning home with his uncle, Jalâl leaves for school. He always had to get to school before the other boys because of a special problem he faced as a stern cleric's son. The government rule stated that boys had to wear short pants at school. Because Jalâl's father was against the policy, his mother sewed buttons inside his trouser pantlegs so that he could walk to school in long pants and then, before the other boys and the principal reached school, tuck and button the bottom half of his long pants up and under so they would become short pants.

After school that day, Jalâl had to take firewood home to the bath, which his father had installed right after Rezâ Pahlavi outlawed châdors so that his wife would not have to leave the house without a châdor to go to a public bath. Jalâl did not like the chore, which was almost a daily occurrence since all the family's female relatives had started coming to Jalâl's house to bathe rather than go to a public bath.

That night Jalâl's father again did not go to the mosque. Someone knocked on the courtyard door, which Jalâl opened. A military officer entered, and behind him a young woman in high heeled shoes with only a small kerchief on her head. It was the first time a woman had ever entered their house without a châdor.

Jalâl hears bits and pieces of the grownups' conversation. The young lady is to become his father's temporary wife for two hours so he can take her to a reception and not have to take his real wife without a châdor.

A second, more serious experience for Al-e Ahmad was the death of his older sister at age thirty-five.(110) She was married but childless and thus had to give permission to her husband to marry again and subsequently put up with a rival wife at home. Then she becomes ill, in fact is stricken with breast cancer. Her husband, whom Jalâl never liked, brings her back to her parents' home. She is bedridden, but has refused to submit to a medical examination and treatment by a male physician on the grounds that it would constitute a religious impropriety. Instead, she finally submits to a home remedy. One day Jalâl is sent to the bazaar to bring back a bucket of lead filings. After he brings them home, not understanding how they are to be used, a local woman expert in folk remedies places them red hot on the breasts of Jalâl's sister, who dies almost immediately thereafter.

After Jalâl finished elementary school, his father sent him to work in the bazaar as an apprentice in watch and electrical repair, and leather goods. At night, Jalâl surreptitiously attended Dârolfonun, Tehrân's oldest and most famous secondary school. In 1943, he finished high school, having kept at electrical repair work on the side with one of his brothers-in-law.

Then came the trip to Karbalâ. Apparently Al-e Ahmad's father and the other clerics in the family were hoping that Jalâl would be inspired to pursue theological studies at Najaf and follow in their footsteps. But a misunderstanding ensued, with Al-e Ahmad breaking off relations with his father some time after his return to Tehrân. Al-e Ahmad stopped praying and otherwise observing Moslem regulations at this time, during his first years at college. Also connected with his break from religion is the mysterious death of his older brother, the cleric who became Ayatollâh Hosayn Borujerdi's (d. 1961) representative in Mecca for two years and died there. His brother's death stayed on Al-e Ahmad's mind as much if not more than his sister's.

Such a sequence of events in Al-e Ahmad's personal life may imply for some readers that his involvement as a young man in Marxist activities and a secular life-style was less the result of reasoned intellectual choices than the need to express personal independence and rejection of his father's Shi'i traditionalism. According to Sâ'edi, Al-e Ahmad was never able to shake his attachment to his traditional religious upbringing despite his efforts, in part inspired by his break with his father, to become a secular intellectual, writer, and social critic.(111) At the same time, however, Sâ'edi does not think that Al-e Ahmad at any time in his adult life was deeply religious or, for that matter, believed in Allâh, heaven and hell, or the Shi'i Emâms. Rather, as a response to increasing Pahlavi control over Iranian life during the 1960s with the manifold threats which Pahlavi Westernization posed for Iranian cultural identity, Al-e Ahmad saw in Shi'i Islam a cultural banner that Iranians might wave as a rallying point, as a means of assuring cultural survival. In the same fashion, according to Sâ'edi, Al-e Ahmad was not an advocate of Ruhollâh Khomayni's political ideas, even though he travelled to Qom in 1963 to see Khomayni and present him with a copy of *Weststruckness* and even though he included the text of Khomayni's famous 1964 speech, which Al-e Ahmad asserts was the specific cause of Khomayni's exile later that year, in the *Addenda: On the Services and Treasonable Activities of Intellectuals*. Rather, according to Sâ'edi, Al-e

133

Ahmad saw in Khomayni merely the strength of opposition to the Pahlavi government.

In short, the first dilemma Al-e Ahmad faced in his life and career was between a possible lack of personal faith in Shi'i Islam and his assertion of its deleterious effects as an institution and traditional force in Iranian society and culture, on the one hand, and the unifying power which Shi'i Islam could represent for the country of Iran as well as religion's potential strength as both a check to absolute monarchical control and a bulwark against the threats the West posed for the long-term survival of Iranian culture. If Al-e Ahmad never resolved his personal sense of dilemma in this regard, one can say that the attempts at resolution by Iranian society at large have been equally unsuccessful: the pendulum swings of Pahlavi secularization and Westernization, on the one hand, and the Khomayni theocracy, on the other.

The critic Rezâ Barâheni, another Al-e Ahmad friend and follower during the 1960s, views Al-e Ahmad's break from his family, his Tudeh Party years, and, for that matter, the other important events in his adult life as a series of attempted escapes on Al-e Ahmad's part from patriarchal forces: first, from his patriarchal religious family; second, from the patriarchy of the Central Committee of the Tudeh Party; and third, from his political mentor and personal "patriarch" Khalil Maleki. But eventually, according to Barâheni, Al-e Ahmad himself became in the 1960s that from which he had expended so much energy earlier trying to escape. In Baraheni's words,

> I met Jalâl when he was about forty years old; but when he talked with those about him, you'd think he was eighty . . . he perforce thought of younger writers around him as his own children. The behavior which his father had displayed in the family toward him (commands and prohibitions), and the behavior which the Tudeh Party exhibited toward its members . . . Al-e Ahmad transferred to his association with younger writers around him.(112)

Barâheni seems thus to be agreeing in his psychological analysis with Sâ'edi's view that Al-e Ahmad remained a prisoner of his background and upbringing. Although both views are interesting in that they come from persons very sympathetic to Al-e Ahmad, they are no more than speculation concerning issues which Al-e Ahmad has himself discussed rather straightforwardly, especially in *A Stone on a Grave* and *Lost in the Crowd*.

Next to his distinctive religious upbringing, his falling out with his father, and his inner conflict with his inherited traditions, the most important subsequent event and permanently influential feature of Al-e Ahmad's intellectual character was Marxism. The list of writers and intellectuals of Al-e Ahmad's generation to flirt with Marxism or join the Tudeh Party is almost endless, among them: Akhavân-e Sâles, Bozorg 'Alavi, M.E. Beh'âzin, Hushang Ebtehâj, Golestân, Nâderpur, Siyâvash Kasrâ'i, and Shâmlu. But if it turned out to be only a stage, it nevertheless had lasting effects on such writers as Âl-e Ahmad. Or in other words, they never outgrew it and its clear, black-and-white analyses of issues that rendered their judgments often simplistic and politically naive in comparison with the live social issues of the day. Moreover, the contradition between Iranian nationalist aims and Moscow-aligned values became evident in the Azarbâyjân crisis when many intellectuals abandoned Moscow alignment then represented by Tudeh Party leadership. Still they seemed not ever to abandon the half-digested philosophy of Marxism which for Iran's heterogeneous agrarian society may never have been an appropriate framework.

In any case, Âl-e Ahmad's youthful experience with Marxism left him with at least two symptoms. He had an almost paranoic fear of material comfort and aversion to people of wealth, as if wealth might somehow corrupt him or render him useless. Ironically, he and his wife were self-conscious about their own limited means and referred constantly in print to money problems and in disparaging terms to their home, summer cottage, and other possessions. Throughout the 1960s, Tehrân intellectuals remained sensitive to references to their being bourgeois. A second symptom was Âl-e Ahmad's suspicion of things American. As late as 1967, he refused an invitation to speak at Tehrân's Iran-America Society precisely because it was American, although he had felt no such aversion at speaking at the parallel Russian institute three years earlier.(113)

If his religious upbringing and Marxist reaction to it can be assigned to his youth, Âl-e Ahmad's most important decision as an adult was his marriage at twenty-seven to Simin Dâneshvar, according to whom they were friends, lovers, confidants, and kindred spirits during their nineteen years together. Âl-e Ahmad himself refers to Simin over and over again in his writings as a partner. But he also represents her in other ways in print that seem to bespeak culture-specific attitudes toward women. For example, in his 1968 autobiographical essay, Âl-e Ahmad matter-of-factly observes on the aftermath of leftist defeats in Iranian politics: "Also during this period I got married. When one comes up short in the big world, you build a smaller one with the four walls of a house. Flight from the paternal home to the society of the party and from that to one's own home." He may imply here that he got married as something one does when one loses in the grand arena: one establishes control or victory in the smaller arena of domestic life; i.e., one gets a wife.

But here too, if one can surmise on the basis of Âl-e Ahmad's own writings, there was a conflict in Âl-e Ahmad of cultural significance. One is struck, for example, at the role played by the title character's wife in the presumably autobiographical novel *The School Principal*. The first person narrator-protagonist describes most of a school year in which he serves as a new school principal in a relatively new elementary school. Home is not part of the narration, and his wife goes unmentioned until the crisis of the novel occurs: the rape of a smaller boy by a larger boy. Then the reader sees

135

the protagonist, who has lost control for a moment and badly beats the sodomizer, going home to a protecting, domestic wife who is there behind the door to offer him a cigarette and solace. One wonders if this traditionally raised Al-e Ahmad can have thought of any woman as an equal in public.

Another illustration of this conflict in Al-e Ahmad is offered in his reported disapproval of Forugh Farrokhzâd, whose attempt to live an independent life of her own and to reveal her feelings and thoughts in writing in an open, natural way would seem to parallel Al-e Ahmad's own goals for himself. Only Al-e Ahmad thought that Farrokhzâd was using sexuality in her verse and her sex in life sensationally, that is to gain attention as a poet. Al-e Ahmad, who thus apparently was unable to accept the same outspokenness and individualistic behavior on the part of a woman that he exhibited in his own personality, seems to exemplify the male chauvinism and double standards that critic Mahmud Azâd Tehrâni asserts were typical of Tehrân intellectuals of the day.(114) Al-e Ahmad admits an awareness of shortcomings in this regard in the posthumously published essay on the childlessness of his marriage called *A Stone On a Grave*. There he asserts that there are really two men in his personality. One is an educated, modern mid-twentieth century social critic and writer. The other is:

> An eastern man, full of tradition and history and desires, all of them in accordance with religious and common law. My father was one, and so was my [older] brother. My brothers-in-law are [eastern men] too, and so are my neighbors and my fellow teachers and cabinet ministers and every merchant and villager. Even the Shâh. And all in accordance with religious regulations and common law.(115)

As described in detail in *A Stone On a Grave* (a volume whose publication in 1981 by Shams Al-e Ahmad surprised Dâneshvar because Jalâl had reportedly not intended for it to appear without rewriting which he did not apparently live to undertake), Al-e Ahmad discovered after two or three years of marriage that his sperm count was too low for Simin to conceive a child. After attempts at divers remedies and recourse to experts of all sorts, Al-e Ahmad learns that he might be able to father a child with a woman other than Simin, or at least the chances of pregnancy would be enhanced in sexual relations with other women, in particular younger women. According to Al-e Ahmad, at this point the "eastern man" in him-- Mohammad Rezâ Shâh Pahlavi took a third wife because his first two were not able to produce a male heir for him--feels that being a father, the father of a male child, takes precedence over any considerations (on the part of the modern man in him) of his wife's rights, feelings, or needs. Al-e Ahmad proceeds in *A Stone On a Grave* to reveal that during his 1962 trip to Europe he had sexual relations with a stewardess in Switzerland, a girl he picked up on a street in Hannover, and a recent divorcée his own age who, after a week with Al-e Ahmad in Amsterdam, accompanied him to London for ten days. He tells this woman at their parting that he will marry her if she should happen to get pregnant, which she does not.

Barâheni sees the personal revelations in *A Stone On a Grave* and *One Well and Two Pits*, another posthumously published collection of essays describing Âl-e Ahmad's errors in judging people, as an indication that "with respect to himself, Jalâl was more courageous than many other writers. Iranian writers were afraid to admit to their own weaknesses . . . Jalâl . . . had the courage to confront the moral problems in his own life."(116) Other Iranian intellectuals, however, have found the revelations in *A Stone On a Grave* foolish, pathetic, or embarrassing.(117) Dâneshvar's judgment is that the book is a valuable account, its ultimate nihilism being particularly remarkable.(118) It proved too controversial for the Islamic Republic of Iran, which finally banned it. In any case, the fact of such cultural conflicts in Âl-e Ahmad is the point to the foregoing comments on the book.

By the late 1950s, Âl-e Ahmad's attention had focussed on the modernization and Westernization that the Pahlavi monarchy promoted as its basic economic and social program for Iran. The upshot of his thinking on the subject was *Weststruckness*, a monograph that circulated clandestinely throughout Iran from 1962 to the end of the Pahlavi era and was the best known non-fictional work of the age. Aside from important thematic thrusts enumerated earlier, *Weststruckness* sheds special light on several conflicts and dilemmas in Âl-e Ahmad's thinking and personality that were common to many Iranian intellectuals in the 1960s.

First and foremost is Âl-e Ahmad's conspiratorial view of history and international affairs. For example, he asserts that "Behind the scenes of every riot, coup d'état or uprising in Zanzibar, Syria, or Uraguay, one must look to see what plot by what colonialist company or government backing it lies hidden." For Âl-e Ahmad, the world, especially the third world and its markets, are manipulated by the White House and the Kremlin. (He does not share the still popular Iranian view that behind the White House lurks still dominant and insidious British power.) Moreover, since Âl-e Ahmad argues in various contexts that the potential political force of Islam in Iran should not be overlooked, he might not have subscribed to a view current among some Iranian professionals and intellectuals that the West engineered the overthrow of the Pahlavi monarchy and the establishment of the Islamic Republic of Iran both because Mohammad Rezâ Pahlavi was behaving independently and because an Islamic Republic might serve more dependably as a barrier against Soviet expansion. In any case, the dilemma for Âl-e Ahmad is that he refuses to suggest that Iran submit to such external power even when he argues it is almost limitless.

Second, Âl-e Ahmad voices disgust at what he sees as a sense of inferiority on the part of his fellow countrymen vis-à-vis the West. However, in his own representation of fear of machines and his constant recourse to Western works and figures to buttress his arguments, Âl-e Ahmad seems not immune to these same feelings himself.

Third, Âl-e Ahmad exhibits a typical conflict between Pahlavi era intellectuals or educated people in general who received their education in Iran as opposed to those who received it abroad. As a member of the former group, Âl-e Ahmad is suspicious of the latter group, sensitive about his own limited acquaintance with foreign languages, and xenophobic about foreign goods and Western machinery; in other words, he has feelings that a foreign-trained Iranian might not have. Throughout the 1960s, these two groups were often at odds, not being able to unite in efforts for social reform and progress.

Âl-e Ahmad argues, fourthly, that for Iran to emerge from its Weststruck situation, it must itself be a master of machines, but that ironically may lead Iran in his view to the diseased machine-struck situation in which he feels the West is mired, the situation he argues that Albert Camus is describing allegorically in *The Plague* and Eugène Ionesco in *The Rhinoceros*. But he asserts that there is more to the diseased condition of the West than this and concludes *Weststruckness* by drawing parallels between Ingmar Bergman's *The Seventh Seal* and his view that "the end to the age of faith will usher in a time of punishment. When the age of belief ends there will be an era of experimentation. Experimentation will lead in turn to the atomic bomb."

Fifth, Âl-e Ahmad implies that traditional religious values may constitute the last bastion against Weststruckness, but argues that religion itself has perpetuated superstition, ignorance and the like.

However, the ultimate dilemma for Âl-e Ahmad in *Weststruckness* is that he does not know what to do or suggest. He asks: "Should we close the doors of our lives to machines and technology and withdraw into the distant past, with national and religious traditions? Or is there a third alternative?" The answer to his rhetorical question is hardly an answer at all. He says: "A third alternative . . . is to put the genie of machines back in his bottle and make him work for us, like a beast of burden . . . Machines are a means . . . The aim is to eliminate poverty and to see to the spiritual and material welfare of all humanity."

Âl-e Ahmad's *Weststruckness* does not stand up well to scholarly scrutiny. One critic in the mid-1960s rightly pointed out that Iranian culture had for nearly 1,400 years been more essentially altered by "Arabstruckness" in the form of religious and linguistic influences than by Weststruckness in the twentieth century.(119) One prominent Iranian historian, writing in the late 1970s, demonstrates the tenuousness of many of Âl-e Ahmad's historical arguments.(120) But the fact remains that the book struck a chord in the minds of many educated Iranians--it warned of real dangers. And as for its shortcomings in the context of its value, a 1984 interview with an expatriate Iranian writer provides the fairest view.

The interviewee was Eslâm Kâzemiyeh (b. 1932), a former high school student, follower, and colleague of Âl-e Ahmad's. The conversation focussed on the emotional conflicts and contradictions in the latter's personality and writings. There was not a little irony in the facts that Kâzemiyeh was now working for the Amini-Bakhtiyâr coalition which began supporting the elder son of Mohammad Rezâ Pahlavi as the Shâh of Iran and that the conversation took place in Paris at Deux Magots Café on Boulevard St. Germain, just tables away from where Jean-Paul Sartre used to sit. Sartre, of course, introduced Al-e Ahmad to many of his dilemmas: social responsibilities of the writer, non-Moscow-aligned communism and socialism, and literature and society issues. Kâzemiyeh was saying that Al-e Ahmad's strident, belligerent voice was actually a life-long cry for help. Then Kâzemiyeh took out a felt-tipped pen and on a napkin drew likenesses of Notre Dame Cathedral, Place de la Concorde, Arc de Triomphe, and the La Défense complex along a single horizontal axis. He talked about there being four hundred years between Notre Dame and La Défense, observing that the French people at least had that amount of time to proceed from Notre Dame and what it symbolizes to Place de la Concorde, Arc de Triomphe, and finally to La Défense. He then drew an X on the diagram between Notre Dame and Défense and a curved line around it. This, he said, was Al-e Ahmad, reaching for the twenty-first century, but having had to leap from the sixteenth century or earlier without the benefit of time and gradual stages in between. As he fell to his emotional destruction, he at least dared a desperate scream to apprise those who would follow of the abyss in front of them.

Consequently, Al-e Ahmad may deserve special respect because he set out from the shores of the traditional past when he need not have; and he struggled to reach today while maintaining his Iranianness, which he likewise need not have. Many other intellectuals have avoided such a fall to the depths by renouncing traditions or by in effect abandoning them. The trip Al-e Ahmad took is also one that one can take only alone, so to speak. He describes the journey and cries out as he falls, from his earliest short stories to his latest essays. But nowhere is the description more pointed or the cries more gripping than in *Lost in the Crowd* (1966). This book demonstrates clearly that the crux of Al-e Ahmad's cultural conflicts and dilemmas was Shi'i Islam which, as a result of serving as the basis of the religious state established with the Islamic Republic of Iran in the spring of 1979, is at the cultural vortex for all Iranian intellectuals. In the most simplistic terms, the culturally nationalistic Iranian intellectual is caught in a dilemma: an Iranian religious solution, by which fear of mortality and individual insignificance can be assuaged, means acceptance of a religion of seventh-century Arab invaders; whereas a secular solution, whether stressing the significance of the individual or that of one's society means acceptance of Western orientations toward life, human perfectibility, progress, and the like. As Akhavân-e Sâles puts it in "The Ending of the *Shâhnâmeh*," Iranians may thus be people after their time. With their own history and culture weighing heavily on their shoulders, they can not turn to available balms because such seem traitorous to Iranianness.

Politically nationalistic Iranian intellectuals face an equally harsh dilemma, with potentially much greater prices to pay for their convictions. First, secular nationalists are obliged to make use of Western forms in speaking and writing and to hope for some Western sophistication in their audience in attempting through non-native media to decry the very sources of that media. Then, the very concepts involved in secular political nationalism are not only Western but little appreciated by the bulk of the Iranian population if popular support of the Islamic Republic of Iran during its first decade is any indication.

Al-e Ahmad's case, as the foregoing sketch of family and personal relationships and experiences shows, is both especially significant and relevant to post-Pahlavi Iran. For in honoring his memory, the Islamic Republic implicitly imputes anachronistic sympathy for its policies on Al-e Ahmad's part. At the same time, some anti-Khomayni intellectuals assert that Al-e Ahmad was somehow instrumental in paving the way for the Islamic Republic of Iran. For example, an October 1982 report in *Irân va Jahân*, an anti-Khomayni weekly published in Paris, describes attention given in Iranian newspapers on the thirteenth anniversary of Al-e Ahmad's death in these words:

> *E'tesâm Magazine* writes about Al-e Ahmad--'He was a Marxist, then [he found] socialism and after that [he was] in the National Front organization, but eventually he realized that his lost soul belonged in righteous Islam, period. He tried to become alienated from himself and drown himself in the abyss of intellectualism. Motivated by confrontation with his pure Islamic mentality and his authentic Islamic nature, he returned to his true self.' Alas that Al-e Ahmad did not live to see the exaltation of his beloved [Islamic] culture.(121)

As another example, Shâmlu, still an *opposé* writer and still in Tehrân, is on record as having denied that his previously quoted poem was composed in memory of Al-e Ahmad at all. He asserts that readers merely assumed a connection. Shâmlu now reportedly curses Al-e Ahmad's memory.(122)

Dâneshvar herself has lent credence to speculation about Al-e Ahmad's hypothetical approval of the Islamic Republic of Iran by asserting that her husband toward the end of his life

> turned to religion . . . [as] the result of his wisdom and insight after he had previously experimented with Marxism, socialism, and, to some extent, existentialism . . . his relative return to religion and the Hidden Emâm was a way toward deliverance from the evil of imperialism and toward the preservation of national identity, a way toward human dignity, compassion, justice, reason, and virtue. Jalâl had need of such a religion.(123)

140

In other words, Al-e Ahmad may have found a resolution to his cultural conflicts and dilemmas in Shi'i Islam. Perhaps Dâneshvar's view implies something less than such a resolution. But the popular view, held by admirers and detractors of Al-e Ahmad alike, is that during his last years he found in religion answers to personal, cultural, social, and political questions and dilemmas.(124)

Any final assessment as to Al-e Ahmad's religiosity or, better, how Shi'i Islam contributed to his cultural conflicts and dilemmas or to their resolution must be based on *Lost in the Crowd*, the most directly religious of his writings.

A record of Al-e Ahmad's two-week trip to Saudi Arabia in the spring of 1964 as a pilgrim on the hajj religious pilgrimage--and, interestingly, a book which even the most critical of Al-e Ahmad's contemporaries find appealing--, *Lost in the Crowd* is particularly significant in literary terms. As a *safarnâmeh* [travel diary], it is the most prominent modern example of a traditional Persian literary form that goes back at least to Nâser Khosrow (1004-c.a.1088), the important literary figure and Isma'ili propagandist whom Al-e Ahmad mentions several times in *Lost in the Crowd*. Nâser Khosrow's *Safarnâmeh*, which describes its author's seven-year travels begun in 1045, including five pilgrimages to Mecca, has served as a model for Persian *safarnâmehs* for nearly a thousand years. In turn, Al-e Ahmad's *Lost in the Crowd* has influenced or inspired more recent *safarnâmehs*, among them volumes by Baraheni and 'Abbâs Pahlavân, another Al-e Ahmad follower and then editor of the important weekly *Ferdowsi*.

A second significance to *Lost in the Crowd* relates to Al-e Ahmad's perspective on travel in general, which he views as "another way of knowing the self, of evaluating it and coming to grips with its limitations and how narrow, insignificant, and empty it is, in the proving ground of changing climes, by means of encounters and human achievements." Given Al-e Ahmad's characteristic candor and directness in writing, his perspective on travel makes *Lost in the Crowd* almost unprecedented in Persian literature in terms of self revelation of personal and cultural doubts, misgivings, and dilemmas.

In *Lost in the Crowd*, Al-e Ahmad presents himself as an unlikely and almost unwilling hajj pilgrim. At the outset, he admits that he is unclear as to why he is going. It is a question he repeats again and again through some fifty-seven entries in the diary covering the period from Friday, 10 April 1964 through Sunday, 3 May 1964. Not having prayed for the previous twenty-or-so years, he is self-conscious about performing ritual prayers at the beginning of the pilgrimage. In addition, he reveals in several places his recognition that secular intellectual confrères in Tehrân will think his going on the pilgrimage foolish--some diary entries seem self-consciously to have them on Al-e Ahmad's mind. While on the pilgrimage itself, Al-e Ahmad hardly contemplates or mentions Allâh, sin, heaven, human souls, or the like. His participation in hajj events is represented as much less

141

spontaneous than that of his fellow pilgrims; he is much more observer than participant, as his taking notes from the very beginning reveals (he presumably planned from before the hajj to write a book on the experience). Even in his reports of hajj events and ceremonies, Al-e Ahmad's focus is far different from what one would expect from most pilgrims; his primary interest seems to lie in presenting ironies and conflicts that the fact of the pilgrimage and its events raise in his mind.

First is Al-e Ahmad's urge as a contemporary Iranian to represent Islam as an essentially non-Arab force worthy of respect and adherence in a twentieth-century world. As a nationalistic Iranian, Al-e Ahmad seems to need to find in early Islam such Iranian connections as Salmân the Persian, one of Mohammad's earliest followers, and in contemporary Islam an Iranian association with Shi'i Islamic doctrine as opposed to Arab association with Sunni doctrine. Time and again he expresses irritation at Sunni belittling of Shi'i practices and views. More interesting in this regard is Al-e Ahmad's animus toward the Arabs, a feeling he had expressed in several early short stories inspired by his trip in 1943 to Karbalâ. In his xenophobic view toward the Arabs and feeling of Iranian superiority, Al-e Ahmad expresses typical twentieth-century Iranian intellectual feelings, as earlier discussions of Akhavân-e Sâles' "Ending of the *Shâhnâmeh*" and Hedâyat's *The Blind Owl* clearly reveal. The same holds for Al-e Ahmad's constant criticism in *Lost in the Crowd* of the Saudi Arabian government for its alleged inefficiency, greed, and other shortcomings, another manifestation of his nationalistic, anti-Arab sentiments (these are the same Arabs with whom Al-e Ahmad's family in claiming to be sayyeds asserted kinship). But his criticism in this regard may have the equally important further dimension of serving as indirect criticism of the Pahlavi regime as well: Al-e Ahmad criticizes the Saudi Arabian government as a monarchy, attacking the institution there as he was never able openly to do with respect to the Pahlavi monarchy, implying through indirection that eventually monarchy itself must disappear everywhere, for example, in Saudi Arabia and in Iran.

Although Al-e Ahmad's firm, cultural and political nationalism makes it impossible for him to accept the notion of a future in which a world government might emerge, he argues throughout *Lost in the Crowd* for internationalization of control of the hajj pilgrimage sites and of Islam as a social force. Interestingly, the Islamic Republic of Iran argued forcefully in its first years for internationalization of the hajj, asserting that the Arab Sunnis are prejudiced against Iranian Shi'is. Of course, Khomayni's political philosophy included the goal of a world-wide Islamic government.

In any case, one must not read too much into anachronistic connections and other similarities between Al-e Ahmad's views and positions of the Islamic Republic of Iran. Al-e Ahmad's Iran in mid-1964 when he made the hajj and wrote *Lost in the Crowd* was a distinct and separate age in comparison with post-Pahlavi Iran in the 1980s. Mohammad Rezâ Pahlavi was firm on his throne, not to be challenged for another fourteen years following the monarchy's successful suppression of religious uprisings in June 1963 fomented by Khomayni himself, who would be exiled in the fall of 1964 to Turkey and then to Iraq. In 1964, the Pahlavi reform program known as The White Revolution, promulgated in early 1963, was in full swing. Iran's economic boom of the late 1960s and early 1970s was just ahead at this time, as was subsequently substantial American business involvement in Iran: a decade later, upwards of 40,000 Americans were living and working there. Two decades later, no more than a handful of American men would be residing in the Islamic Republic of Iran.

In short, the mid-1960s' intellectual perspective from which Al-e Ahmad speaks in *Lost in the Crowd* developed in and relates to an age significantly different both from the early and mid-1970s of Pahlavi suzerainty and from the Islamic Republic of Iran which came into existence in early 1979. Nevertheless, in his participation in the hajj, which tens of thousands of Iranian Moslems have annually undertaken for centuries, Al-e Ahmad perforce speaks from other Iranian perspectives which transcend both the Islamic Republic of Iran and the Pahlavi monarchy before it and which extend back from the Qâjâr era (1796-1925) and earlier dynastic epochs to the Arab Moslem conquest of the Iranian region in the middle of the seventh century. In other words, Al-e Ahmad raises both timely and almost timeless Iranian issues in *Lost in the Crowd*, perhaps none more thought-provoking for Iranian intellectuals today than the dilemma of feeling significant and distinctive as individual Iranians while being asked by their historical religion to be no more than a chip in a wood pile, a Moslem believer lost in the Moslem crowd. Iranians supportive of the Islamic Republic of Iran naturally argue that Al-e Ahmad was such a believer, while former colleagues and followers of his who are opposed to the Islamic Republic assert that he had no such belief. Judgement on the issue seems less significant than the appreciation of Al-e Ahmad's multifaceted dilemmas as typical of many educated Iranians today. Furthermore, if one supposes that Al-e Ahmad himself actually forged an internal alliance between modernist intellectualism and religious authority implied as possible or desirable in some of this writings, who is to say that in the paradox-laden world of Iranian culture such an alliance may not lead to a resoluton of Iran's perennial and contemporary plights?

From the Persianist perspective, however, that alliance is not easy to imagine. In other words, Al-e Ahmad's great attraction to the Persian language, his tireless dedication of time and energy to become a skillful writer of Persian, and his conviction of the special significance of imaginative Persian literature, on the one hand, together with his unequivocal Iranian nationalism, on the other, are attitudes and values not wholly consonant with the attitudes and demands of the religion of his birth. Twelver Shi'i Islam would appear to demand of its Iranian followers that they feel loyalty to the nation of Islam rather than to their Iranian homeland and that they temper attraction for imaginative literature and love of the

Persian language with the realizations that literary writing other than in the service of Allâh is potentially misleading and evil and that no literary language deserves wholehearted acceptance in the face of the divine origin of the Arabic Koran. For the Persianist, Al-e Ahmad would appear to have been an Iranian writer of Persian, first, and perhaps a Shi'i Moslem, second.

6

AN IRANIAN FINALLY SPEAKS AS A WOMAN
AND AS AN INDIVIDUAL

Women are important in a man's life only if they're beautiful
and charming and keep their femininity . . . . This business of
feminism for instance. What do these feminists want? You
say equality. Oh! I don't want to seem rude, but . . . You're
equal in the eyes of the law but not, excuse my saying so, in
ability . . . You've never produced a Michelangelo or a Bach.
You've never even produced a great chef. And if you talk to me
about opportunity, all I can say is, are you joking? Have you
ever lacked the opportunity to give history a great chef?
You've produced nothing great, nothing.

Mohammad Rezâ Pahlavi, 1975(125)

It is highly recommended that a girl be married off as soon as
she reaches the age of puberty. One of the blessings of man is
to have his daughter experience her first menstrual period not
in her father's house, but in that of her husband.

Ruhollâh Khomayni(126)

For many Iranians, the most important woman in history lived during the
early days of Islam. That would be the Arab woman called Fâtemeh,
daughter of the Moslem prophet Mohammad (c.570-632). Fâtemeh became
the wife of 'Ali (d. 661), the fourth Moslem caliph and first Shi'i Emâm,
and the mother of Hasan and Hosayn, the second and third Emâms. It was
Hosayn's unsuccessful military revolt against the forces of the Omayyad
caliph Yazid near Karbalâ in today's Iraq that afterwards became the core
religious saga for Shi'i Moslems who commemorate Hosayn's martyrdom in
680 on the ninth and tenth days of the lunar month of Moharram every year.
The holiest and saddest days in the Shi'i calendar, those days coincided in
1978 with the monumental demonstrations in Tehrân on December 10th and

145

11th, which proved to the television world that Iranians were determined to overthrow Mohammad Rezâ Pahlavi in favor of Ruhollâh Khomayni. As for Fâtemeh, she remains important because of who her father, husband, and sons were. She serves as a consequent symbol of feminine perfection--as in the writings of the social reformer 'Ali Shari'ati (1933-1977)--because of how true she was to her menfolk.(127)

For these same Moslem Iranians, the second most significant woman in history may be Ma'sumeh Fâtemeh (d. 816), who is buried in Qom, the city ninety miles south of Tehrân that became the important pilgrimage and religious center it remains today because of her tomb and shrine there. Of Ma'sumeh's life, little is known except that she was the sister of Rezâ (d. 818), the eighth Shi'i Emâm who died and was buried in Mashhad, which got its name, grew, and is a major city today primarily because of the shrine there in his honor as the sole Shi'i Emâm buried in Iran. Iranians revere Ma'sumeh only because she was the seventh Emâm's daughter and the eighth Emâm's sister.

As for literary Iranian women, during the classical period of Persian poetry from Rudaki (d. 940/1) to Jâmi (1414-1492), several women's names appear as poetesses, chief among them Râbe'eh and Mahsati.(128) But little beyond apocryphal, anecdotal stories is known about them. Furthermore, such Iranian scholars as Heshmat Moayyad consider them insignificant as literary artists.(129)

More interesting evidence on the status of women in Iranian cultural history is their role as characters in classical Persian poetry, for example in already discussed works by Ferdowsi, Khayyâm, Khâqâni, Rumi, Sa'di, and Hâfez, among others.

In lyric verse, the most highly developed and highly regarded classical literary mode, women have almost no role at all. Poetic speakers are male, of course. But so, for the most part, are the beloveds addressed and described. As pointed out earlier in conjunction with Sa'di's famous "Caravan Ghazal" and several Hâfezian ghazals, Iranian critics assume that boys and young men are the models for the love poets. In other words, what Sir William Jones renders as "sweet maid" in his "Persian Song" version of "Turk of Shirâz" ghazal is a stock male character with a lengthy history in Persian poetry. In addition, a male figure often serves as the ideal beloved. For example, the beautiful Joseph is an irresistible temptation for Potiphar's wife Zolaykhâ, who serves as a one-dimensional reminder of how smitten one can be by perfect beauty.(130)

As for narrative verse (in which romantic love is heterosexual), Ferdowsi's story of Rostam and Sohrâb seems typical enough. In it, Tahmineh, the daughter of the king of Samangân, falls in love with Rostam who proceeds to spend only a single night with her and that without strong feelings of his own. The other female character in the tale is the warrior Gordâfarid who early on engages Sohrâb in combat. But their encounter is an episode that does not figure in the main action. Furthermore, Gordâfarid achieves significance and attention only because she disguises herself as a man and participates in the male arena of warfare.(131)

Khâqâni's "Ode on the Palace at Ctesiphon" gives voice to another dimension of the status of women in traditional Iranian literary culture. At one point in the poem, while pondering human mortality, the speaker says: "this hungry-eyed earth never becomes sated. / This white-browed mother with black sagging breasts / makes her rouge with children's heart's blood." In associating femininity with the earth and mortality (as opposed to the association of masculinity with spirituality and immortality), Khâqâni exhibits a masculine bias which at least one Iranian critic has argued is a fundamental premise and inspiration for imagery in Persian poetry from its very beginnings.(132)

In post-medieval Iranian culture, women remained mostly anonymous or invisible. Iranians are hard put to cite a single Iranian woman by name from the Safavid Era (1501-1736), whose most famous monarch, Shâh 'Abbâs the Great (ruled 1587-1629), "honored" his own wife by naming the famous Shaykh Lotfollâh mosque on his famous Shâh Square in Esfahân after his father-in-law! 'Abbâs's own ambitious mother was summarily assassinated for her attempts to achieve power.

In Qâjâr Iran (1796-1925), a handful of women achieved some recognition, mostly as a result of family connections. For example, a daughter of Nâseroddin Shâh Qâjâr (ruled 1848-1896) called Tâjossaltaneh was sensitive to the plight of Iranian women and addresses this and related issues in her *Memoirs* (although the book was completed in 1914, it was not published until 1982).(133) However, the most famous nineteenth-century Irânian woman was an anti-establishment figure named Tâhereh whom Nâseroddin Shâh ordered executed for heresy in 1852. Better known by her sobriquet Qorratol'ayn, this Bâbi devotee was a knowledgeable, determined, and courageous religious apologist and is a saintly heroine in the eyes of members of the Bahâ'i Faith today. But, as one Iranian scholar has noted, although her bold public actions were perhaps unprecedented for an Iranian woman, Qorratol'ayn was a follower of a male leader and seems to have been motivated by conventional religious faith rather than by a sense of her rightful personhood as a woman.(134)

By the end of the nineteenth century, numbers of Iranian women were beginning to emerge from behind domestic walls and to respond to the traditional culture in which they had subordinate roles. Women participated in the successful boycott of tobacco products called for by Shi'i clerical authorities in response to the Shâh's signing of a concession in 1890. Although female motivation in this case was apparently for the most part religious, such was not the case in their participation in the Constitutional Movement (1905-1911). Shortly thereafter, women's societies came into being, as well as later magazines by and for women. Zanddokht Shirâzi (1909-1952) and Zhâleh Qâ'em'maqâmi (1884-1946) are the best known among such women. Both exhibited feminist consciousness and produced verse as well, although their collected poems did not appear until much later.(135)

Also very conscious of the lamentable situation of Iranian women was a more famous woman called Parvin E'tesâmi (1907-1941), who became the best known Iranian woman in the arts in history up to the mid-1950s. A poetess much praised in traditionalist circles in part because she was a model of traditional decorum and circumspectness in both her personal life and her verse, E'tesâmi lived her life in the shadow of her family's protection. More to the point, although she composed poems lamenting the oppression of women, her verse lacks distinguishable feminine personae. She speaks as male poets would.(136) Still, E'tesâmi's very participation in the male world of Persian poetry had special significance, according to Simin Dâneshvar, insofar as she thus demonstrated to Iranian men and women alike that an Iranian woman could actually compose competent verse.(137) After all, prior to E'tesâmi no Iranian woman had achieved any real success as a poet in a thousand years of Persian poetry.

A generation later came Forugh Farrokhzâd (1934/5-1967), perhaps the most controversial Iranian woman in history and without question the première Persian poetess.(138) Farrokhzâd thought of herself as unprecedented as an Iranian woman speaking out as a woman in poetry; and she does not acknowledge any putative debts to the likes of Zanddokht Shirâzi, Zhâleh Qâ'em'maqâmi or Parvin E'tesâmi.(139) In a monograph called *A Lonely Woman: Forugh Farrokhzâd and Her Poetry* (1987), I have concurred with the poet's self-assessment in presenting her as "Iran's First Feminine Voice," an assertion to which several Iranian critics take exception.(140) My view is that the Iranian women who composed verse prior to Farrokhzâd either used poetic personae indistingushable from men or when they composed verse on female issues did not stand on their own as women. E'tesâmi lived under the protective wings of her father and then her brother, who handled the publication of her verse. Zhâleh Qâ'em'maqâmi is almost invariably introduced not as a poetess in her own right, but as the mother of Hosayn Pezhmân Bakhtiyâri (a traditionalist poet and literary scholar). In contrast, Farrokhzâd achieved prominence in Persian literature without dependence upon a relationship with a man. Most importantly, unlike her female predecessors, Farrokhzâd had a poetic voice that was and remains heard (whereas a voice not heard may be no voice at all). In fact, it has probably been because of Farrokhzâd's speaking out poetically as an Iranian woman that the verse of Zanddokht Shirâzi and Zhâleh Qâ'em'maqâmi eventually saw the light of printed day in the late 1960s.

Forugh Farrokhzâd was born in Tehrân into a middle class family of seven children. She attended public schools through the ninth grade, thereafter received some training in sewing and painting, and married when she was seventeen. Her only child, the boy addressed in "A Poem for You," presented in translation below, was born a year later. Within less than two years after that, her marriage failed, and Farrokhzâd relinquished her son to her ex-husband's family in order to pursue her calling in poetry and independent life style. She clearly voices her feelings in the mid-1950s about conventional marriage, the plight of women in Iran, and her own situation as a wife and mother no longer able to live a conventional life in such poems presented in translation below as "The Captive," "The Wedding Band," "Call to Arms," and "To My Sister."

As a divorcée poet in Tehrân, Farrokhzâd attracted much attention and considerable disapproval. She had several shortlived relationships with men-- "The Sin" describes one of them--, found some respite in a nine-month trip to Europe, and in 1958 met Ebrâhim Golestân (b. 1922), a controversial film-maker and writer with whom she established a relationship that lasted until her death in an automobile accident at thirty-two years of age in February 1967. Golestân, already married with two children and Farrokhzâd's employer at his Tehrân film studio, is presumably the beloved described or addressed in such poems below as "Conquest of the Garden" and "Another Birth."

These poems, as well as earlier autobiographical poems treating her marriage and later poems voicing views of life in general, exhibited unprecedented candor and outspokenness on the part of an Iranian woman. And although Farrokhzâd's importance as a poet derives from remarkable artistic achievements in her poetry qua poetry, nevertheless the fact that she was a woman composing poetry in the man's world of Persian literature has great cultural significance. In other words, if one accepts Rezâ Barâheni's reading of the Iranian past and traditions as basically a "masculine history," one can call Farrokhzâd the founder of "feminine culture" in Persian poetry and the originator of a new literary gender with which subsequent Iranian poets and readers will always have to deal.(141)

In describing this feminine gender in Iranian culture and in defining Farrokhzâd's unprecedented outspokenness as an Iranian woman, one should scrutinize her eventful life as she strove against great odds and social pressure to be an individual, to be her own person. Her biography may be one of the culturally most telling Iranian lives ever, as the cursory sketch in *A Lonely Women* suggests.

But this chapter is a characterization of Farrokhzâd as a literary woman who nevertheless paradoxically epitomizes essential traits and ideals of individuality which Iranian male literary figures also hold dear. To this end, twelve culture-specific poems, from among nearly 130 poems she composed between mid-1954 and her death less than thirteen years later, are here presented in straightforward translations, accompanied by commentary designed to highlight salient cultural features. These translations allow Farrokhzâd to speak for herself and, together with the commentaries, demonstrate remarkable differences between her Iranian voice and such prominent masculine voices as those of Ferdowsi, Khayyâm, Sa'di, Hâfez, Hedâyat, and Al-e Ahmad.

The most obviously different theme in Farrokhzâd's verse is her female and feminist sensitivity to the plight of Iranian women and her encouragement to her female readers to understand their state of oppression and then to do something about it. In the first poem presented below, Farrokhzâd presents a female character who learns through experience that marriage is not necessarily a partnership or a relationship based on trust. Called "The Wedding Band," the poem does not reflect Farrokhzâd's own experience with marriage, which ended in divorce for very different reasons, but rather her sense of typical situations in which married Iranian women find themselves. The next two poems, also products of the mid-1950s, are self-explanatory feminist appeals called respectively "Call to Arms" and "To My Sister." The final poem in this first group is a longer and more famous poem composed around 1960. Called "The Windup Doll," it is a comprehensive indictment of the lives which Farrokhzâd sensed the majority of Iranian women live.

The Wedding Band

The girl smiled and said: What
is the secret of this gold ring,
the secret of this ring that so tightly
embraces my finger,
[5]the secret of this band
that sparkles and shines so?
The man was startled and said:
It's the ring of good fortune, the ring of life.

Everyone said: Congratulations and best wishes!
[10]The girl said: Alas
that I still have doubts about its meaning.

The years passed, and one night
a downhearted woman looked at that gold band
and saw in its gleaming pattern
[15]days wasted in hopes of husbandly fidelity,
days totally wasted.

The woman grew agitated and cried out:
O my, this ring that
still sparkles and shines
is the band of slavery and servitude.(142)

Call to Arms

Only you, o Iranian woman, have remained
in bonds of wretchedness, misfortune, and cruelty;
if you want these bonds broken,
grasp the skirt of obstinacy.

[5]Do not relent because of pleasing promises,
never submit to tyranny;
become a flood of anger, hate and pain,
excise the heavy stone of cruelty.

It is your warm embracing bosom
[10]that nurtures proud and pompous man;
it is your joyous smile that bestows
on his heart warmth and vigor.

For that person who is your creation,
to enjoy preference and superiority is shameful;
[15]woman, take action because a world
awaits and is in tune with you.

Sleeping in a dark grave is happier for you
than this abject servitude and misfortune;
where is that proud man . . . ? Tell him
[20]to bow his head henceforth at your threshold.

Where it that proud man . . . ? Tell him to get up
because a woman is here rising to battle him;
her words are the truth, in which cause
she will never shed tears out of weakness.(143)

To My Sister

Sister, rise up after your freedom,
why are you quiet?
Rise up because henceforth
you have to imbibe the blood of tyrannical men.

[5]Seek your rights, sister,
from those who keep you weak,
from those whose myriad tricks and schemes
keep you seated in a corner of the house.

How long will you be the object of pleasure

151

[10]in the harem of men's lust?
How long will you bow your proud head at his feet
like a benighted servant?

How long for the sake of a morsel of bread,
will you keep becoming an aged hâji's temporary wife,
[15]seeing second and third rival wives.
Oppression and cruelty, my sister, for how long?

This angry moan of yours
must surely become a clamorous scream.
You must tear apart this heavy bond
[20]so that your life might be free.

Rise up and uproot the roots of oppression.
Give comfort to your bleeding heart.
For the sake of your freedom, strive
to change the law, rise up.(144)

   The Windup Doll

More than this, ah yes,
one can remain silent more than this.

For hours and hours
with the vacant stare of a corpse,
[5]one can gaze at cigarette smoke,
at the shape of a tea cup
at a faded flower in a carpet,
at an imaginary line on the wall.

With stiff fingers one can
[10]draw aside the curtain and
watch the rain pouring down onto the alley,
a child standing under an arch
colored balloons in hand,
a rickety cart noisily and hastily
[15]leaving the empty square.

One can remain perfectly still
both blind and deaf, next to the curtain.

One can exclaim,
with a voice patently false and alien,

[20]"I love . . . "
In the powerful embrace of a man,
one can be a beautiful, healthy female commodity
with two large, firm breasts,
with a body like a smooth leather table cloth.
[25]In bed with a drunk, a mad man, a vagrant,
one can contaminate the purity of a love.

One can cleverly ridicule every startling mystery.
One can solve crossword puzzles only
and with the discovery of a useless answer
[30]keep oneself occupied, a useless answer,
yes, in five or six letters.

One can genuflect a whole lifetime
with bowed head at the foot of a saint's cold sarcophagus,
one can find God in a nameless grave,
[35]one can find faith with an insignificant coin,
one can rot in the precincts of a mosque
like an old prayer reader.

Like zero in addition, subtraction, and multiplication,
one can always achieve a constant result.
[40]One can see the depths of your pupils
as a faded button on an old shoe.
Like water in its own container, one can dry up.
One can hide the beauty of a moment with embarrassed shame
like an unbecoming black-and-white snapshot
[45]at the bottom of a trunk.
In the empty frame of a day
one can hang the image of a person condemned, defeated, or crucified.
One can cover cracks in the wall with images;
one can merge with even more useless designs and pictures.

[50]Exactly like a windup doll,
one can see one's own world with two glass eyes.
With a body filled with straw
one can sleep for years
in a felt-lined box
[55]on lace and tinsel.

In response to every obscene squeeze of a hand,
one can exclaim without reason:
"Oh, I'm so happy!"(145)

In these four feminist poems, Farrokhzâd would appear to speak for all Iranians with similar feelings. This role of the poetic speaker as spokesperson is explicit and obvious in "The Windup Doll," in which Farrokhzâd vividly depicts the middle class, urban Iranian woman's potentially lifeless status as wife who waits at home for her man with nothing much to do and seems no more than an object for that man's sexual gratification. The Iranian woman can be "exactly like a windup doll": seeing "one's own world with two glass eyes," sleeping "for years in a felt-lined box on lace and tinsel," and exclaiming "in response to every obsecene squeeze of a hand . . . 'Oh, I'm so happy!'"

The next poem also presents Farrokhzâd as a spokesperson, as a critic of life in Westernized North Tehrân in the 1960s. Its title, "O Jewel-studded Land," was the title of an official Pahlavi-era anthem, which Farrokhzâd here satirizes along with the modernized and westernized culture the Pahlavi monarchy fostered. References in the poem to Iranian identity cards, national lottery drawings on Wednesday afternoons, traditionalist poets searching in the refuse heap of history for inspiration, and the traditionalist versifier Ebrâhim Sahbâ (Abraham, the western form of his given name deliberately given) make the poem very culture-specific. The poet even uses her own name for the speaker, although the poem's details are not personally autobiographical. Farrokhzâd expresses in "O Jewel-studded Land" the critical view shared by many non-establishment, secular-minded intellectuals of her day.

O Jewel-studded Land

I've won,
I registered myself,
adorned myself with a name, an identity card,
and my existence has become defined with a number.
[5]Therefore, long live 678, resident of Tehrân,
        long live 678, issued at precinct 5.
My worries are over now
in the homeland's loving bosom,
my pacifier: glorious historical traditions,
my lullaby: civilization and culture,
[10]my toy rattle: the rattle box of law.
Ah,
my worries are over now.

Overjoyed,
I went to the window, and eagerly 678 times
[15]inhaled air compacted with dung dust
        and the odor of garbage and urine.

154

And on 678 bills
and on 678 job applications I have written: "Forugh Farrokhzâd."
In the land of poetry and roses and nightingales,
it is a blessing to live, especially
[20]when the reality of your existence
is acknowledged after years and years,
a place where
through the curtains with my first offical look
I see 678 poets,
[25]charlatans, all of them, a strange beggarly company,
searching in the garbage for rhymes and meters.
And at the sound of my first official steps,
suddenly from the dark slime, 678 furtive nightingales,
who for fun
[30]have transformed themselves into 678 old black crows,
fly lazily toward the edge of day.
And my first official breath
is impregnated with the odor of 678 stemmed red roses
products of the great Plasco factories.

[35]Yes, it is a blessing to live
in the birthplace of Sheikh Abu Dalqak,
        the opium-addict *kamâncheh* player,
and Sheikh Ay Del Ay Del, the lute-playing descendant of drums,
the city of superstar legs and derrieres and breasts
        and cover pictures and *Art* magazine,
cradle of authors of the philosophy
        "so what? what's it to me? forget it,"
[40]cradle of IQ olympics--o my!
a place where when you touch any transmitter of picture and sound,
from it the brilliant blare of a young genius blurts out.
And when the nation's intellectual elite
put in an appearance at an adult education class,
[45]their chests are decorated with 678 electric kabob cookers,
and on both wrists 678 Seiko watches; and they are certain
that weakness drives from empty pockets, not from ignorance.

I won, yes I won.
Now in celebration of this victory
[50]in front of the mirror, with pride,
I light 678 candles bought on credit
and leap onto the mantle so that, with your permission,
I might address a few words to you
        concerning the legal advantages of life
and to the resonance of enthusiastic applause

[55]I break ground with the pickaxe on the part at the top of my head
for the lofty edifice of my life.

I'm alive, yes, like Zendeh Rud River that was alive one day
and from all that is exclusively
        the right of living people I'll drive benefit.

As of tomorrow,
[60]in the city's side streets brimming
with national blessings
and in the lighthearted shadows of telegraph poles,
I'll stroll along
and proudly write 678 times on public lavatory walls:
[65]"I wrote this line to make donkeys laugh."
As of tomorrow,
like a zealous patriot,
I'll have in heart and mind
a share in the great ideal which society
[70]every Wednesday afternoon
follows with anxious excitement,
a share of those thousand-desire-nurturing, 1000-riyal notes
which can be used for refrigerators, furniture, and curtains
or which for 678 natural votes
[75]can be donated one evening to 678 patriotic men.

As of tomorrow,
at the back of Khâchik's shop,
after inhaling several snorts of a few grams of first hand pure stuff
and consuming several not-so-pure pepsis
[80]and uttering several Sufi exclamations,
I'll officially join the association of prominent pensive
        learned people and enlightened erudite excrement
and followers of the school of la-dee-da,
and scribble the plot outline of my first great novel
which around year 1678 Shamsi-ye Tabrizi
[85]will be formally submitted to a bankrupt press
on both sides of 678 packs of genuine Oshno Special cigarettes.

As of tomorrow
with complete confidence
I'll treat myself to one velvet-covered seat for 678 sessions
[90]in the assembly of assembling and guaranteeing the future
or the assembly of gratitude and praise
because I read *Art and Science*
and *Flattering and Bowing*,

and I know the "correct writing"method.

[95]I have strode into the arena of existence
       in the midst of a creative populace
whose great scientific strength has brought them
to the threshold of manufacturing artificial clouds
and inventing neon lights
of course in the research and laboratory centers
       of chicken kabob stands.
[100]I have strode into the arena of existence
       in the midst of a creative populace
who although they have no bread
have instead an open and spacious vista
presently bounded
on the north by verdent Tir Square
[105]and on the south by historic E'dâm Square
and in those overcrowded neighborhoods reaching Tupkhâneh Square.
And in the shelter of the shining sky and secure in its security
from morning till night 678 big plaster swans
accompanied by 678 angels,
[110]angels made of mud and clay,
are busy advertising plans for inaction and silence.
I won, yes I've won.
Therefore long live 678, resident of Tehrân,
       long live 678, issued at precinct 5,
who by dint of determination and perseverance
[115]has reached such a lofty station that
she now stands in the frame of a window
       678 meters above the ground
and now has the honor of being able
from that very window, not by way of the stairs,
to hurl herself madly down
       into the affectionate bosom of the motherland.
[120]And her final will and testament is this:
that, for 678 coins, the honorable master Abraham Sahba
compose an elegy in the rhyme of sing song eulogizing her life.(146)

The next three poems, "The Captive" (1954), "The Sin" (1954), and "A Poem for You" (1957), exhibit some of the qualities that brought Farrokhzâd immediate fame when she began publishing her poems in the mid-1950s. The poems are frank, intense, and straightforward representations of very personal experiences, conflicts, and dilemmas couched in everyday images and vocabulary. Such poems were almost unprecedented in Persian in their autobiographical candor, that is, in their poet's refusal to don a mask or to veil real concerns in the garb of conventional literary decorum.

The Captive

I want you, yet I know that never
can I embrace you to my heart's content.
You are that clear and bright sky.
I, in this corner of the cage, am a captive bird.

[5]From behind the cold and dark bars
directing toward you my rueful look of astonishment,
I am thinking that a hand might come
and I might suddenly spread my wings in your direction.

I am thinking that in a moment of neglect
[10]I might fly from this silent prison,
laugh in the eyes of the man who is my jailer
and beside you begin life anew.

I am thinking these things, yet I know
that I can not, dare not leave this prison.
[15]Even if the jailer would wish it,
no breath or breeze remains for my flight.

From behind the bars, every bright morning
the look of a child smiles in my face;
when I begin a song of joy,
[20]his lips come toward me with a kiss.

O sky, if I want one day
to fly from this silent prison,
what shall I say to the weeping child's eyes:
forget about me, for I am captive bird?

[25]I am that candle which illumines a ruins
with the burning of her heart.
If I want to choose silent darkness,
I will bring a nest to ruin.(147)

The Sin

I sinned a sin full of pleasure,
in an embrace which was warm and fiery.
I sinned surrounded by arms

158

that were hot and vengeful and iron.

[5]In that dark and silent seclusion,
I looked into his secret-full eyes.
My heart shook anxiously in my breast
in response to the requests of his pleading eyes.

In that dark and silent seclusion,
[10]I sat distressed at his side.
His lips poured passion on mine,
I escaped from the sorrow of my crazed heart.

I whispered in his ear the tale of love:
I want you, o sweetheart of mine,
[15]I want you, o life-giving embrace,
o crazed lover of mine, you.

Desire sparked a flame in his eyes;
red wine danced in the cup.
In the soft bed my body
[20]drunkenly quivered on his chest.

I sinned a sin full of pleasure,
next to a trembling, unconscious body;
O God, who knows what I did
in that dark and quiet seclusion.(148)

A Poem for You

I am composing this poem for you
on a parched summer dusk
halfway down this road of ominous beginning
in the old grave of this endless sorrow.

[5]This is the final lullaby
at the foot of the cradle where you sleep.
May the wild sounds of my screaming
echo in the sky of your youth.

Let the shadow of me the wanderer
[10]be separate and far from your shadow.
When one day we reach one another,
standing between us will be none other than God.

159

Against a dark door I have rested
my forehead tight with pain;
[15]I rub my thin, cold fingers
against this door in hope.

That person branded with shame who used to laugh
at foolish taunts was I.
I said I would be the cry of my own existence;
[20]but o, alas that I was a "woman."

When your innocent eyes glance
at this confused, beginningless book,
you will see a deep-rooted, lasting rebellion
blooming in the heart of every song.

[25]Here the stars are all dim,
the angels here all weep.
The blooms of the tuberose here
have less value than desert thorns.

Here, seated along every road
[30]is the demon of duplicity, disgrace and deceit.
In the dark sky I do not see
a light from the bright morning of wakefulness.

Wait until once again my eyes
overflow with drops of dew.
[35]I have taken it upon myself to unveil
the "pure" faces of the holy Marys.

I have cast away from the shore of good name;
in my heart lies a storm star.
The place of my anger's flame,
[40]alas, is the prison's dark space.

Against a dark door I have rested
my forehead tight with pain.
I rub my thin, cold fingers
against this door in hope.

[45]Against these ascetic hypocrites
I know this fight is not easy.
My city and yours, my sweet child,
has long been Satan's nest.

A day will come when your eyes
[50]will sadly quiver at this painful song.
You will search for me in my words
and tell yourself: My mother, that is who she was.(149)

The remaining poems constitute a fourth sort of Farrokhzâdian poetic statement, and perhaps the key to her preeminence as a contemporary Iranian poet. These are four poems in which the female poetic speaker deals with what poetic art means to her. In an interview conducted in 1964, Farrokhzâd was asked why she wrote poetry. Part of her answer was:

I cannot explain why I write poetry. I think all those who are involved in creative work have as their motive, or at least one of their motives, a sort of need to struggle with and confront annihilation. These are individuals who love and understand life more, and likewise death. Creative work is a kind of struggle to maintain existence, or else to perpetuate "self" and negate the meaning of death. Sometimes I think it is right that death is one of the laws of nature; it is only in the face of this law that humanity feels humiliated and small. This is one dilemma about which nothing can be done. One cannot even fight to eliminate it.(150)

The following poem, called "Green Delusion," is described by the feminist critic Farzaneh Milani as "Forugh's eloquent statement of all the sacrifices she has had to make for her art."(151) In this poem, which Milani entitles in translation "Green Terror," the ever honest poet reveals that her decision to live as an individualistic female and artist is not without its price.

Doubts, questions, and twinges of regret remain as to roads not taken and more conventional, more acceptable roles rejected. The speaker in "Green Delusion" recognizes that nature can no longer be a comforting idyllic force in her life, that she is far beyond being able to seek refuge in comfortable maternal and other domestic female roles, and that her steadfast search for life's meaning has deprived her of the comfort of religious faith.

Green Delusion

I cried all day in the mirror.
Spring
had entrusted my window to the trees' green delusion.
My body would not fit in the cocoon of my loneliness.
[5]And the odor of my paper crown had polluted the air
    of that sunless realm.

I couldn't anymore, I just couldn't:
street sounds, the sound of birds,
the sound of felt balls being lost,
and the fleeting clamor of children,
[10]and the dance of balloons
bobbing upward at he end of their string stems
like soap bubbles,
and the wind, wind which seemed
to be breathing in the depths
     of the deepest dark moments of lovemaking,
[15]were exerting pressure
on the ramparts of the silent fortress of my confidence
and through old cracks in the walls were calling my heart by name.

All day my gaze was fixed
on my life's eyes,
[20]at those two anxious fearful eyes which avoided my stare
and sought refuge in their lids' safe seclusion like liars.

Which peak, which summit?
Do not all of these winding roads
reach the point of converence and termination
[25]in that cold sucking mouth?

O simple words of deception and renunciation of bodies and desires,
what did you give me?
If I stuck a flower in my own hair,
would it not be more alluring
[30]than this fraud, than this paper crown?

How the spirit of the desert got me
and the moon's magic led me from the flock's faith!
How the incompleteness of my heart grew large
and no half completed this half!
[35]How I stood and saw
the ground beneath my two feet vanish,
and no warmth of my mate's body
fulfill the futile anticipation of my body!

Which peak, which summit?
[40]Give me refuge, o apprehensive lights,
o bright doubting houses
on whose sunny roofs sway
clothes laundered in the embrace of scented smoke.

Give me refuge, o simple, whole women
[45]whose slender fingertips
trace
the exhilarating movement of a foetus beneath the skin
and in whose opened blouses
the air always mingles with the smell of fresh milk.

[50]Which peak, which summit?
Give me refuge, o hearthsful of fire--o goodluck horseshoes--,
and o song of copper pots in the blackened kitchen,
and o somber humming of the sewing machine,
and o day-and-night struggle between carpets and brooms.
[55]Give me refuge, o insatiable loves,
whose painful desire for immortality
adorns your bed of conquests
with magical water and drops of fresh blood.

All day, all day,
[60]forsaken, forsaken like a corpse on water,
I floated towards the most terrifying rocks,
toward the deepest sea caves.
And the most carnivorous of fish
and the thin vertebrae of my back
[65]twinged with pain at sensing death.

I couldn't any longer, I just couldn't.
The sound of my feet arose from the denial of the road,
and my despair had become vaster than my spirit's capacity to endure.
And that spring season and that green-colored delusion
[70]passing by the window said to my heart:
"Look,
you never progressed,
yours has been a descent."(152)

Many of Farrokhzâd's later poems exhibit undercurrents of loneliness and near-despair, even if the sadness and doubts do not reach the surface as in "Green Delusion." At the same time, Farrokhzâd's capacity to follow her heart's bidding and her faith in the meaningfulness of artistic expression brought her some remarkably ebullient moments as well, moments when she soared as a poet and as a person. One of the most famous of these poems, and the other side of the proverbial coin in tandem with "Green Delusion," is called "Conquest of the Garden."

"Conquest of the Garden" is Farrokhzâd's manifesto of rejection of societal conventions and determination to follow the dictates of her heart. The speaker here knows that a relationship of love has little to do with signing a

163

marriage certificate, but a lot to do with ignoring what "everyone" will think. It means overcoming the fears that most people have when faced with the opportunity to be totally open. The issues in "Conquest of the Garden" are age-old in Persian literature, nowhere more stylishly voiced than in Hâfez's ghazals. In the "Cup of Jamshid" ghazal (pages 87-90, above) the speaker searches for this cup, which is synonymous with the capacity to experience and express love, a pearl-like jewel obtainable only if one risks all and dives into the deep, the only place where pearls exist. In "Conquest of the Garden," Farrokhzâd gives a personal cast to the timeless realization of the significance of true love.

In Iranian terms, Farrokhzâd's invitation is a modernist echo of FitzGerald's "Oh, come with Old Khayyâm," who asserts that "wilderness were Paradise enow . . . / With me along the strip of Herbage strown/ That just divides the desert from the sown." Both Khayyâm and Farrokhzâd see the good life in the age-old Iranian vision of an idyllic, natural garden, the ideal environment for people whose lives actually take place in "the desert" of Iran's harsh and brown plateau lands and "the sown" of the patriarchal order of kings, which for Khayyâm means images of Mahmud of Ghazneh and which for Farrokhzâd manifests itself in the city and its authoritative, conventional moral order.

Ferdowsi, Hâfez, and Hedâyat can also be viewed in these garden terms. Ferdowsi's *Shâhnâmeh* shows readers an Iranian "sown" world eventually in shambles, but promises the Koranic gardens of heaven to those who accept Allâh as a just and providential god. Hâfez sustains his lyric garden ghazal patterns and their garden content in a remarkably consistent corpus of over five hundred ghazal poems. As for Hedâyat, his narrator in *The Blind Owl* struggles desperately and unsuccessfully to keep himself in an innocent green world.

Conquest of the Garden

That crow which flew over our heads and
descended into the disturbed thought of a vagabond cloud
and the sound of which traversed the breadth
    of the horizon like a short spear
will carry the news of us to the city.

[5]Everyone knows,
everyone knows
that you and I have seen the garden
from that cold sullen window
and that we have plucked the apple
[10]from that playful branch beyond reach.

Everyone is afraid
everyone is afraid, but you and I
joined with lamp, water and mirror,
and we were not afraid.

[15]I am not talking about the flimsy linking of two names
and embracing in the old pages of a ledger.
I'm talking about my fortunate tresses
with the burnt anemone of your kiss
and the intimacy of our bodies,
[20]and the glow of our nakedness
like fish scales in the water.
I am talking about the silvery life of a song
which the small fountain sings at dawn.

We asked
[25]wild rabbits one night in that green flowing forest
and shells full of pearls in that turbulent coldblooded sea
and young eagles on that strange overwhelming mountain
what should be done.

Everyone knows,
[30]everyone knows
we have found our way into the cold and quiet dream of phoenixes.
We found truth in the garden
in the embarrassed look of a nameless flower,
and we found immortality in an endless moment
[35]when two suns stared at each other.

I am not talking about timorous whispering in the dark,
I am talking about daytime and open windows,
and fresh air,
and a stove in which useless things burn,
[40]and land which is fertile with a different planting,
and birth and evolution and pride.
I am talking about our loving hands
which have built across nights a bridge
of the message of perfume and light and breeze.

[45]Come to the meadow
to the grand meadow,
and call me, from behind the breaths of silk-tasseled acacias,
just like the deer calls its mate.

The curtains are full of a hidden rancor,

[50]and innocent doves
look to the ground
from their white tower heights.(153)

In her bold poem, Farrokhzâd is in part confronting Khayyâmic dilemmas
and is voicing moods and views which FitzGerald's character entertains
during the day depicted in his *Rubaíyát.* That individualistic Saljuq Iranian
and Victorian Englishman realized too that he could not transform natural
"wilderness" into a paradise: the prospect of physical mortality and the
realization of the capriciousness of fate make prolonged enjoyment of nature
almost impossible. Religion and science as well cannot provide either
adequate answers or adequate comfort. Ultimately, one must rely on him- or
herself and make the best of a bad bargain. Khayyâm's is a difficult way to
have to live. But his may have been the easier chore, because he at least did
not have to fight Farrokhzâd's battle to be an independent **woman** as well.

Actually Farrokhzâd's struggle was even more difficult because she refused
to take refuge or solace in Ferdowsi's Islam, Khayyâm's skepticism and
stoic resignation, or Hedâyat's despair and misanthropy. Unlike Khayyâm
and Hedâyat who removed themselves from the fray in one way or another,
Farrokhzâd dared to begin each day of poetry with a resolve to live and
represent life as if her world could truly be a Persian garden. She did not
romanticize her situation or engage in self-deception: on balance, "green
delusions" outweighed "victories over gardens"; and she, who felt more and
more that she was a lonely woman or a woman alone, sensed the truth of
her situation. Nevertheless, she refused to be vanquished. So had Hâfez,
whose consistent display of confidence must have been a subliminal part of
what Farrokhzâd found so uniquely appealing about him. Hers was a similar
quest and endeavor, although in a modernist context. Accordingly, she
represents her vigorous efforts to make and maintain a garden out of her
world in the very individual terms of personal experiences as they happened
for her. Because she had no Hâfezian mask and because she thought of her
poetry as a mirror and intimate companion, Farrokhzâd felt duty-bound to
present in her poetry the truth of her many failures to find her garden or keep
it green, as well as her few, brilliant successes such as "Conquest of the
Garden." If Hâfez's victory over life lies in his never letting down his guard
and never removing his mask in classic poems that have achieved
immortality (the only true victory for the literary person), Farrokhzâd's is a
matter of her refusal to surrender to despair as a poet on any given day
despite a setback or defeat on the day previous.

Another of Farrokhzâd's victories over or in life is her epoch-making
"Another Birth." The title poem of the collection published in early 1964,
which is as an important a single volume of verse as anything else
published in the Persian language since Hâfez's *Divân* and one of the most
discussed and appreciated modernist Persian poems, "Another Birth" is a

brilliant statement of Farrokhzâd's convictions as to the purpose and significance of poetry. It is also a love poem and an evocative glimpse down the poet's memory lane. The translation which follows may be closer to the voice of the poet than the other translations in this chapter, because it is the fruit of collaboration between Farrokhzâd and the critic and translator Karim Emâmi.

Another Birth

My whole being is a dark chant
that perpetuating you
will carry you to the dawn of eternal growths and blossomings
in this chant I sighed you, sighed
[5]in this chant
I grafted you to trees, to the water, to fire.

Life is perhaps
a long street through which a woman holding a basket
     passes every day
life is perhaps a long rope with which a man
     hangs himself from a branch
[10]Life is perhaps a child returning home from school.

Life is perhaps lighting up a cigarette in the narcotic
     repose between two love-makings
or the absent gaze of a passerby
with a meaningless smile and a good morning.

Life is perhaps that enclosed moment
[15]when my gaze destroys itself in the pupil of your eyes
and it is in the feeling
that I will put into the Moon's perception
     and the Night's impression.
In a room as big as loneliness
my heart
[20]which is as big as love
looks at the simple pretexts of its happiness
at the beautiful decay of flowers in the vase
at the saplings you planted in our garden
and the song of canaries
[25]that sing to the size of a window.

Ah . . .
this is my lot

this is my lot
a sky that is taken away at the drop of a curtain
[30]my lot is going down a flight of disused stairs
to regain something amid putrefaction and nostalgia
my lot is a sad promenade in the garden of memories
and dying in the grief of a voice that tells me
I love your hands.
[35]I will plant my hands in the garden
I will grow, I know, I know, I know
and swallows will lay eggs
in the hollow of my ink-stained hands.

I shall wear twin cherries as earrings
[40]and I shall put dahlia petals on my fingernails.

There is an alley
where the boys who were in love with me
still loiter with the same unkempt hair, thin necks and bony legs
and think of the innocent smiles of a little girl
[45]who was blown away by the wind one night.

There is an alley that my heart has stolen
from the streets of my childhood.

The journey of a form along the line of time
and inseminating the line of time with the form
[50]a form conscious of an image
returning from a feast in the mirror.

And it is in this way
that someone dies
and someone lives on.

[55]No fisherman shall ever find a pearl
     in a small brook that empties into a pool.

I know a sad little fairy
who lives in an ocean
and ever so softly
plays her heart into a magic flute
[60]a sad little fairy
who dies with one kiss each night
and is reborn with one kiss each dawn.(154)

Several years later, in her last major poem, Farrokhzâd again proclaims her dedication to her art. But the proclamation is tense and defiant, and not lyric and joyful, as in "Another Birth." Called "It Is Only Sound That Remains," the poem reads:

Why should I stop, why?
The birds have gone in search of the blue direction.
The horizon is vertical,
the horizon is vertical, and movement fountain-like;
[5]and at the limits of vision,
shining planets spin.
The earth in elevation reaches repetition,
and air wells change into tunnels of connection;
and day is a vastness,
[10]which does not fit into the narrow mind of newspaper worms.

Why should I stop?
The road passes through the capillaries of life,
the planting environment of the uterus-like moon
will kill the corrupt cells;
[15]and in the chemical space after sunrise
there is only sound,
sound that will be drawn to the particles of time.
Why should I stop?

What can a swamp be,
[20]what can it be but the spawning ground of corrupt insects?
Swollen corpses scrawl the morgue's thoughts,
the unmanly one
has cloaked his lack of manliness in darkness,
and bugs . . . ah,
[25]when bugs talk,
why should I stop?
Cooperation of lead letters is futile,
and cannot rescue miserable thoughts.
I am descended from trees.
[30]Breathing stale air depresses me.
A bird which died advised me to commit flight to memory.
The ultimate extent of all powers is union, joining
with the bright principle of the sun
and pouring into the consciousness of light.
[35]It is natural for windmills to fall apart.
Why should I stop?
I clasp to my breast
the unripe bunches of wheat

and breast-feed them.

[40]Sound, sound, only sound,
the sound of the limpid wish of water to flow,
the sound of the falling of starlight
     on the layer of earth's femininity
the sound of the binding of meaning's sperm
and the expansion of the shared mind of love.
[45]Sound, sound, sound, it is only sound that remains.

In the land of dwarfs,
the critieria of comparison
have always traveled in the orbit of zero.
Why should I stop?
[50]I obey the four elements;
and the job of drawing up the constitution of my heart
is not the business of the local government of the blind.

What is the lengthy wild whimpering
in the sexual organs of animals to me?
[55]What to me is the worm's humble movement
     in its fleshy vacuum?
The bleeding ancestry of flowers has committed me to life:
are you familiar with the flowers' bleeding ancestry?(155)

In Iranian culture, for people whose personal lives and history have
routinely included invasions, earthquakes, epidemics, oppression at the
hands of monarchs, harsh climatic conditions, and a host of other factors
that persuade many to retire to the sidelines or behind courtyard walls,
Forugh Farrokhzâd's persistence and refusal to knuckle under make her an
ideal Iranian personality type. But hers is not a mythologized personality as
are those of Ferdowsi, Khayyâm, and Hâfez, who were essentially
establishment figures bound professionally to serve the patriarchal system
their artistic personalities may have privately opposed. Farrokhzâd's is not a
romantic personality either, one that achieves idealization only through self-
destruction as Hedâyat did. Farrokhzâd stands as an ideal Iranian type because
she strove for personal and artistic personhood and individuality in an
everyday Tehrân world through words and deeds for which many other
Iranians might easily find analogous behaviors in their own lives. This is
what essentially makes her an exciting and unprecedented Iranian model.
Perhaps not wholly unprecedented. For example, there is the mythical hero
Sohrâb, Rostam's son.
    Sohrâb seeks to place on the Iranian throne a man he believes, incorrectly
it turns out, deserves to be there: his own father. He plans to share in the
rule of the Iranian empire and to install his mother as queen. As an actor in

a mythological monarchial age in a narrative composed in another monarchical age, Sohrâb necessarily envisions justice and reform within the parameters of the world view familiar to him and to his poet. Nevertheless, his belief that the good and the strong should have a voice in who rules and that only one who deserves by behavior, rather than by birth, to rule should be king, may make him a kindred spirit and mythological forebear of Farrokhzâd.

The parallels between the character Sohrâb in Ferdowsi's *Shâhnâmeh* and Forugh Farrokhzâd are striking. Sohrâb is loyal to neither God nor king. Farrokhzâd professed not to believe in God and thought the Pahlavi monarchy so much foolishness. Love is at the center of Farrokhzâd's life and Sohrâb's. He loves his mother and his father, and is about to fall in love with Gordâfarid. The posturing patriarch Rostam, on the other hand, is incapable of such emotions. Sohrâb is killed by patriarchy, at the hand of his father on orders from the king, with at least one Iranian critic thinking it was no accident. Farrokhzâd was harassed continually by similar forces throughout her short life. And they might have overwhelmed her had she lived on. The root of Sohrâb's problem may be that he was raised by a woman and naturally did not learn masculine religion and loyalty to the throne. As for Farrokhzâd, having deliberately chosen at sixteen years of age to escape from her father's home through marriage and then choosing to escape from that second paternal situation before the age of twenty, she too looked at the world through her own, woman's eyes. That many of her poems do not treat obvious political issues of the day is not the result of presumed feminine myopia. For her, such issues were best left to blustering, self-important male poets who, in her view, had done nothing for her culture in centuries. Male critics still refuse to see her satirical poem "O Jewel-studded Land" as a woman's indictment of masculine culture, in which it makes sense for a woman to despair and consider suicide.

Yet, as either an ideal Iranian or as a model for others, Farrokhzâd is not sufficiently typical to warrant realistic emulation. Although Iranian to the depths of her psyche and artistic soul, she does not embody Iranianness in as characteristic a fashion as does Al-e Ahmad. As an individualistic and modern woman, she hardly looks back on Shi'i Islam and Persian monarchy. Common sense bade her to abandon both in youth. As a woman whose sex was allowed no serious role in Iranian cultural history, she need not agonize over historical dilemmas and ties, as does Al-e Ahmad.

No woman in Iran today can possibly emulate Farrokhzâd as a person or as an artist, and survive. And it is unclear how Iranian males might translate her actions into analogues for their lives. In short, the implication here is that the Persianist perspective on Iranian culture fails to find a beacon in the dark or an inspiration that will work. In addition, comparative consideration of such literary figures as Ferdowsi, Khayyâm, Sa'di, Hâfez, Hedâyat, Sâ'edi, Al-e Ahmad, Farrokhzâd, and others may even imply that the small percentage of the Persian-speaking population throughout history which is

171

intellectually curious, questioning of received values, and dedicated to literature may not be as culturally homogeneous as would seem to be the case at first glance.

EPILOGUE:
AN IRANIAN IDENTITY CRISIS PAST AND PRESENT

"Comment peut-on être persan?"
Montesquieu, *Lettres persanes*(1721)

From the early years of the twentieth century, Persian literary works have treated Iranian self-identity as much as, if not more than, any other issue or concern. For example, from Sâdeq Hedayat's *The Blind Owl* (1937) to Esmâ'il Fasih's *Sorayya in a Coma* (1983), narrative fictions have depicted consternation on the part of individual Iranians trying to fathom and feel at home in their culture.

The tortured main character of Hedayat's still influential masterpiece finds the cultural burden of his Iranian past unbearable and cringes in terror from both the Iranian present and identification with other Iranians. Fasih's novel describes a group of Iranian expatriates who express great love for their homeland, yet seem curiously at home in Paris in the early 1980s. The narrator, who is visiting that city to see after a hospitalized niece, does not know what to make of his compatriots there or of the war with Iraq back home or of back home in general. His niece Sorayya is actually in a coma which seems to worsen by the end of the novel, when the reader comes to feel that she may represent Iran for the narrator as well as the author.(156)

In Persian poetry, from Nimâ Yushij's "O Night" (1922)(157) to Nâder Naderpur's "Blood and Ashes" (1984), lyric speakers have routinely expressed deep-seated, cultural and political alienation from the Iranian mainstream. Nimâ's still much quoted 1941 poem called "Ahoy There, People" depicts a lone individual struggling desperately to keep afloat in a heavy sea. He calls out to people on the shore, who are either too busy enjoying themselves or too preoccupied with self-enhancing endeavors to hear or heed him. In his poem, Nimâ communicates a general cultural malaise and the Iranian intellectual's longstanding, near-desperate sense of alienation.

Nâderpur's poem, although equally indefinite in terms of specific references to Iran, describes both the post-Pahlavi environment in the Islamic Republic, which the speaker cannot tolerate, and his forced residence

173

in a foreign clime which can never be home for him. Nâderpur composed the poem in Nice almost two years after leaving Iran for good. In part it reads:

That earthquake . . . one night
turned everything upside down . . .
and bloodied the ash gray of dawn.
It galloped over princes' tombs
and smashed ancient artists' images . . . .
It . . . extinguished the poet's lantern of imagination . . .
and buried the treasure of sweet days
beneath the dirt of past sorrow.
. . . That earthquake carried out a hundred night raids
on my home and memories.

[So] I turned my face toward exile,
. . . the chain of misfortune around my neck.

. . . Here where I am may be heaven on earth,
but what can I do? It is not my home . . . .
The moon shining on this shore
is not that which shone down
from the ever enchanting Alborz heights . . . .
That earthquake which shook the house,
it is impossible to say what it did to my heart.(158)

In drama as well, with such plays of premier dramatist Gholâmhosayn Sâ'edi as *Long 'A,' Short 'A'* and *Clubwielders of Varazil* constituting graphic examples, conflict after conflict deals with Iranianness in the face of American influence and other presumed threats during the 1960s and 1970s to the cultural integrity of the country.

Moreover, much of pre-modern Persian literature implicitly voices concerns and complexities of Persian and Iranian identity. Ferdowsi's *Shâhnâmeh* and Khâqâni's "Ode on the Palace at Ctesiphon" are the most obvious examples. Persian literary culture as a whole seems energized and enriched by such concerns and complexities.

In short, no other question seems more appropriate as an epiloque to a Persianist scrutiny of Iranian culture than a consideration of issues of cultural identity in Persian literature, to discern how Iranian writers themselves answer the question as to who they culturally are and to test the hypothesis that an identity crisis may be a perennial and paradoxically natural or salutory condition for literary Iranians.

But another question of long standing may need asking first. It is a question which highlights at least one factor in why Iranian self-identity is such a burning issue today. It was first posed in 1721 in Montesquieu's *The Persian Letters*, in which a fictional Parisian asks an Iranian visitor: "Ah, oh! So Monsieur is an Iranian! What an extraordinary thing! How can anyone be Iranian?"(159) For the French of Montesquieu's day, Iranians were curious and uncivilized. To what they assumed was a rhetorical question, the obvious richness of Iranian culture as manifested for millennia in divers arenas and forms, chief among them imaginative literature from Rudaki (d. 940/1), the 'father' of Persian poetry, to the prolific novelist Mahmud Dowlatâbâdi (b. 1940), whose most recent work is a ten-volume saga called *Klidar* (1986), offers a resounding, unequivocal rebuttal. Accordingly, one should feel justifiable pride in being Iranian and also feel that one's culture, in the manifold voices of Ferdowsi, Khayyâm, Nâser Khosrow, Khâqâni, Nezâmi, 'Attâr, Rumi, Sa'di, Hâfez, Hedâyat, Nimâ Yushij, Shâmlu, Al-e Ahmad, Chubak, Sâ'edi, Farrokhzâd, Golshiri, Akhavân-e Sâles, and scores of other literary artists, has undauntingly addressed essential human issues of love, death and the rest and created great and culture-specific art in the process.

But in the final years of the twentieth century, Montesquieu's question deserves posing again, this time in serious consternation, in terms neither ethnocentric nor patronizing. For as the voices of Akhavân-e Sâles in "The Ending of the *Shâhnâmeh*" and Al-e Ahmad in *A Stone on a Grave* and *Lost in the Crowd* testify, being Iranian can be a difficult business today indeed, for at two reasons: the continuing lack of reconciliation with the fact of the Moslem Arab conquest of Iran in the seventh century and a sense of powerlessness or inferiority vis-à-vis the West.

In his 1957 poem, Akhavân wonders what has happened to Iran's pre-Islamic glory and warns today's poets not to play the tunes of yesteryear. At the same time, he cannot make peace with Islam, that overwhelming force which brought the Sâsânid dynasty and pre-Islamic Iranian culture to their end. Such concerns which secular-minded writers continue to voice about their Islamic heritage cannot be overemphasized, nor should the complexities of the situation be underestimated. For example, a leading Pahlavi-era journalist addresses one aspect of the question in these words:

> The advent of Islam in Iran nearly fourteen centuries ago led to what some Iranian thinkers describe as "our national multiple schizophrenia." Nowhere is this schizophrenia more evident than in the Persian language. An Indo-European language, Persian is, nevertheless, written in the borrowed Arabic alphabet. It is a language eminently suited to poetry; it has found its best expression in the writing of poetry. At the same time, it is Islam's second most important language and the Mohammedan faith has a traditional dislike of poets and poetry in general . . . poetry and poets [do not] have a legitimate place in the Islamic society. (160)

In other words, potential tension exists for Iranian writers by their mere devotion to their craft. Not that all of them see their art, as Hedâyat and

175

Farrokhzad do, as their real religion. Yet their use of language in literary art is something by official cultural definition less valuable than and perhaps perceived as competing with the perfect use of language and the same Arabic script in the Arabic Koran, Allâh's very words to humankind. The standing of imaginative literature in Iranian religious circles and among other conservative elements is an issue which has yet to receive due attention.

In his autobiographical *A Stone on a Grave*, Al-e Ahmad also struggles with his Islamic heritage, or as he puts it, the conflict in him between his traditional "Eastern" self and the modern intellectual he likewise is. He feels naturally uncomfortable with his culture's Islamic monarchy. In addition, he has difficulty making sense of his life in a patriarchal order when he cannot accept the views of his own father, a Shi'i cleric, and when he is unable personally to father a son. At the same time, in his polemic essay *Weststruckness*, Al-e Ahmad decries infatuation with things Western, yet exhibits their pervasive influence in his own mind set and argumentation.

History and tradition are at the vortex of Iranian cultural identity today. The mere fact that Iran has a lengthy, continuous cultural history may make dealing freshly and nonconventionally with the present and its unprecedented issues potentially problematic. That this history, as Ferdowsi's *Shâhnâmeh* demonstrates on an epic scale and Khâqâni's "Ode on the Palace at Ctesiphon" on a lyric scale, inevitably culminates in Iran's defeat at the hands of foreign invaders can make one's sense of pride ambiguous. In addition, as Sâ'edi relates in his short story "Dandil" and as Al-e Ahmad depicts a generation earlier in a story called "The Mobilization of the Nation," humiliating latterday invasions by the Russians, the British, and the Americans are as much a part of the Iranian experience today as those of the Greeks, the Moslem Arabs, and the Mongols in the distant past.

In Al-e Ahmad's 1945 story, the scene is a World War II air raid on Tehrân. Patrons of a neighborhood public bath are frightened--the whole country is shown as not having a say in its destiny--; so the people, some of them half-naked, run from the bath, as if they might find some place else safer.(161) As for Sâ'edi's story, written in 1966, townspeople associated with a local brothel think that a foreign soldier stationed at a nearby base must be someone of consequence and wealth merely because he is American. So they invite him to partake of the pleasures of their establishment and locate an attractive virgin for the occasion. They are hoping for a big spender. But the soldier, oblivious to everything, leaves without paying.(162)

But history, recent and distant, offers more than the lesson of defeat, nostalgic *ubi sunt* or a(n unwarranted) sense of inferiority. It presents also an almost endless array of contradictions and conflicts which literary Iranians must continually face. As potential anti-monarchists, they no doubt realize that their history is primarily the story of the monarchical glory which Ferdowsi immortalizes in his *Book of Kings*. Iran's greatest pre-modern artists, among them Sa'di and Hâfez, have served monarchs, often unquestioningly. The point and problem for Iranians today is two-fold: one cannot easily reject one's cultural past out of hand; yet the Iranian monarchy never evolved during its twenty-five centuries--it remained patriarchally absolutist and, in its own view, infallible, from the Achaemenids (559-330 BCE) to the Pahlavis (1926-1979), the temporary "aberration" of the short-lived Constitutional Era notwithstanding.

As for the most part secular-minded, Iranian writers likewise cannot deny the essentially religious core to their culture, historically and contemporarily, a core which likewise seems not to have evolved. In other words, leaders and supporters of the Islamic Republic of Iran appear to them to have the same world view that supporters of Shi'i Emâm Hosayn had at Karbalâ in 680. Although nothing received stronger criticism in modernist Persian literature from 1921 to 1979 than religious institutions, practices, and the Shi'i clergy,(163) nevertheless no force played a greater role than the religious in bringing down a monarchical regime that writers were either indifferent to, thought little of, or despised. Subsequently, these writers have had to deal with an official religion that has become the basis for a religious state.

As potentially or inclinationally individualistic, these same Iranians also find themselves part of traditions in which the individual counts for little unless he is a patriarch or one of latter's representatives. Heroic individuals from the legendary Sohrâb to the very real Samad Behrangi, the educational and social reformer from Tabriz whose career was cut short by a bizarre drowning in 1968,(164) are overwhelmed precisely because of their individuality, a quality sometimes as apparently fatal as it is revered.

These Iranians, as Herodotus first noted, have long been flexible and adaptable in their historial crossroads towards goods and ideas from abroad. Yet they are often justifiably suspicious of things foreign and sometimes feel guilty at their attraction toward them. The Iranian writer who takes pride in competence in Arabic and who speaks and writes with a cultivated Arabic diction may detest Arabs themselves, as Hedâyat did, or Arab states, as Al-e Ahmad did. The intellectual who becomes deeply familiar with Western literatures and displays their pervasive influence in his or her own writing may nevertheless, like the reformer 'Ali Shari'ati (1933-1977), decry Weststruckness and call quixotically for a purist authenticity of culture.(165)

All of these contrary tugs at their cultural psyches make some Iranians potential loners, alienated from both past and present. The poet Nimâ Yushij sought refuge in the Caspian region of his birth, both in his imagination and in person when he could find the time to return there. In the post-World War II era, he sought thrice daily refuge in opium as well, that unsociable, traditional Iranian narcotic.(166) Hedâyat's misanthropy drove him into a pessimistic, private world of fiction and finally to suicide. The writers who sought some release or escape through drugs, alcohol, and the like from the stresses of being Iranian during the post-Mosaddeq, pre-

Khomayni era (late 1953-1978) are numerous, reportedly among them Shâmlu, Akhavân-e Sâles, and Sâ'edi.

Those writers who have sought to escape what they sense as unbearable burdens or irresolvable dilemmas spotlight through such behavior a perhaps essential fact of literary Iranian cultural identity, its already alluded to dynamics of dipolarity and duality.(167) In that sense, there has always been an Iranian identity crisis: modern nationalism has just made it more dilemma-ridden than ambivalence-laden.

No Iranian literary figure more clearly embodies traditional cultural dualism than the fourteenth-century poet Hâfez. Because interest today in Iran's premier lyric poet in history is primarily neither academic nor dilettantish, but rather as a poetic voice of assumed enduring relevance and inspiration, he is not out of place in a cultural overview of the contemporary literary scene. In fact, Hâfez is a cultural hero for such otherwise different literary figures as the poet Forugh Farrokhzâd, the East Berlin-based writer Bozorg 'Alavi, the activist poet and dramatist Sa'id Soltânpur (whom the Islamic Republic of Iran executed in 1981), and for leading modernist poet Shâmlu, who devoted years to editing Hâfez's poems. For Al-e Ahmad, Hâfez epitomizes "the Iranian world view." Reminding readers that "we do not seek all these auguries from Hâfez for nothing," Al-e Ahmad sees Hâfez's quintessential Iranianness in his expression of pairs of opposites: protest and submission, ingenuousness and cleverness, faith and apostacy, endeavor and nonchalance, determinism and free will.(168)

Such dualism is apparent in Ferdowsi's *Shâhnâmeh* between the poet's expression of personal faith in Arab Islam and equally firm reverence for pre-Islamic Iranian culture. In the case of 'Omar Khayyâm, dualism takes the form of his outwardly orthodox and establishment career and views vis-à-vis the individualistic and heterodox defiance Khayyâmic quatrains voice. In addition, the Khayyâmic view as illustrated in FitzGerald's *Rubaíyát*, exhibits that particularly Iranian conflict between the harsh, brown, inimical real world and the vision of the perfect garden, which springtime approaches and which the Iranian New Year celebrates. Of course, the fact that many of the same readers accept both Ferdowsi and Khayyâm, with their contrary world views, is but another instance of this dualism, which is to say, a cultural capacity to hold almost mutually exclusive views almost simultaneously.

Some contemporary writers have sought to resist the dualistic cultural tide by finding answers or resolving dilemmas. Others seek personally, although not artistically, to avoid facing the true situation, as did Yushij and Hedâyat through opium and suicide, respectively. However, those who remain in the dilemma-ridden Iranian arena may discover no answers. On the contrary, many of them will awaken on the morrow, like FitzGerald's Khayyám, to face their dilemmas anew. In other words, in Iranian literary culture no bottom line or resolution of conflicts seems to exist from the Persianist perspective. Rather, the conflicts and tensions themselves constitute the culture-specific nature of things. The past is always grander and unbearable in retrospective comparison. The present, in turn, is always terrifying when one senses that it is leading inevitably to another "ending of the *Shâhnâmeh*." The monarchy and aristocracy cannot be trusted; yet, one cannot take solace in or be hopeful with respect to the people at large either, because the masses never understand the writer's sensitivity. Iran's is obviously a superior culture, yet Iran seems just as obviously, and inexplicably, somehow not as efficient as many other nation-states. The national religion may deserve nostalgic and fraternal sympathy, but certainly not commitment. The heroic seems manifested in monarchical history, however much one loathes monarchy. Nothing is more sacred than individual aspirations and views, even if they can never be expressed openly. On and on.

The Pahlavi monarchy seemed to threaten the pendular balance and dipolar tensions characteristic of Iranian culture through its unenlightened, unconstitutional authoritarianism and its naive and insensitive imposition of Western modernization. Of course, in its own eyes, the Pahlavi regime was endeavoring to transform Iran into an efficient, "bottom-line" society that might subsequently compete favorably in the West-dominated world. It failed miserably in the unequivocal, dramatic way a monarchy can, with the ignominious flight of the royal family from the country in January 1979.

However, the Pahlavi threat to cultural integrity was not as grave as many writers thought in 1978 when they temporarily joined forces with the Shi'i religious majority, whose own values had seemed in grave danger of succumbing to Rezâ Pahlavi and his son Mohammad Rezâ. In the aftermath of the establishment of the Islamic Republic in the spring of 1979, as the cultural pendulum has seemed to cease swinging, some Iranians feel that great dangers exist for their country's future as the backdrop and social context for continuing cultural richness, particularly of literary expression. This sense of gloom itself may be in great measure the result of perennial Iranian sadness and pessimism, of expecting the worst, of assuming that yet another "ending of the *Shâhnâmeh*" lies ahead. In any case, the revolutionary upheaval in Iran and its aftermath are the chief reason for consternation at Iranianness today and the wonderment at exactly what Iranians are all about.

Further delineation of an answer to the latter question makes appropriate prior consideration of how comprehensive any definition of Iranianness can be, an issue which Mohammad 'Ali Jamâlzâdeh (b. 1892), Iran's first short story writer of note, implies in his most famous work. That would be "Persian Is Sugar," an anecdotal tale written in 1920 or thereabouts and narrated by a middle-aged, world-wise Iranian just back from Europe.(169) He is inexplicably detained in a customs-house cell at the Caspian port of Enzeli along with two other persons: a young Iranian male whose dress and manner make it obvious that he is returning from school in France, and a bearded, turbaned mulla. Suddenly, a fourth person is thrown into the cell, a young man called Ramazân, whose accent and dress mark him as a native of the Caspian province of Gilân.

Upset at the injustice of being jailed for no apparent reason, Ramazân rants and raves for some minutes. When he calms down, he turns to the mulla and begs for an explanation of their incarceration. The mulla replies at some length, beginning with *jazâkum allâh, mu'min* [may God reward you, o believer] and *al-sabr miftâh al-faraj* [patience is the key to comfort]. With further Arabic phrases and allusions punctuated by a Persian verb or noun, the mulla thoroughly confuses Ramazân, who understands literally nothing of what is said to him. So, stunned by the reply and now desperate to fathom what is transpiring, Ramazân turns to the Frenchified student and says: "Sir . . . this sheikh is obviously a jinn . . . who doesn't understand our language . . . he's an Arab . . . so, would you please tell me why they've thrown us into this tomb." To this the student warmly replies, his explanation full of such terms as *possibilité, despotisme*, and *décadence*. All are equally incomprehensible to Ramazân, who thereupon cries out for help, begging the guards as fellow Moslems to torture him or do whatever else they wish, as along as they get him "out of the clutches of these madmen . . . who do not even understand human speech." Naturally sympathetic to Ramazân's plight, the narrator now steps forward and begins talking to him. The latter becomes almost ecstatic at hearing Persian that he can understand. In a paternal tone, the narrator explains to him that "these other two people are not mad or jinns; they're Iranians and fellow Moslems." Ramazân begins to laugh and begs the narrator: "Please, sir, don't put me on. If they're Iranians, why do they speak languages that don't even slightly resemble human speech?" The narrator starts to tell Ramazân that the mulla and the student were speaking Persian; but he realizes that Ramazân would never believe him.

At this point, the four cellmates are released. As they leave the customs house, guards are bringing in another person who, in a thick Azarbâyjâni accent with numerous Turkish words and phrases, is begging his captors to listen to him. Ramazân overhears the conversation and remarks to the narrator how amazing it is that on this particular day every imaginable lunatic is being sent to Enzeli. The narrator thinks better of explaining to Ramazân that the newcomer, obviously from Khoy or thereabouts, is just as much Iranian as anyone else, and that what he is speaking is also Persian. The story draws to a close with the narrator, the mulla, and the student sharing a carriage to Rasht. Ramazân says goodbye to the narrator and marvels at his courage in his choice of traveling companions.

Seventy years later, the cast of characters in "Persian Is Sugar" is still very much a part of the Iranian scene, with the Iranian educated in the United Kingdom or North America the most visible, indigenous addition to it. The story itself is also as instructive today as it was in the 1920s. It, first, provides a caveat to any generalization that one might make about Iranians, insofar as the characters in the story seem not to have much in common but their plight. The fact of heterogeneity presents yet another dilemma for nationalistic Iranian writers who feel compelled to speak for their society through their art and yet who realize that they cannot honestly speak for many of their fellow countrymen. Secondly, it illustrates how limited and specific a Persianist focus is in an investigation of Iranian culture. In other words, the mulla, Ramazân, and the young Azarbâyjâni are not the Persianist's subject of study except as characters in literary works which they either cannot or choose not to read. For the Persianist, Iranian culture is that of Jamâlzâdeh's narrator and of the student returning from France, the culture of Persian-speaking Iranians with a modern or Western-style education, the culture, in short, of a minority of the Iranian population.

It is for that minority, and not for the peasantry, the urban proletariat, or Iranians with a religious education, that in the aftermath of the establishment of the Islamic Republic a long-standing identity crisis has intensified, with withdrawal, despair, and self-exile as three of its chief symptoms or consequences. And the facts that cause such poems as those which Shâmlu presents in his collection called *Little Songs of Alienation* (1980) bespeak a culture perhaps at a dangerous brink. The very title implies an ironic sense of exile on Shâmlu's part even though he lives in Tehrân. The most famous poem in the collection, a 1979 composition called "In This Dead End," is a dramatic representation of this sense. It reads:

They smell your breath.
You better not have said, "I love you."
They smell your heart.
These are strange times, darling . . .
And they flog love at the roadblock.
We had better hide love in the closet . . .
In this crooked dead end and twisting chill,
they feed the fire
with the kindling of song and poetry.
Do not risk a thought.
These are strange times, darling . . .
He who knocks on the door at midnight
has come to kill the light.
We had better hide light in the closet.
Those there are butchers
stationed at the crossroads
with bloody clubs and cleavers.
These are strange times, darling . . .
And they excise smiles from lips
and songs
from mouths.
We had better hide joy in the closet . . .
Canaries barbecued

on a fire of lilies and jasmine,
these are strange times, darling . . .
Satan drunk with victory
sits at our feast.
We had better hide God in the closet.(170)

This defiant, desperate cry implies a fear that Iranians such as the speaker and his beloved, as well as their culture, may not survive the new social order in their land. In other words, by juxtaposing powerful, contrary images, Shâmlu implies that Iran's characteristic cultural dualism no longer exists. Unlike the familiar milieu of continuing tension and combat between light and dark, good and evil, and the sorts of conflicts and ambivalences depicted throughout this study, Shâmlu's Iran embodies not just the opposite of the values he holds dear, but even their extermination. Light, love, and lyricism--eternal Iranian values--must be hidden or face annihilation at the hands of the authorities.

As a secular vision, Shâmlu's poem is naturally very subjective. In addition, there are contrary literary views. One is that of the American-trained poetess Tâhereh Saffârzâdeh (b. 1937), who has seen in Islam the path to salvation for Iranian culture and has even composed paeans to Ruhollâh Khomayni.(171) Nevertheless, the vast majority of Iranian writers would seem to share Shâmlu's view.

More significantly in cultural terms, Iran again has a political system which threatens to remove one of the poles of the pendulum, to remove balance and vital dilemmas from Iranian life, while ignoring the fact that Iran, as a quintessential land bridge and crossroads land, thrives culturally when adaptability and xenophobia live hand in hand, when flexibility and inveterateness are mates, when thinking Iranians love and adapt the foreign forces they abhor and decry.

Most significant, however, is the specific ideology of the Iranian political system of the 1980s, especially vis-à-vis the world of Iranian literary art. The latter needs the nurturing of a national culture and a national home, whereas Iranian Islam owes no loyalty to any specifically or exclusively Iranian state or culture. Iranian literary art has thrived in situations of establishment patronage, support, or lipservice, whereas Iranian Islam has traditional, theological grounds for suspicion of, if not antagonism toward, literary expression. The Koranic chapter on "The Poets" and authoritative sayings attributed to Mohammad are the dramatic bases for hostility on the part of some Moslem authorities toward Persian literature.(172) In the theocratic Iranian state of the 1980s, it is no wonder, then, that some writers and readers fear for the very existence of their favorite art in the future. (Such fears may be groundless in the light of Persian literary activity in Tehrân, Paris, London, Washington, D.C., and Los Angeles and the dramatic increase in readership during the 1980s throughout Iran. Still, literary

182

Iranians feel that in the present circumstances total censorship in Iran is always only a *fatvâ* [religious edict] away.)

Imaginative Persian literature has always been the mirror *par excellence* for Iranian cultural tension, balance, and dipolarity. In the most general terms, classical poetry combined Iranian genius with Arabic rules and gave voice to Moslem faith tinged with perennial skepticism and individualism. Modernist literature, on the other hand, has combined contemporary Iranian concerns and impulses with Western forms and species, and the past and the present as dynamic poles of imagination.

Imaginative Persian literature has survived as Iranian culture's proudest and preeminent voice during the strangest and worst of times. For this reason, Persian Iranian culture may survive even if an Iranian polity might not. The culture may survive for as long as writers in Persian follow literary and intellectual traditions, dating back to the emergence of the New Persian language as a literary vehicle in the ninth century, of viewing the world and life in terms broader than what today are subsumed under nationalism and broader than those used to describe life and human goals according to specific ideologies.

But of course, Iranian literary figures and works do not speak for all of Iran. It bears repeating that the only Iran for which they speak is the minority Iran of literate, Persian-speaking Iranians. Even in the more limited realm of modernist, secular, literary figures, such prominent writers as Hedâyat, Âl-e Ahmad, Farrokhzâd, and Sâ'edi do not begin to exhaust the possibilities.

An example is the controversial writer and cinematographer Ebrâhim Golestân (b. 1922), whose cultural personality differs greatly from that of Hedâyat, Farrokhzâd, and Âl-e Ahmad. Interestingly, he knew Hedâyat well, was Farrokhzâd's employer and lover for the last eight years of her life, was a close acquaintance of Âl-e Ahmad and named by the latter as an executor to his estate, and was a supporter of such other figures as Akhavân-e Sâles and the prominent nature painter and poet Sohrâb Sepehri (1928-1980). After over two decades of literary activity and filmmaking, Golestân apparently became frustrated with what he saw as the ignorance of the Iranian audience, the superficiality and hypocrisy of the intelligentsia, and the incompetence and corruptness of the Pahlavi government.(173) All of this contributed to his decision to abandon writing, filmmaking, and Iran itself in the mid-1970s for a gentleman's life in London and Sussex. In a sense, Golestân exemplifies those Iranian intellectuals whose country is not "good enough" or ready enough for their art and wisdom and who are motivated by neither a strong political nationalism nor apprehensions about being able to survive outside of the homeland. A major literary work by Golestân, of which his collections of short stories, translations, and films hint that he is capable, may yet be forthcoming in the form of his own memoirs, should he decide to publish them. But cut off from Iran since the mid-1970s, whatever he now produces in Persian will likely rehash the past or exhibit telltale signs of expatriate art, as the works of Jamâlzâdeh and 'Alavi have for years.(174) In any case, Golestân may represent the Iranian cosmopolite whose native land need not be his homeland.

Other figures as well represent other literary facets of Iranian culture. For example, the painter and poet Sepehri espoused a latter-day gnosticism in his art. Almost from its beginnings, literary Sufism was characteristically Iranian in its dipolarity. In addition, it has long served thinking Iranians as a banner of hypothetical priorities and desiderata. But it has rarely proved to be a viable alternative in everyday living in the world of practical familial, social and political realities. In Sepehri's case, he understandably could not sustain the mood and philosophy once he discovered that he had contracted a fatal form of leukemia.(175) More significant is Sepehri's use of Sufism in his art (176) and life as a means of avoiding a confrontation with the stresses of cultural tensions and dipolarities. For that matter, medieval Sufism itself did not embody ambivalence or dipolarity in its orthodox forms. Like mainstream Sunnism, it rejected this world, for which reason Sepehri may need to be termed gnostic, rather than Sufic or neo-Sufic. In any case, Sepehri's paintings, which often enough exhibit American and Japanese influences in style and composition, are recognizable as very Iranian in color and subject matter. Bright springtime flowers appear in brown settings, including buildings. But it is what does not appear in his paintings that intimates a denial of cultural facts of his day: he paints no people or urban life into the scenes. Sepehri chose not to face the dilemmas which those two elements embody and voice.

Golestân, Sepehri, and such others as the retired novelist and short story writer Sâdeq Chubak (b. 1916), who quietly forsook Iran and writing upon early retirement and a new life in a San Francisco suburb in the mid-1970s, stand in sharp contrast with more typical personalities because of their avoidance of confrontation with or reduction of the dipolar complexities of being Iranian to a single mind set or focus. In other words,--and more power to them--they may have resolved to their own satisfaction ambivalences, tensions, conflicts, paired contradictions, and dilemmas that underscore and provide the creative, culture-specific dynamics for such classical authors as Ferdowsi, Khayyâm, and Hâfez, and for such major modernists as Hedâyat, Âl-e Ahmad, and Farrokhzâd.

Of course, in one way or another, these three modernists were casualties in the forbidding, inhibiting, and harsh climate and environment which Iranian culture calls home. However, even if such individuals seem more often than not to fail to survive, much less change or overcome, their Iranian social environment, their Iranian culture from a Persianist point of view has itself always seemed paradoxically assured.

The same holds for the values of Ferdowsi, Khayyâm, Sa'di and Hâfez, who centuries earlier likewise failed appreciably to influence the system in which they lived. Yet, despite the fact that Ferdowsi's Shâhnâmeh tells a tale of national defeat, speaks on behalf of traditional patriarchy, and explains Iranian life through an initially alien Islamic faith system, Ferdowsi displays concomitant individuality of spirit in finding significance in having a Persian heritage during an age controlled by an Arab religion and a Turkic state. Despite the fact that Khayyâm dutifully served the powers that be as an establishment scientist, scholar, and teacher during another Turkic age, he too felt the need to express things in an Iranian cultural language, and to voice the most serious doubts of all about the faith system which the establishment of the day promulgated and supported. Hâfez, as well, can be seen as a poet whose skills were for the main put in the service of local rulers and their courts. But he was able brilliantly to express the medieval equivalent of modern individualistic heterodoxy given the constraints within which he had to operate.

Nevertheless, despite the arguable continuity in Iranian culture from Hâfez to the present, more than the remove of history dissuades the Persianist from grounding a definition of Iranianness in the past. It is not just that the Islamic Republic and the religious fervor behind it have changed the complexion of Iranian life in the 1980s. Other differences between past and present in terms of Iranianness are equally essential. The post-medieval inequality of relations between Iran and the West, which, as Âl-e Ahmad notes in *Weststruckness*, arose subsequent to the discovery of sea routes around Africa and Iran's loss of centrality as a crossroads along silk and other routes, has paved the way for the uniquely modern threat to Iran on the part of the potentially overwhelming complex of forces called the West. Another peculiarly modern situation derives from the Safavid imposition of a Twelver Shi'i Moslem culture as a core element in Iranian identity. The more recent phenomena of nationalism, novel twentieth-century roles for the writer vis-à-vis society, a new literary audience consisting potentially of the general public, and modern modes of censorship are further differences of consequence between past and present. In all of these regards, Iranians today face dilemmas their pre-modern forbears did not.

Hedâyat sought to escape the historical dilemma which tormented him. Mortally fearful of it, he sought to resolve cultural ambivalence, ambiguity, and internal contradictions by rejecting the Arab Moslem invasion and its cultural heritage, something no more possible than Âl-e Ahmad's dream of putting the genie of Westernization back into its proverbial bottle. In addition, Hedâyat attempted to deny his oneness with other Iranians and his patriarchal destiny as he strove to become the individual of his modernist ideals. Although the perennial dilemmas vitalized and energized his art, his suicide, an act which some intellectuals applaud and respect while naturally never considering it as an option in their own lives, shows that at the end he was not a quintessential Iranian personality, but rather a sensitive Iranian genius who could not live up to Iranian standards or live down Iranian facts of life. As for who could, two names come to mind for this Persianist, Jalâl Âl-e Ahmad and Forugh Farrokhzâd.

Farrokhzâd likewise renounces her patriarchal inheritance, but not like Hedâyat, because she can not ever actually become a patriarch and because abject intellectual surrender did not occur to her as a personal option despite lessons on this score which her culture offered her. Rejecting the whole tradition while living fully in its midst, Farrokhzâd almost accomplishes in the twentieth century what Ferdowsi's Sohrâb attempted in that martial and mythological age when he joined battle in the arena of patriarchal values and died for his non-patriarchal feelings.(177) Unfortunately, Farrokhzâd, who tried to bear up under the opprobrium fostered in people espousing those values, failed physically to survive that automobile accident felling her at thirty-two years of age. It is tempting, although not fair, to say that her death serves as a symbol of the inevitable failure in Iranian culture of non-patriarchal values. It is equally tempting, and equally unfair, to use Farrokhzâd as a model representation of essential Iranian cultural dimensions. Although she may represent ideals many Iranians cherish, that she was a woman, that she was able to put her culture's religion out of her mind, and that she was able to live on her own terms as an individual all disqualify her from representativeness. In other words, she would appear not to have been ultimately caught in the middle, where her crossroads, land-bridge culture has always been, and where literary Iranians have always found themselves, straddling dilemmas.

In these terms, the most representative, prominent Iranian writer has to be Al-e Ahmad. If Hedâyat endeavors both to avoid recognizing that he is like everyone else and to deny the dilemmas which the Arab Moslem invasion brought to Iranian culture and if Farrokhzâd simply is not like many others, Jalâl Al-e Ahmad accepts the fact that he is like everyone else and, often enough, has the integrity not to rationalize that fact or explain away the contradictions it raises for him. He flat out asserts that, like it or not, three factors make one Iranian: the Persian language, Twelver Shi'i Islam, and the physical experience of the Iranian environment from childhood.(178) In addition, he is not so naive as Hedayat to reject his patriarchal inheritance, that is, to refuse either to become a patriarch or to take comfort in Islamic cultural values. He accepts such facts of Iranian life and tries to remember to talk candidly. Of course, Al-e Ahmad faced a further dilemma insofar as he was unable to become a natural father. He was, thus, ironically not able to be like everyone else in the one sense he strongly desired. It was a deprivation which he took to his grave, along with Iranian tensions and dipolarities within himself. He joins Ferdowsi, Khayyâm, Khâqâni, Hâfez, Nimâ Yushij, and scores of other literary Iranians in having done so. Others will no doubt continue the tradition in the future.

It often seems to be the winter of the Iranian writer's discontent, or just "Winter," as Akhavân-e Sâles calls his brilliant, early 1956 poem.

> They do not want to answer your hello;
> heads are in collars.

Nobody wants to look up to answer or to see friends.
Eyes see only one step ahead,
[5]for the road is dark and slippery.
And if you extend a hand of love toward another,
a hand will unwillingly emerge from a pocket;
for it is bitter cold.

The breath that comes out of the chest's warm space
            becomes a dark cloud, and
[10]stands like a wall before your eyes.
When breath is this, then how can you expect a look
from the eyes of acquaintances and friends?

My noble Messiah! O old Christian in dirty clothes!
The weather is so ignobly cold . . . Hey . . .
[15]Be of good health and good cheer!
Answer my greeting, open the door!

It is I, your nightly guest, the sad, gypsy-like one.
It is I, the sick, kicked stone.
It is I, creation's abject curse, the discordant melody.
[20]I'm not from Turkey or Africa, I'm just plain colorless.
Come, open the door, open up, my spirits are low.
Friend! Host! Your monthly and yearly guest is shivering
            like a wave behind the door.
There's no hail out here, no death.
If you hear a sound, it's the story of cold and teeth.

[25]I've come tonight to pay my bill,
to put what I owe beside the cup.

What do you mean, it's past time, it's morning, dawn has come?
It's playing a trick on you,
            this isn't the redness of the sky after dawn.
Friend! This is an ear smitten by cold,
            it's a memento of winter's cold slap.
[30]And the lantern of the narrow sky, dead or alive,
is hidden in the thick, nine-folded, death-covered coffin of darkness.
Friend, go light the wine lamp; night and day are one.

They do not want to answer your hello.
The weather depressing, doors closed, heads in collars, hands hidden,
[35]breaths short, hearts tired and sad,
the trees crystalline skeletons,
the earth lifeless, the roof of the sky low,

187

dusty the sun and the moon.
It is winter.(179)

In reacting to the despairing note which Akhavân's poem strikes, one might take comfort in the fact that Akhavân must know that spring follows winter, however long and pervasive the latter may seem. Countless Persian poems past and present have extolled spring and perfect garden settings. Yet, a part of the Persian literary soul, for example, from Ferdowsi's *Shâhnâmeh* to Rumi's exordium to his *Spiritual Couplets* and throughout Hedâyat's fiction, seems always in a spiritual state of winter, of exile from the season of spring or the perfect garden and from the necessary warmth of a true love.

FURTHER READING

Arranged according to foregoing chapter divisions, this list of essays, monographs, and translations presents published English-language materials utilized in this study and other materials which readers unfamiliar with the Persian language will find useful in pursuing a particular topic or subject of interest. Persianist and Iranologist readers will find extensive Persian language sources in the following "Backnotes."

On Iran and Iranian Culture in General (Introduction)

Abrahamian, Ervand. *Iran between Two Revolutions*. Princeton, New Jersey: Princeton University Press, 1982.

Arjomand, Said Amir. *The Turban for the Crown*. New York, New York: Oxford University Press, 1988.

Beeman, William O. *Language, Status, and Power in Iran*. Bloomington, Indiana: Indiana University Press, 1986. [To be read with the caveats in Hamid Dabashi's review in *Iranian Studies* 21 (1988): 122-127.]

Chelkowski, Peter J. Editor. *Ta'ziyeh: Ritual and Drama in Iran*. New York, New York: New York University Press and Sorush Press, 1979.

Hillmann, Michael C. "Language and Social Distinctions in Iran." *Modern Iran: The Dialectics of Continuity and Change*. Edited by Michael Bonine and Nikki Keddie. Albany, New York: State University of New York Press, 1981. Pp. 327-340 and 438-439.

_____. *Persian Carpets*. Austin, Texas: University of Texas Press, 1984.

"Iran, History of." *Encyclopaedia Britannica* 9 (1986): 829-861.

Lazard, Gilbert. "The Rise of the New Persian Language." *The Cambridge History of Iran*. Volume 4. Cambridge, England: Cambridge University Press, 1975. Pp. 595-632.

Meskoub, Shahrokh. *Iranian Nationality and the Persian Language*. Washington, D.C.: Mage Publishers, 1990. [English and Persian texts of a revision of *Melliyat va Zabân*, 1983.]

Said, Edward. "The Latest Phase." *Orientalism*. New York, New York: Random House, 1978. Pp. 284-328 and 348-350.

189

Singer, Milton. "The Concept of Culture." *International Encyclopaedia of the Social Sciences* 3 (1968): 527-543.

On *Rostam and Sohrâb*, Iranian Patriarchy and Persian Sadness (Chapter 1)

Arnold, Matthew. "Sohrab and Rustum." *Poetical Works*. Edited by C.B. Tinker and H.F. Lowry. Oxford, England: Oxford University Press, 1969 (first published in 1950). Pp. 61-87.

Chubak, Sâdeq. *The Patient Stone*. Translated by M.R. Ghanooonparvar. Costa Mesa, California: Mazdâ Publishers, 1989.

Ferdowsi, Abolqâsem. *The Epic of the Kings*. (Abridged prose) translation by Reuben Levy. Chicago, Illinois: University of Chicago Press, 1967.

Golshiri, Hushang. *Prince Ehtejâb*. Translated by Minoo R, Buffington et al. *Major Voices in Contemporary Persian Literature*. Compiled and edited by Michael C. Hillmann. *Literature East & West* 20 (1980): 250-303.

Hanaway, William, L., Jr. "The Iranian Epics." *Heroic Epics and Sagas: An Introduction to the World's Great Folk Epics*. Edited by Felix J. Oinas. Bloomington, Indiana: Indiana University Press, 1978. Pp. 76-98.

Hillmann, Michael C. "Ferdowsi's *Shâhnâmeh* after a Thousand Years." *The Epic and Asian Literatures--Literature East & West* 26 (1990).

Lerner, Gerda. *The Creation of Patriarchy*. New York, New York: Oxford University Press, 1986.

Sâ'edi, Gholâmhosayn. *Dandil: Stories from Iranian Life*. Translated by Robert Campbell, Hasan Javadi, and Julie Scott Meisami. New York, New York: Random House, 1981. Pp. 29-56.

Wickens, G.M. "The Imperial Epic of Iran: A Literary Approach." *Iranian Civilization and Culture*. Edited by Charles J. Adams. Montreal, Canada: McGill University Institute of Islamic Studies, 1972. Pp. 133-144.

Yarshater, Ehsan. "Iranian National History." *The Cambridge History of Iran*. Volume 3, Part 1. Cambridge, England: Cambridge University Press, 1983. Pp. 359-479.

On Khayyâm, Sa'di, Iranian Skepticism, Individualism and Gardens (Chapter 2)

Avery, Peter, and John Heath-Stubbs, translators. *Ruba'iyat of Omar Khayyam*. Harmondsworth, Middlesex, England: Penguin Books, 1985 (first published in 1979).

Boyle, J.A. "Omar Khayyam: Astronomer, Mathematician, and Poet." *The Cambridge History of Iran*. Volume 4. Cambridge, England: Cambridge University Press, 1975. Pp. 658-664.

Cadbury, William. "FitzGerald's *Rubáíyát* as a Poem." *Journal of English Literary History* 34 (1967): 541-563.

Dashti, 'Ali. *In Search of Omar Khayyam*. Translated by L.P. Elwell-Sutton. London, England: Allen & Unwin, 1971.

Draper, John W. "FitzGerald's Persian Local Color." *West Virginia University Bulletin: Philological Papers* 14 (1963): 26-56.

FitzGerald, Edward. *Rubáíyát of Omar Khayyám*. First and fifth editions. Edited and introduced by Dick Davis. New York, New York: Viking Penguin, 1989.

Sa'di. *The Gulistan or Rose Garden of Sa'di*. Translated by Edward Rehatsek. Edited with a preface by W.G. Archer. Introduction by G.M. Wickens. London: George Allen & Unwin, 1964.

Schenker, Daniel. "Fugitive Articulation: An Introduction to the *Rubáíyát of Omar Khayyám*." *Victorian Poetry* 19 (1981): 49-64.

Sonstroem, David. "Abandon the Day: FitzGerald's *Rubáíyát of Omar Khayyám*." *The Victorian Newsletter*, no. 36 (Fall 1969): 10-13.

Yohannan, John D. "The Fin de Siècle Cult of FitzGerald's *Rubáíyát of Omar Khayyám*." *Review of National Literatures* 2, no. 1 (1972): 74-91.

_____. *The Poet Sa'di: A Persian Humanist*. Lanham, Maryland: University Press of America, 1987.

On Hâfez, Sufism, and Persian Classicist Aesthetics (Chapter 3)

Burgël, Johann Christoph. "The 'Licit Magic' of Poetry." *The Feather of Simurgh: The "Licit Magic" of the Arts in Medieval Islam*. New York, New York: New York University Press, 1988. Pp. 53-88.

Hillmann, Michael C. "Afterword." *Hafez, Dance of Life*. Washington, D.C.: Mage Publishers, 1988. Pp. 95-104.

_____. "Hâfez and Poetic Unity through Verse Rhythms." *Journal of Near Eastern Studies* 31 (1972): 1-10.

_____. "Manûchihrî: Poet or Versifier?" *Edebiyat* 1 (1976): 93-110.

Hospers, John. "Aesthetics, Problems of." *Encyclopaedia of Philosophy* 1 (1967): 35-56.

Meisami, Julie Scott. *Medieval Persian Court Poetry*. Princeton, New Jersey: Princeton University Press, 1986.

Olson, Elder. *On Value Judgments in the Arts and Other Essays*. Chicago, Illinois: University of Chicago Press, 1976.

Pope, Arthur Upham. *Persian Architecture: The Triumph of Form and Color*. New York, New York: George Braziller, 1965.

Rumi, Jalâloddin. *This Longing*. Translated by John Moyne and Coleman Barks. Putney, Vermont: Threshold Books, 1987.

_____. *The Mathnawi of Jalaluddin Rumi*. Eight volumes. Translated by Reynold Nicholson. London, England: Luzac, 1925-1940.

Schimmel, Annemarie. "Poetry and Calligraphy: Thoughts about Their Interrelation in Persian Culture." *Highlights of Persian Art*. Edited by Richard Ettinghausen and Ehsan Yarshater. Delmar, New York: Caravan Press (for Bibliotheca Persica), 1979. Pp. 177-212.

_____. *The Triumphal Sun: A Study of the Works of Jalaloddin Rumi*. London, England: Fine Books, 1978.

Yarshater, Ehsan. "Affinities between Persian Poetry and Music." *Studies in Art and Literature of the Near East*. Edited by Peter Chelkowski. Salt Lake City, Utah: Middle East Center at the University of Utah and New York University Press, 1974. Pp. 59-78.

_____. "Cultural Development in Iran." *Iran: Past, Present and Future*. Edited by J.W. Jacqz. New York: Apsen Institute for Humanistic Studies, 1976. Pp. 407-419.

On *The Blind Owl*, Hedâyat, and Sâ'edi
(Chapter 4)

Beard, Michael. *A 'Blind Owl' Companion*. Princeton, New Jersey: Princeton University Press, 1990.

_____. "Psychology and Character in *The Blind Owl*." *Edebiyat* 1 (1976): 207-218.

Fischer, Michael M.J. "Towards a Third World Poetics: Seeing through Short Stories and Films in the Iranian Cultural Arena." *Knowledge and Society: Studies in the Sociology of Culture Past and Present*. Volume 5. JAI Press, 1984. Pp. 171-241.

Hedayat, Sadeq. *The Blind Owl*. Translated by D.P. Costello. New York: Grove Press Evergreen Black Cat Edition, 1969.

_____. *Sadeq Hedayat: An Anthology*. Edited by Ehsan Yarshater. Boulder, Colorado: Westview Press, 1979.

Hillmann, Michael C. "Hedâyat's *The Blind Owl*: An Autobiographical Nightmare." *Irânshenâsi* 1, no. 1 (Spring 1989): 1-21 (English section).

_____. Compiler and editor. *Hedayat's 'The Blind Owl' Forty Years After*. Austin, Texas: The Center for Middle Eastern Studies at The University of Texas at Austin, 1978.

Howe, Irving. Editor. *The Idea of the Modern in Literature and the Arts*. New York, New York: Horizon Press, 1967.

Kamshad, Hasan. "Part Two" [on Hedâyat]. *Modern Persian Prose Literature*. Cambridge, England: Cambridge University Press, 1966. Pp. 135-208.

Sâ'edi, Gholâmhosayn. *The Cow: A Screenplay*. Translated by Mohsen Ghadessy. *Sociology of the Iranian Writer*. Compiled and edited by Michael C. Hillmann. *Iranian Studies* 18, nos. 2-4 (1985): 257-323.

_____. "O Fool! O Fooled!" *Modern Persian Drama: An Anthology.* Translated by Giselle Kapucinski. Lanham, Maryland: University Press of America, 1987. Pp. 107-173.

On Âl-e Ahmad and Iranian Intellectual Dilemmas (Chapter 5)

Âl-e Ahmad, Jalal. *Gharbzadegi* [Weststruckness]. Translated by John Green and Ahmad Alizadeh. Costa Mesa, California: Mazdâ Publishers, 1982.

_____. *Iranian Society: An Anthology of Writings.* Compiled and edited by Michael C. Hillmann. Costa Mesa, California: Mazdâ Publishers, 1982.

_____. *Lost in the Crowd.* Translated by John Green et al. Introduced by Michael C. Hillmann. Washington, D.C.: Three Continents Press, 1985.

_____. *By the Pen.* Translated by M.R. Ghanoonparvar. Introduced by Michael C. Hillmann, Austin, Texas: The Center of Middle Eastern Studies at The University of Texas at Ausitn, 1988.

Daneshvar, Simin. *The Mourners of Siyâvash.* Translated by M.R. Ghanoonparvar. Washington, D.C.: Mage Publishers, 1990.

Mottahedeh, Roy. *The Mantle of the Prophet: Religion and Politics in Iran.* New York, New York: Simon and Schuster, 1985.

Shils, Edward. "Intellectuals." *International Encyclopaedia of the Social Sciences* 3 (1968): 527-543.

On Farrokhzâd, Individuality, and Iranian Feminine Views (Chapter 6)

Baraheni, Reza. "Women and Their Position in Masculine History." *The Crowned Cannibals: Writings on Repression in Iran.* New York, New York: Random House Vintage Books, 1977. Pp. 45-64.

Daneshvar, Simin. *Daneshvar's Playhouse.* Translated by Maryam Mafi. Washington, D.C.: Mage Publishers, 1989.

E'tesami, Parvin. *A Nightingale's Lament.* Translated by Heshmat Moayyad and Margaret Madelung. Costa Mesa, California: Mazdâ Publishers, 1985.

Hillmann, Michael C. Compiler and editor. *Forugh Farrokhzâd A Quarter-Century Later--Literature East & West* 24 (1988).

_____. "Forugh Farrokhzâd's Autobiographical Voice." *Women's Biographies and Autobiographies in Contemporary Iran.* Compiled and edited by Afsaneh Najmabadi. Cambridge, Massachusetts: Harvard University Center for Middle Eastern Studies, 1990.

_____. *A Lonely Woman: Forugh Farrokhzâd and Her Poetry.* Washington, D.C.: Mage Publishers and Three Continents Press, 1987.

Mahdavi, Shirin. "The Position of Women in Shi'a Islam: Views of the 'Ulama." *Women and Family in the Middle East: New Voices of Change.* Edited by Elizabeth Warnock Fernea. Austin, Texas: University of Texas Press, 1985. Pp. 255-268.

Milani, Farzaneh. "Power, Prudence, and Print: Censorship and Simin Dâneshvar." *Iranian Studies* 18 (1985): 325-347.

Tabari, Azar. "The Enigma of the Veiled Iranian Woman." *MERIP Reports*, no. 103 (February 1982): 22-27.

Weintraub, Karl. "Autobiography and Historical Consciousness." *Critical Inquiry* 1, no. 4 (June 1975): 821-848.

_____. *The Value of the Individual.* Chicago, Illinois: University of Chicago Press, 1978.

On Literary Iranian Cultural Identity (Epilogue)

Alishan, Leonardo P. "Ahmad Shâmlu: The Rebel Poet in Search of an Audience." *Iranian Studies* 18 (1985): 375-422.

_____. "From The Waste Land to the Imam." *Literature and Society in Iran.* Compiled and edited by Michael C. Hillmann. *Iranian Studies* 15 (1982): 181-210.

Bakhash, Shaul. "The Outcasts of Iran." *The New York Review.* 10 May 1984. Pp. 33-36.

Cottam, Richard W. "Book Review--*Major Voices in Contemporary Persian Literature* (1980)." *Iranian Studies* 14 (1981): 123-125.

Fasih, Esmail. *Sorayya in a Coma.* London, England: Zed Press, 1985.

_____. "The Status: A Day in the Life of a Contemporary Iranian Writer." *Third World Review* 9 (1987): 825-847.

Hillmann, Michael C. Compiler and editor. *False Dawn: Persian Poems by Nader Naderpour--Literature East & West* 22 (1986).

_____. "Iranian Nationalism and Modernist Persian Literature." *Nationalism and Asian Literatures--Literature East & West* 23 (1987): 69-89.

_____. "Revolution, Islam, and Modern Persian Literature." *Iran: Essays on a Revolution in the Making.* Edited by Robert Olson and Ahmad Jabbari. Costa Mesa, California: Mazdâ Publishers, 1980. Pp. 121-142.

Yarshater, Ehsan. Compiler and editor. *Persian Literature.* Albany, New York: State University of New York Press, 1988.

BACKNOTES

These notes provide explanatory material for readers not expert in Iranian culture as well as information on Iranian sources of potential use to expert readers. As a reminder of Persian pronunciation, â (as in Tehrân, similar to "a" in "father") is distinguished from a (as in Mashhad, similar to "a" in "cat") in these notes and throughout the volume.

1.   As implied in the "Chronology of Iranian Culture" (pages 7 and 8, above) and as described in the opening chapters of *Persian Literature*, edited by Ehsan Yarshater (Albany, New York: State University of New York Press, 1988), the story of imaginative literature in Iran begins long before Rudaki (d. 940/1) and other early New Persian [= *Fârsi*] language poets. But because appreciation of pre-Islamic Iranian literature requires competence in languages other than Persian, Iran's chief language since the ninth century, the Persianist view which this study describes does not treat earlier literature.

As for Ferdowsi's *Shâhnâmeh*, since the mid-1930s the "Berukhim" edition called *Shâhnâmeh--Ferdowsi* (Tehrân: Berukhim, 1966, reprinted; first published in 1934 in conjunction with the 1,000th anniversary of Ferdowsi's birth) has been the most popular text. Then came the more scholarly *Shâhnâmeh-ye Ferdowsi* (Moscow: Enstitu-ye Melal-e Asiyâ, 1966-1971), edited by E. Bertels, 'Abolhosayn Nushin, et al. Bertels argues in his introduction that even a minimally satisfactory text of the *Shâhnâmeh* is a long way off. Djalâl Khâleqi Motlaq's new edition, the first volume of which appeared in early 1988 (Albany, New York: State University of New York Press for Bibliotheca Persica), promises to be the standard text of Ferdowsi's work from the Iranian perspective for as long as there are no further and unexpected manuscript discoveries.

For many reasons, serious textual problems exist in the case of almost all the major poets of the classical period of Persian literature from Rudaki (d. 940/1) to Jâmi (d. 1492). One is the fact of handwritten manuscript transmission, which naturally led to mistakes by scribes from generation to generation. Some scribes altered and expanded texts deliberately to suit their own tastes and views. Second is the fact of repeated invasions and depredations wreaked by one group after another from the Ghaznavids and Saljuqs to the Mongols and Timurids, with some of the recorded knowledge of the vanquished ruling families and their courts being destroyed in each case. The earliest, complete *Shâhnâmeh* manuscript dates from 1276, two and a half centuries after Ferdowsi's death. A third reason is that printing presses did not come into serious use for Persian literary publications until the twentieth century. Fourth is the perennially relevant factor of official censorship of literary works.

The first English translation of the *Shâhnâmeh* was *The Shah Nameh of the Persian Poet Ferdowsi*, translated and abridged in prose and verse by James Atkinson (London: Oriental Translation Fund, 1832). The only complete English version is *The Shahnama of Firdausi*, 9 volumes, translated by Arthur George and Edmond Warner (London: Kegan Paul, 1905-1925). A more recent and readily available translation is Reuben Levy's *The Epic of the Kings* (London: Routledge and Kegan Paul, 1967). However, this prose version is not error-free and arbitrarily omits or summarizes important passages, among them, in Levy's words, "some of the poet's moralizings" (p. xxvii). The exordium to Ferdowsi's story about Rostam and his son Sohrâb, quoted in translation on page 31 above, is an example of material Levy omits. In so doing, he effects very different reader responses from that which Ferdowsi attempts to effect in what Rezâzâdeh Shafaq, *Farhang-e Shâhnâmeh* [Culture of the *Shâhnâmeh*] (Tehrân: Châpkhâneh-ye Irân, 1941), pp. 23-27, shows as the essentially didactic-moral nature of the *Shâhnâmeh*.

2.   In an introduction to pre-Islamic Iran called *The Persians* (New York: Time--Life Books, 1975), pp. 106-131, Jim Hicks and the Editors of Time-Life Books provide a handy description of Persepolis. The word "Persepolis" is a corruption of the Greek term "Perseptolis," which means "destroyer of cities," a title given in tribute to the destruction which the Achaemenids had in earlier campaigns wrought on the Greeks. In the Persian language, Persepolis is called "Takht-e Jamshid" [throne of Jamshid] in honor of the mythological King Jamshid whose reign is described early in the *Shâhnâmeh*.

3.   The word "Pahlavi" denotes the Middle Persian language, which came into use after Old Persian, the language of the Achaemenid Era (559-330 BCE), and before New Persian , which came into existence after the Moslem Arab invasion of the Iranian region in the 640s CE. Various dialects of Middle Persian or Pahlavi were current during the Parthian (240s BCE-224 CE) and Sâsânid (224-651) empires. Although a rich literature seems to have existed in the Pahlavi language, almost all that remains today are religious texts, among them Zoroastrian writings in redactions from the early Islamic era.

4.   Amin Banani, "Ferdowsi and the Art of Tragic Epic," *Persian Literature*, pp. 109-119.

5.   Mehdi Akhavân-e Sâles, "Shush-râ Didam" [I Saw Susa] *Ferdowsi*, no. 1098 (December 1972), translated by Leonardo P. Alishan, *Major Voices in Contemporary Persian Literature*, compiled and edited by Michael C Hillmann, *Literature East & West* 20 (1980): 141-143.

6.   Idem, "Akhar-e *Shâhnâmeh*" [The Ending of the *Shâhnâmeh*], *Akhar-e Shâhnâmeh* [The Ending of the *Shâhnâmeh*] (Tehrân: Nil, 1958), pp. 30-46. An earlier and helpful translation and superficial *explication de texte* appear in Sorour Soroudi, "Akhavan's 'The Ending of the *Shâhnâmeh*': A Critique," *Iranian Studies* 2 (1969): 80-96. Idem, "The Iranian Heritage in the Eyes of the Contemporary Poet Mehdi Akhavân-e Sâles," *Towards a Modern Iran: Studies in Thought, Politics, and Society*, edited by Elie Kedourie and Sylvia G. Haim (London: Frank Cass, 1980), pp. 132-154, discusses Akhavân-e Sâles' special interest in Iranian history.

A number of culture-specific allusions in "The Ending of the *Shâhnâmeh*" deserve glossing. In line 5, the reference to Zoroaster is to the great Iranian prophet who had established the Zoroastrian religion by the sixth century BCE. In line 9, the word *mehrâb* refers to the arch or niche shape in that mosque wall which faces Mecca and, as such, shows Moslems the direction which they should face in performing obligatory ritual prayers. In line 23, the atomic bombs dropped on Nagasaki and Hiroshima by American armed forces at the end of World War II are behind the image of "fantastic excrement of a far-flying bird." In line 45, "demons' life bottles" are cited in accordance with an Iranian folklore belief that demons cease to exist if the containers from which their lives emerged could be found and smashed. In lines 73 and 75, two Rostams are cited: first is the legendary hero of the *Shâhnâmeh*, the son of the albino warrior-hero Zâl; second is the ill-starred general, son of Farrokhzâd, who led the Sâsânid forces to catastrophic defeat at the hands of the Arab Moslems. The image in line 93 of "cave companions' sleep" alludes to the legend of the persecution of Christians by the Roman emperor Decius in the third century. Six of the former sought refuge in a cave where they slept for several centuries. When they awakened and returned to their native city, they discovered that they no longer understood life there, not even the language. Consequently, they begged God for death. In line 96 appears the image of Daqyânus, the word being an Arabicized form of Decius. In Persian, the phrase "age of Daqyânus" is proverbial, meaning a very long time ago. Here, Akhavan's point is in reference to the just cited legend and the parallel between the situation of Iranians today and those Christians who awakened after their long sleep, finding themselves living after their time.

7. Sâdeq Chubak, *Sang-e Sabur* (Tehrân: Jâvidân-e 'Elmi, 1966), translated by M. R. Ghanoonparvar as *The Patient Stone* (Costa Mesa, California: Mazdâ Publishers, 1989).

8. *Sohrâb* is the title given this episode of Ferdowsi's *Shâhnâmeh* in the Macan, Mohl, Vullers-Landauer, Berukhim, and Moscow (Bertels et al.) editions. P.N. Khanlari's student edition is called *Rostam va Sohrâb* [Rostam and Sohrâb] (Tehrân: Amir Kabir, 1965, seventh printing). Mojtabâ Minovi's edition called *Dâstân-e Rostam va Sohrâb* [The Story of Rostam and Sohrâb] (Tehrân: Amir Kabir, 1973) is a standard text and is utilized in the commentary by Ja'far She'âr and Hasan Anvari called *Ghamnâmeh-ye Rostam va Sohrâb* [The Tragedy of Rostam and Sohrâb] (Tehrân: Nashr-e Nâsher, 1984). Atkinson's translation of the story, done in 1814, is available as *Sohrâb and Rustam: A Facsimile Reproduction*, with an introduction by Leonard R. N. Ashley (Delmar, New York: Scholar's Facsimiles & Reprints, 1972). *The Tragedy of Sohrâb and Rostam* (Seattle, Washington: University of Washington Press, 1988), translated by Jerome Clinton, features the Moscow Persian text and an English version in unrhymed iambic pentameter on facing pages. Clinton's useful translation is reviewed in "Translation as Interpretation: The Case of Ferdowsi's *Sohrâb*," *Irânshenâsi* 1, no. 3 (Fall 1989): 1-25 (English section), and further discussed in "Ferdowsi's *Shâhnâmeh* after a Thousand Years," *The Epic and Asian Literatures-- Literature East & West* 26 (1990). I have used my own translations in the text.

Among pertinent discussions in English on the subject of the Sohrâb episode are: Hasan Javadi, "Matthew Arnold's *Sohrâb and Rustum* and Its Persian Original," *Review of National Literatures 2*, no. 1(Spring 1971), pp. 65-86; and Minoo S. Southgate, "Fate in Firdawsi's 'Rustam va Suhrab'," *Studies in Art and Literature of the Near East*, edited by Peter Chelkowski (Salt Lake City: Middle East Center, University of Utah, 1974), pp. 149-159. In Persian, Mortazâ Saqibfarr, "Negâreshi bar Terâzhedi-ye Rostam va Sohrâb" [Writing on the Tragedy of Rostam and Sohrâb], *Jahân-e Now* 24, no. 3 (1969): 33-45, examines the story in terms of narrative plausibility and demonstrates the clear motivation in the behavior of Sohrâb, Kâvus, Hojir, and Humân, but fails to consider the motivation behind Rostam's prevarication and refusal to identify himself in answer to Sohrâb's queries.

9.   The text of *Sohrâb and Rustum* here quoted from is Matthew Arnold, *Poems*, second edition (London; Longman, Greene, and Longmans, 1858). Besides the famous "Preface to the First Edition," this edition includes excerpts from Sir John Malcolm's *The History of Persia*, 2 volumes (London: John Murray, 1815), and C.A. Sainte-Beuve's *Causeries du lundi*, I (Paris: Garnier, n.d.). Arnold, who did not know Persian, asserted that he had not read any of the available translations of Ferdowsi's story, but fleshed out his narrative inspired by discussions in Malcolm and Sainte-Beuve. The attraction which the story had for him is not unrelated to Edward FitzGerald's interest in Persian quatrains attributed to 'Omar Khayyam, since, as M. A. Eslâmi Nodushan shows in "Khayyâm va Ferdowsi" [Khayyâm and Ferdowsi], *Yaghmâ* 19 (1966/67), reprinted in *Jâm-e Jahânbin* (Tehrân: Ebn-e Sinâ, 1970, third printing), pp. 168-215, the two poets shared attitudes about the human condition which struck chords of familiarity, through the works of Arnold and FitzGerald in Victorian England.

A good modern edition of Arnold's poetry is Tinker and Lowry's *The Poetical Works of Matthew Arnold* (Oxford: Oxford University Press, 1969, first published in 1950), which includes variant readings in footnotes and has the virtue, observed by the editors, of following the 1888 Library Edition, "the last which would have had the advantage of the poet's arrangement of the material in it." Among discussions of Arnold's poem are: W. P. Anderson, *Matthew Arnold and the Classical Tradition* (Ann Arbor: University of Michigan Press, 1965); A Dwight Culler, *Imaginative Reason: The Poetry of Matthew Arnold* (New Haven, Connecticut: Yale University Press, 1966); W. Stacy Johnson, *The Voices of Matthew Arnold* (New Haven, Connecticut: Yale University Press, 1961); Jennie E. MacNeill, "'Sohrâb and Rustum', The Orient in Matthew Arnold's Poetry," University of Toronto M.A. Paper, 1935, pp. 29-56; William A. Madden, *Matthew Arnold: A Study of the Aesthetic Temperament* (Bloomington, Indiana: Indiana University Press, 1967); and M. A. Potter, *Sohrâb and Rustum: The Epic Theme of a Combat between Father and Son* (London, 1902), which traces similar father-son narratives in world literature.

10.   Westerners have had very mixed feelings about the *Shâhnâmeh*'s appeal as an epic. For example, Edward G. Browne, *A Literary History of Persia*, volume 2 (Cambridge, England: Cambridge University Press, 1969, first edition 1906), pp. 142-143, asserts that the *Shâhnâmeh* "has certain definite and positive defects. Its inordinate length is, of course, necessitated by the scope of its subject, which is nothing less than the legendary history of Persia from the beginning of time until the Arab Conquest in the seventh century of our era; and the monotony of its metre it shares with most, if not all, other epics. But the similes employed are also . . . unnecesssarily monotonous: every hero appears as 'a fierce, war-seeking lion,' a 'crocodile', 'a raging elephant', and the like; and when he moves swiftly, he moves 'like smoke', 'like dust', or 'like the wind.' The beauty of form in any literary work is necessarily lost in translation . . . but beauty and boldness of ideas there should be less difficulty in preserving . . . . But the *Shâhnâmeh* . . . defies satisfactory translation, for the sonorous majesty

of the original . . . is lost, and the nakedness of the underlying ideas stands revealed." More recently, G. M. Wickens, "The Imperial Epic of Iran: A Literary Approach," *Iranian Civilization and Culture*, edited by Charles J. Adams (Montreal: McGill University Institute of Islamic Studies, 1972) adds to Browne's list of *Shâhnâmeh* flaws stylized language, dullness and lack of humor, asserting that "not a single Western scholar has approached *Shâhnâmeh* with real respect or laid it aside with keen pleasure" (p. 133). In my juxtaposition of Arnold's poem and Ferdowsi's episode and liberal quotation from Arnold's, I mean to imply my sense of the greater poetic appeal of the former and the greater cultural significance of the latter. As for a typically laudatory Iranian view in English, there is Amin Banani, "Ferdowsi and the Art of Tragic Epic."

11.   Gerda Lerner, *The Creation of Patriarchy* (New York: Oxford University Press, 1986), p. 239.

12.   Mostafâ Rahimi, "Del az Rostam Âyad beh Khashm" [The Heart Grows Angry at Rostam], *Alefbâ*, no. 3 (Tehrân, 1973): 1-18.

13.   Hushang Golshiri, *Shâzdeh-ye Ehtejâb* [Prince Ehtejâb] (Tehrân: Zamân, 1969), translated by Minoo R. Buffington et al., *Major Voices in Contemporary Persian Literature*, pp. 250-303. The translation is prefaced by a bio-bibliographical note and a short autobiographical note by Golshiri, one of Iran's leading active writers of fiction. M.R. Ghanoonparvar, "Hushang Golshiri and Post-Pahlavi Concerns of the Iranian Writer of Fiction," *Iranian Studies* 18 (1985): 349-373, describes Iranian writers as having "long been fighting against two social 'demons,' one political and the other religious, which their work can be viewed as attempting to exorcise from Iranian society." The two demons are monarchy and religion, both seen as oppressive patriarchal forces.

14.   Gholâmhosayn Sâ'edi, "Bâzi Tamâm Shod" [The Game Ended], which first appeared in *Alefbâ*, the already cited and important, short-lived, non-establishment periodical that appeared in six issues from September 1973 through March 1974. Sâ'edi's story has been translated by Minoo S. Southgate as "The Game Is Up," *Modern Persian Short Stories* (Washington, D. C.: Three Continents Press, 1980), pp. 180-201, and also in Robert Campbell's version called "The Game is Over," *Dandil: Stories from Iranian Life* by Gholamhosayn Sâ'edi (New York: Random House, 1981), pp. 29-56.

15.   'Abdolhosayn Zarrinkub, *Az Chizhâ-ye Digar: Majmu'eh-ye Naqd . . .* [Of Other Things: A Collection of Criticism . . .] (Tehrân: Jâvidân, 1977), p. 283.

16.   This quatrain is stanza 26 in the first edition of Edward FitzGerald's *Rubaíyát of Omar Khayyám*, which contained seventy-five quatrains and was published anonymously in 1859. In the third and subsequent editions of *The Rubaíyát*, which were expanded to 101 quatrains and constitute the poem's standard text, the stanza is number 63, revised as follows:

> O threats of Hell and Hopes of Paradise!
> One thing at least is certain--This Life flies;
> One thing is certain and the rest is lies:
> The Flower that once has blown forever dies.

The revision seems more effective both *in vacuo* and in the context of the overall Khayyâmic monologue. The images of Hell and Paradise are immediate and meaningful as opposed to the ambiguous or unfocussed invitation of Stanza 26 in the first edition (line 1). "This life" is more immediate and personal in comparison with the generalized "That life" (line 2). The revision also avoids the fourth edition, which was published in 1879 and was the last edition Fitzgerald himself saw to press. A convenient reprinting of the famous first edition is *FitzGerald's Rubáíyát: Centennial Edition*, edited by Carl J. Weber (Waterville, Maine: Colby College Press, 1959). The first and fifth editions are presented in Dick Davis' edition called *Rubáîyât of Omar Khayyâm* (New York: Viking Penguin, 1989).

17. Edward Heron-Allen, *Edward Fitzgerald's Rubáíyát of Omar Khayyám with their Original Persian Sources* (Boston: L.C. Page, 1899) parallels FitzGerald's 101 stanzas with popular Persian quatrains which may have inspired him.

In general, Western efforts at determining Persian quatrains attributable to the historical figure of 'Omar Khayyâm have been unproductive. Arguing that the discovery of old manuscripts will resolve the problem of establishing an authoritative text of Khayyâm's poetic output, A.J. Arberry published the texts and English translations of poems asserted to be in a manuscript dated 1259/60 in *The Ruba'iyat of Omar Khayyam* (London: Walker, 1949). Three years later, Yale University published *Omar Khayyam: A New Version Based upon Recent Discoveries*, in which, on the authority of what the editor-translator Arberry takes to be an even earlier manuscript dated 1208, English versions of 252 quatrains are given. The Persian text and facsimile are available in Rostam Aliyef and Mohammad Nur Osmanoff, *Omar Khayyam: Robaiyat*, 2 volumes (Moscow: Enstitu-ye Khâvarshenâsi, 1959). In a lengthy introduction, Arberry argues that since all the quatrains in the 1259/60 manuscript appear in this 1208 manuscript, a larger collection earlier than the latter must have existed, from which later collections were drawn. This would destroy "the chief argument used by scholars challenging Omar's authorship of the *Rubáíyát*," that being that "of the manuscripts of his poems hitherto known, the earlier their date the fewer the verses they contained." Arberry's conclusion is that the two manuscripts and their obvious relationship argue to the "inescapable" surmise that Omar did compose a large number of quatrains, since "there would hardly have been time in seventy-five years to build up an almost mythical figure into an author of perhaps seven hundred seventy-five quatrains." Also in 1952, in an article entitled "Omar Again," *Bulletin of the School for Oriental and African Studies* 14 (1952): 413-419, Arberry reports the discovery of another collection of quatrains, 247 of them, which, when compared to the 1208 and 1259/60 manuscripts, lead him to assert that "there is no shadow of doubt that" the three manuscripts "belong the same family." But Arberry here also reveals misgivings about the authenticity of the manuscripts insofar as the colophons of 1216 and 1208 manuscripts are nearly identical.

In Iran, both Jalâloddin Homâ'i, as quoted by Vladimir Minorsky, "The Earliest Collections of O. Khayyam," *Yadnameh-ye Jan Rypka* (Prague: Academia, 1967), pp. 107-118, and Mojtabâ Minovi, "Towzih" [Explanation], *Râhnemâ-ye Ketâb* 6 (1964/5): 238-240, flatly declared that the manuscripts were forgeries. In the West, both L.P. Elwell-Sutton and Minorsky expressed suspicion at the coincidence of the discovery of four or five, supposedly thirteenth-century manuscripts within a period of less than ten years. Minorsky argued that there was no sense talking about the manuscripts without technical tests of paper and ink.

18. Joanna Richardson, *Edward FitzGerald* (London: Longmans, Green & Company, 1960), on which the following biographical sketch is largely based,

is a handy starting point. Robert Bernard Martin's *With Friends Possessed: A Life of Edward FitzGerald* (New York, 1985) is the most comprehensive biography.

The man who made 'Omar Khayyâm a household word throughout the world has generally been viewed either as a minor literary figure whose fame rests on the stroke of good luck at having discovered Khayyâm's quatrains or as an inadequate scholar who felt no obligation to produce an accurate translation of his model. The facts are that FitzGerald was singularly equipped and prepared to undertake an English rendering of Khayyâmic quatrains, that, in his own words, "very few people have ever taken Pains in Translation as I have," and that in terms of the relative and enduring appeal of literary works, the *Rubáíyát of Omar Khayyám* is an indisputably major work in world literature. As for FitzGerald's own name in English literature, if one dispassionately assesses his achievement in the *Rubáíyát* and acknowledges the significance of his published letters, that his place in English literature ought to be permanent becomes obvious.

Born in 1809 the seventh child of a wealthy Irish family, particularly his mother whose last name her husband and their children took, Edward FitzGerald attended the Grammar School at Bury St. Edwards and Trinity College at Cambridge, where he received a degree in 1830. After college, with a permanent income that made it unnecessary for him ever to work for a living, FitzGerald took a short trip to Paris, lived in London, and spent much time in the country as well. When in the city, he spent time on walks and visits with relatives and friends. Reading was a prime activity wherever he was. In addition, he consciously practiced plain living. Thackeray and Tennyson were among his friends, and FitzGerald followed their literary careers closely. The fact that they composed works with Middle Eastern themes, the former producing *The Tremendous Adventures of Major Gahagan* and the latter *Reflections of the Arabian Nights* and *Nadir Shah*, is a good reminder that FitzGerald's subsequent fascination with Persian literature was typical of the great influence things oriental had in nineteenth-century English intellectual and literary life.

In 1837 FitzGerald moved into a cottage by the gates of the family estate near Bredfeld where he lived in apparent serenity, reading, writing, and enjoying the country. There he became friends with the Quaker poet Bernard Barton and George Crabbe, vicar of Bredfeld and the poet's son. In 1840 FitzGerald attended Carlyle's lectures on "Heroes and Hero Worship." In 1845 FitzGerald met Edward Cowell, who at nineteen years of age had already established himself as an orientalist with his translations of Persian poetry. A frequent visitor at the Suffolk cottage of Cowell and his wife, FitzGerald there began to work on Spanish, traditional ballads, and a play by Calderón.

FitzGerald's first published book, an edition of the *Poems and Letters of Bernard Barton*, appeared in 1849. Significantly, it was more a free adaptation than an edition in that FitzGerald reduced nine volumes of writing to two hundred pages. In 1851, again without his name, FitzGerald published *Euphanor, A Dialogue on Youth*, a criticism of contemporary English education in the form of a Platonic dialogue. His next work, which appeared in 1852, was *Polonius: A Collection of Wise Saws and Modern Instances*, an anthology of quotations on such topics as honesty, liberty, vanity, and charity. By the end of 1852, when the Cowells had moved to Oxford, FitzGerald had translated one of Calderón's plays. The following year appeared *Six Dramas of Calderón*, a selection plays. The following year appeared *Six Dramas of Calderón*, a selection designed, in FitzGerald's words, to give a fair idea of Calderón's Spanish life with the English text diverging from the Spanish wherever it suited FitzGerald's taste.

At Oxford in 1853, Cowell recommended to FitzGerald that he begin studying Persian. FitzGerald began with Sir William Jones' *Grammar of the Persian Language*, which features "A Persian Song," the famous free translation of Hâfez's "Turk of Shirâz" ghazal (quoted on pages 70 and 71, above). FitzGerald proceeded to read Hâfez closely. By October 1853 he was translating Sa'di. In the same year, Matthew Arnold's *Sohrâb and Rustum*, the second most famous English poem based on a Persian model, was first published. For the next eighteen months FitzGerald studied Persian and Persian poetry. In 1856 he published his version of the Sufi allegory *Salaman and Absal* by the famous poet Jâmi (d. 1492).

Shortly before Cowell left England for India in 1856, he and FitzGerald together read some Khayyâmic quatrains copied from a Persian manuscript in the Bodleian Library at Oxford. By early 1957 FitzGerald had worked more on Hâfez, read Jâmi's *Joseph and Zolaykhâ* and Nezâmi's *Seven Portraits*, most of 'Attâr's *Conference of Birds*, and had looked at some of Rumi's *Spiritual Couplets*. He seemed to be deciding upon a particular Persian poet on whom to work more deeply. By late March 1857, he narrowed his choice to Hâfez and 'Omar Khayyâm, whom he characterized as ringing like true metal. Shortly thereafter, he prepared over thirty Latin quatrains based on the Bodleian manuscript of quatrains attributed to Khayyâm. In the middle of June 1857, FitzGerald received a copy of a second Khayyâm manuscript which Cowell had discovered in Calcutta.

In the next six months FitzGerald "translated" many of the quatrains in the two manuscripts and was experiencing a real affinity to the Khayyâmic mood and point of view. In March 1859, the first edition of the *Rubáiyát* appeared. After this first edition of the *Rubáiyát*, FitzGerald did not appear publicly in print until Quaritch issued the expanded second edition in 1868. He was not, however, idle during these nine years. He finished his translation of 'Attâr's *Conference of Birds* which remained unpublished until after his death. He also translated two more plays of Calderón, one of them being the famous *La Vida es Sueno*, of which FitzGerald's *Such Stuff as Dreams are Made On* is a radical reconstruction.

FitzGerald's later literary activities included a collection of material for a vocabulary of provincial English, and the printing of glossaries for *Suffolk Sea Words and Phrases*. In 1876 he published a version of the *Agamemnon*. In 1880 and 1881 his translations of Sophocles were privately distributed. In 1882 Quaritch published FitzGerald's *Readings in Crabbe*.

During his last years FitzGerald was working on selections from Dryden's *Prefaces* and a dictionary for Sevigne's correspondence. A projected biography of Charles Lamb went no further than a brief chronology of the essayist's life. A prodigious letter writer throughout his adult life, FitzGerald's letters were posthumously collected and published in several multi-volume editions.

This thumbnail sketch of Edward FitzGerald's life demonstrates that the author of the *Rubáiyát of Omar Khayyám* was a relatively competent Persianist and an intellectual very much in tune with his own age. As for his world-famous poem, one can expect from the poet a fair representation therein of Persianness that he drew from the sources which inspired him and a rich texture of aspects of Iranian culture which his poem transmits.

In his "Introduction" to a new printing of the first and fifth editions of *Rubáíyát of Omar Khayyám* (New York: Viking Penguin, 1989), Dick Davis asserts both FitzGerald's homosexuality and the influence of that sexual orientation on the poem itself. I have not treated the issue in the above sketch because I see no representation of homosexuality in the poem and because the issue has no bearing on FitzGerald's status as a Persianist and poet. In addition, because Davis does not mention the sexual orientation of Ferdowsi, 'Attâr, and the their translators in his writing on those poets, one might question the appropriateness of emphasis on the issue in a critical introduction to the *Rubáíyát of Omar Khayyám*.

19.   Sâdeq Hedâyat, *Tarâneh'hâ-ye Khayyâm* [Songs of Khayyâm], (Tehrân: Amir Kabir, 1963, fourth printing, first published in 1934). Although unavailable in English translation, Hedâyat's seminal study is discussed in Leonard Bogle, "The Khayyâmic Influence in *The Blind Owl*," *Hedâyat's 'The Blind Owl' Forty Years After*, compiled and edited by Michael Hillmann (Austin, Texas: UT Austin Center for Middle Eastern Studies, 1978), pp. 87-98. The collaborative translations by Peter Avery and John Heath-Stubbs called *The Ruba'iyat of Omar Khayyam* (Harmondsworth, Middlesex, England: Penguin Books, 1985, first published by Allen Lane in 1979), pp. 47-82, nos. 1-143, are of Hedâyat's selection of Persian quatrains.

The second important Iranian edition of Khayyamic quatrains is the compilation by Mohammad 'Ali Foraghi and Qâsem Ghani called *Robâ'iyât-e Hakim Khayyâm-e Nishâburi* [Quatrains of Hakim Khayyâm of Nishâpur] (Tehrân: Zavvâr, 1960, first published in 1942). The Persian texts of the *robâis* in this edition together with English prose translations are published in *The Ruba'iyat of Omar Khayyam*, translated and introduced by Parichehr Kasra (Delmar, New York: Scholar's Facsimiles & Reprints, 1975). Avery and Heath-Stubbs in *The Ruba'iyat* ignore Kasra's work and offer new translations of the Foraghi--Ghani selections.

Kasra's work exemplifies the perpetuation of several Khayyam myths and exhibits numerous mistranslations as well as verbal infelicities). In support of the myth of "FitzGerald as Translator," Kasra asserts that over forty quatrains from FitzGerald's *Rubáíyát* are "verse translations" of quatrains in the Foraghi-Ghani collection. At most, then, arguing against her own assertion, Kasra is saying that FitzGerald's *Rubáíyát's* 101 stanzas could be a 40% translation of Khayyâm. Typical of that alleged 40% translation are stanzas 11 and 12 of the *Rubáíyât*. A comparison of those stanzas with the following literal translations of the original Persian quatrains which inspired FitzGerald shows that "translation" is not a correct descriptive term for FitzGerald's work: #43--"I know not at all whether He who molded me made me of the folk of paradise or of ugly hell. A bowl (of wine), a beloved, and a harp, along the fringes of a sown field--these three are cash for me, and for thee a credit-paradise." #175--"If a loaf of wheaten bread could be had, two measures of wine and a leg of mutton, together (with a beloved) with tulip cheeks, and in the corner or a garden; it would be a luxury not in the power of every sultan."

Evidence laying to rest other Khayyâm myths is offered in the Cadbury, Draper, and Sonstroem articles cited in the "Further Reading" section on this chapter (pages 190-1, above), as well as in 'Ali Dashti, *Dami bâ Khayyâm* [A Moment with Khayyâm] (Tehrân: Amir Kabir, 1965/66, revised and expanded in a 1969 edition). L.P. Elwell-Sutton translated the preface to the second edition together with the text of the first edition in a volume called *In Search of Omar Khayyam* (London: Allen & Unwin, 1971). Despite problems with Elwell-Sutton's translation, the subject of Michael Hillmann's review in "Dami bâ Khayyâm" [A Moment with Khayyâm], *Râhnemâ-ye Ketâb* 15 (1970/71): 632-644, *In Search of Omar Khayyam* serves adequately as an English representation of recent Iranian research on the subject.

20. Hedâyat, *Songs of Khayyâm*, pp. 27-28.

21. Ibid.

22. The text on which this translation is based is taken from Mohammad Javâd Shari'at, *A'ineh-ye Ebrat: Sharh-e Qasideh-ye Ayvân-e Madâ'en-e Khâqâni* [Mirror of Admonishment: A Commentary on Khâqâni's Ctesiphon *Qasideh*] (Esfahân: Esfahân University Press, 1969). The following explanatory notes are based on discussions in Shari'at's commentary and Ziyâ'oddin Sajjâdi's commentary in *Gozideh-ye Ash'âr-e Khâqâni-ye Sharvâni* [Selected Poems by Khâqâni of Shervân] (Tehrân: Sherkat-e Sahâmi-ye Ketâbhâ-ye Jibi, 1972/73), pp. 281-287.

Jerome W. Clinton, "The Madaen Qasida of Xaqani Sharvani, I, "*Edebiyat* I (1976): 153-170, and "The Madaen Qasida of Xaqani Sharvani, II: Xaqani and al-Buhtari," *Edebiyat* 2 (1977): 191-206, rejects the culturally nationalistic interpretation of the poem by Hedâyat, Sajjâdi, Shari'at, and other Iranian writers. In Clinton's view, Khâqâni's "Ctesiphon Qasideh" is "a profoundly Islamic work with a clear anti-monarchical and anti-nationalist coloration . . . the sight of the colossal ruins of Madaen sets the poet to lamenting the passing of the noble dynasty of the Sassanians. As he laments, he calls to mind images from that magnificant past--their storied justice, their splendid court, their fearsome majesty. One of these images, that of an imperial execution, recalls to him the present grim fact that time sweeps all away, and that 'The paths of glory lead to the grave.' He consoles himself by calling to mind the eternal quality of Islam. If he submits to the guidance of Islam, as he is doing by undertaking the pilgrimage to Mecca, he will triumph over mortality." In other words, according to Clinton, Khâqâni "has undertaken to instruct us as to what we must do . . . to assure our survival after death."

The contrary Iranian view is that Khâqâni represents a Persian perspective in his poem. For example, the setting of the poem is not that of the speaker undertaking a hajj pilgrimage to Mecca, but rather his return to his home city of Sharvân, the hajj over and done with. That the poet appears to suggest that the pilgrimage to Ctesiphon is more important and potentially more instructive than that to Mecca is what Iranians have always appreciated about the poem: it instructs them as to their place in the cultural scheme of their history. Even the following explanatory notes of culture-specific material in the poem imply that Islamic elements are secondary to other Iranian elements.

Couplet 1: "Ctesiphon" was a capital city of the Sâsânids (224-651), where Shâpur I (241-270), famous also for capturing the Roman emperor Valerian in 260, built a storied palace. Only the façade and grand archway of the palace remain today near the Tigris River in Iraq. In Khâqâni's day, the Palace at Ctesiphon was the most famous pre-Islamic Iranian ruins. **Couplet 8:** "the palace chain" refers to the famous chain of justice the Sâsânid monarch Anusharvân, called "the Just," reportedly had installed by the royal court at Ctesiphon so that any Sâsânid subject not satisfied with other means of seeking justice might pull on the chain at any time of day or night to gain a royal audience. **Couplet 12:** "rose water" was thought to be a remedy for headaches. **Couplet 14:** "court of justice" is a reference to the reputation of the Sâsânids for justice, especially Anusharvân. **Couplet 17:** "Ctesiphon's white-haired woman" had a hovel next to the Palace which she refused to sell, while the story goes that "an old woman of Kufeh" had an oven in her house out of which raged the storm Noah is famous for surviving. **Couplet 23:** "No'mân was an Arab ruler in the days of Sâsânid monarchs Hormoz IV and Khosrow Parviz (591-628). **Couplet 27:** Anusharvân had a crown on which were written pieces of advice. **Couplet 28:** "Parviz" is the last great Sâsânid ruler Khosrow Parviz who captured Alexandria in 617. **Couplet 30:** the quotation is from the Arabic *Koran*, Surah 44, verses 25-27. **Couplet 33:** "Shirin" was the Armenian princess who became Khosrow Parviz's mistress; their relationship, including the unrequited love of Farhâd for her, is one of the most famous stories in Persian literature. **Couplet 36:** "Khâqân" is a title for a Mongol monarch. **Couplet 38:** "Sharvân" is Khâqâni's home city, located in today's Soviet Azarbâyjân. **Couplet 39:** "Hamza" was the paternal uncle of the prophet Mohammad and a leader of the Quraysh tribe just before and during the early years of Islam, while "Salmân" is famous as being the first Iranian to join Mohammad at the very beginning of the Islamic movement.

23.   Hedâyat, *Songs of Khayyâm*, p. 86, no. 56; Dashti, *In Search of Omar Khayyâm*, p. 220.

24.   Fo7rughi and Ghani, *Robâ'iyât*.

25.   Heron-Allen's arrangement of Persian quatrains inspired a famous fraud sixty-some years later when Omar Ali-Shah, brother of the self-styled Sufi guide Idries Shah, duped the English poet Robert Graves (1892-1985) into collaboration on a translation of a supposed thirteenth-century manuscript of the *Rubaíyát*. Their translation, published as *The Rubaiyyat of Omar Khayyam: A New Translation with Critical Commentaries* (London: Cassell, 1968), was demonstrated to be based on a forged manuscript in L.P. Elwell-Sutton, "The Omar Khayyam Puzzle," *Royal Central Asian Journal* 55 (1968): 167-179; idem, "The *Rubaíyát* Revisited," *Delos* 3 (1969): 170-191; and J.C.E. Bowen, *Translation or Travesty? An Enquiry into Robert Graves's Version of Some Rubaiyiat of Omar Khayyam* (Abingdon: The Abbey Press, 1973); and idem, "The Ruba'iyyat of Omar Khayyam: A Critical Assessment of Robert Graves and Omar Ali Shah's Translation," *Iran* 11 (1974): 63-73.

Although the specific claims made by Omar Ali-Shah and Robert Graves have been convincingly refuted, the larger issue of the misrepresentation of aspects of traditional Iranian literary culture by self-styled experts remains a continuing concern for Persianists. In the frankest terms, pseudo-scholars and charlatans exist in the field. The case of Omar Ali-Shah's brother Idries Shah illustrates the problems from the Persianist perspective. Idries Shah has written numerous books, mostly on the subject of Sufism, each exuding authoritative, authorial self-confidence. Although not taken seriously by Persianist scholars, Shah's claims may not be immediately perceived as groundless by non-expert readers. For example, Shah's *The Way of the Sufi* (New York: E.P. Dutton, 1969) contains a section called "Classical Authors," in which Shah identifies 'Omar Khayyâm as one of eight important Sufi authors. He asserts: "Khayyam was an important philosopher . . . and a practical instructor in Sufism . . . Khayyam's teaching poems, and those of other members of his school which have become an accepted part of this material [Shah's writings?], are based upon the special terminology and allegory of Sufism." According to Shah, one reason why Khayyâm is not widely known as a Sufi is "Edward FitzGerald, who in Victorian times published a few of Omar's quatrains in English." FitzGerald's versions of Khayyâm exhibit "poor thinking capacity," and "His interpolation of anti-Sufi propaganda into his rendering of Khayyam cannot be excused even by his most ardent supporters . . . who tend to ignore this amazing dishonesty, and shout about other subjects instead" (p. 58). Shah follows this introductory note about Khayyâm with English translations of quatrains and couplets he attributes to the poet. But none of the translated verse derives from older manuscripts in which it is attributed to Khayyâm. As for Shah's other assertions, he offers no evidence for Khayyâm's alleged standing as a philosopher or Sufi instructor because none exists. In the case of FitzGerald's renderings of Persian quatrains and fashioning of his English poem from Persian sources, the already cited comparative study by Heron-Allen demonstrates FitzGerald's fidelity to the spirit of the original Persian sources and his creation of a new English poem structurally unrelated to anything Khayyâm may or may not have authored. Readers can judge for themselves that such Khayyâmic quatrains as quoted in translation in this chapter do not allow a Sufi interpretation. Finally, no reason has existed for either FitzGerald or Persianists today to "interpolate anti-Sufi propaganda" into writing on Persian literature. Sufi poetry in Persian has constituted a brilliant chapter of Iranian literary culture. The writings of Sanâ'i (d. 1150/1), 'Attâr (d.c.1220), and Rumi (1207-1273), discussed briefly in chapter 3, are acknowledged major works in Persian literature. The issue for the Persianist scholar is simply to designate as Sufi only that for which evidence allows such a designation. On the basis of historial and textual evidence, one is obliged to recognize that Ferdowsi and Khayyam, different in outlook from one another, were two literary figures also not Sufi in orientation. A more interesting and debatable case is Hâfez, the subject of chapter 3. Annemarie Schimmel, "Foreword" for Faridoddin 'Attâr, *The Ilahi-Nama or Book of God*, translated by John Andrew Boyle (Manchester: Manchester University Press, 1976), pp. ix-xvi, presents a thumbnail sketch of the first several centuries of Sufi literature in Persian.

26.   John Andrew Boyle, "Omar Khayyam; Astronomer, Mathematician and Poet," *The Cambridge History of Iran*, volume 4 (Cambridge, England: Cambridge University Press, 1975), pp. 658-664, sketches Khayyâm's life and career; while E. S. Kennedy, "The Exact Sciences in Iran under the Saljugs and Mongols," *The Cambridge History of Iran*, volume 5 (Cambridge, England: Cambridge University Press, 1968), pp. 659-679, surveys Khayyâm's contributions to science.

27.   Nezâmi Samarqandi, *Chahâr Maqâleh* [Four Discourses], manuscript edited by Mohammad Qazvini, edited by Mohammad Mo'in (Tehrân: Zavvâr, 1954/5); translated by E.G. Browne as *Revised Translation of the Chahár Maqála* (London: Cambridge University Press, 1921).

28.   Hedâyat, *Songs of Khayyâm*, p. 85, no. 53, and p. 91, no. 72; Dashti, *In Search of Omar Khayyam*, p. 192, no. 28, and p. 194, no. 44.

29.   According to the poet's son Sheraguime Youchidje in conversation with the author in the summer of 1985 in Austin, Texas.

30.   E.g., Sâ'edi's friend Arshak Tahmasebi, in numerous conversations with the author during 1984 to 1986 in Austin, Texas.

31.   Bozorg Alavi, as quoted in Donné Raffat, *The Prison Papers of Bozorg Alavi: A Literary Odyssey* (Syracuse, New York: Syracuse University Press, 1985), p. 55.

32.   Qatrân Tabrizi, *Divân-e Hakim Qatrân-e Tabrizi* [Collected Poems of Hakim Qatrân of Tabriz], edited by Mohammad Nakhjavâni (Tehrân: Qoqnos, 1983), p. 113, excerpted from a *qasideh* to Abu Nasr Mohammad, the Saljuq governor of Azarbâyjân. The lines quoted follow the arrangement in Hadi Hasan's *A Golden Treasury of Persian Poetry*, second revised edition, edited by M.S. Israeli (New Delhi: Indian Council for Cultural Relations, 1972), pp. 62-65.

33.   Sa'di, *The Gulistan or Rose Garden of Sa'di*, translated by Edward Rehatsek, edited with a preface by W.G. Archer, introduced by G.M. Wickens (New York: Capricorn Books, 1966; London: George Allen & Unwin, 1964).

34.   Forugh Farrokhzâd, as quoted from a letter to Ebrâhim Golestân, *Jâvdâneh Forugh Farrokhzâd* [Immortal Forugh Farrokhzâd], compiled by Amir Esmâ'ili and Abolqâsem Sedârat (Tehrân: Marjân, 1972), p. 17.

35.   Hâfez, *Divân-e Khâjeh Shamsoddin Mohammad Hâfez Shirâzi* [Collected Poems of . . . Hâfez], compiled and edited by Mohammad Qazvini and Qâsem Ghani (Tehrân: Ketâbkhâneh-ye Zavvâr, 1941; reprinted by The Foundation for Iranian Studies, Washington, D.C., 1986). Parviz Nâtel Khânlari, compiler and editor, *Divân-e Hâfez*, 2 volumes, second edition revised (Tehrân: Enteshârât-e Khârazmi, 1983).

36.   E.g., *Kayhân-e Farhangi* 5, no. 8 (Abân 1988), 104 p.

37.   Raffat, *Prison Papers*, pp. 42 and 52.

38.   Francine Timothy Mahak, "A Critical Analysis and Translation of a Modern Persian Novel: *Winter Sleep* by Goli Taraqqi" Ph.D. Dissertation, University of Utah, 1986, p. 5.

39.   Ahmad Kasravi, *Hâfez Cheh Miguyad?* [What Does Hâfez Say?], third printing (Tehrân, n.d.), is not available in translation, but Kasravi's views on the subject are described in M.A. Jazayery, "Kasravi's Analysis of Persian Poetry," *International Journal of Middle Eastern Studies* 4 (1973): 190-203, which details Kasravi's disapproval of Khayyam, Rumi, and Sa'di, as well. Then there is Asghar Fathi's "Kasravi's Views on Writers and Journalists: A Study in the Sociology of Modernization," *Iranian Studies* 19 (1986): 167-182. Idem, "Kasrawi Tabrizi," *Encyclopaedia of Islam: New Edition* 4 (1978): 732-733, provides a thumbnail sketch of Kasravi's life and works. Amin Banani, "Ahmad Kasravi and the 'Purification' of Persian: A Study in Nationalist Motivation," *Nation and Ideology*, edited by Ivo Banac, John G. Ackerman, and Roman Szporluk (Boulder, Colorado: East European Monographs, 1981), pp. 463-479, describes Kasravi's evolving, single-minded and naive determination to improve Iran through reform of the Persian language. A related essay is Ervand Abrahamian's "Kasravi: The Integrative Nationalist," *Middle Eastern Studies* 9 (1973): 271-295. Carol Regan, "Ahmad Kasravi's views on the Role of Women in Iranian Society as Expressed in *Our Sisters and Daughters,*" *Women and the Family in Iran*, edited by Asghar Fathi (Leiden: E. J. Brill, 1985), pp. 60-76, presents Kasravi as against veiling and sexual double standards and for women's education, but also as thinking that women, psychologically weaker than men, should work at home and obey their husbands. M.R. Ghanoonparvar has translated Kasravi's *Dar Pirâmun-e Eslâm* [On Islam] and *Shi'igari* [Shi'ism] as *On Islam* (Costa Mesa, California: Mazdâ Publishers, 1989).

40.   Amir Taheri, *The Spirit of Allah: Khomeini and the Islamic Revolution* (Bethesda, Maryland: Adler & Adler, 1986), pp. 59-61, 94, and 244.

41.   'Ali Dashti, *Naqshi az Hâfez* [A Portrait of Hâfez] (Tehrân: Ebn-e Sinâ, 1970, fifth printing), pp. 203-205.

42.   Jan Rypka, "Sadi--Poets and Prose Writers of the Late Saljug and Mongol Periods," *The Cambridge History of Iran*, volume 5 (Cambridge: Cambridge University Press, 1968), pp. 594-601, offers a handy review of Sa'di's life and works. G.M. Wickens has translated Sa'di's *Bustân* [Flower Garden] as *Morals Pointed and Tales Adorned* (Toronto: University of Toronto Press, 1974). The handiest translation of *Golestan* [Rose Garden] is the already cited version by Edward Rehatsek called *The Golestan Being the Rose Garden of Shaikh Sa'di*. John D. Yohannan, *The Poet Sa'di: A Persian Humanist* (Lanham, Maryland: University Press of America, 1987) surveys the available translations of Sa'di's works and presents an interpretation based on them and critical writing in the West. The only comprehensive treatment of traditional Persian court poetry in English is Julie Scott Meisami, *Medieval Persian Court Poetry* (Princeton, New Jersey: Princeton University Press, 1987). But she chooses not to discuss Ferdowsi and Sa'di and concentrates instead on Fakhroddin Gorgâni, Sanâ'i, Nezâmi, and Hâfez.

43.   Sa'di, *Kolliyât-e Sa'di*, edited by M. A. Foroughi (Tehrân: Amir Kabir, 1961, third printing; first published in 1941), p. 508.

44.   Michael C. Hillmann, *Unity in the Ghazals of Hâfez* (Minneapolis: Bibliotheca Islamica, 1976), pp. 2-3 and p. 154, fn. 12.

45.   A.J. Arberry, "Hafiz and His English Translators," *Islamic Culture* 20 (1946): 118-128 and 229-249, reviews the published translations down to World War II. Parvin Pursglove, "Translations of Hafiz and Their Influence on English Poetry since 1771: A Study and Critical Bibliography," Ph.D. Thesis, University College of Swansea, Wales, 1983, is a comprehensive review of available Hâfez translations. A recent addition to the list are Michael Boylan's versions in *Hâfez, Dance of Life* (Washington, D.C.: Mage Publishers, 1987).

46.   "A Persian Song" first appeared in William Jones, *A Grammar of the Persian Language* (London: W. & J. Richardson, 1771), pp. 137-40, preceded by a literal translation, pp. 135-36. According to G.H. Cannon, Jr., *Sir William Jones, Orientalist: An Annotated Bibliography of His Works* (Honolulu: University of Hawaii, 1952), pp. 21-22: "It was immensely popular at once and continued to be popular for decades . . . and definitely   stimulated . . . Byron . . . Swinburne . . . [and] Moore and Gatty . . . it is one of Jones's most successful poems." In *Oriental Jones: A Biography of Sir William Jones (1746-1794)* (Bombay: Asia Publishing House, 1964), p. 31, Cannon observes: "Today, it is still the third most-famous English rendering from the Persian, being surpassed only by the *Rubaíyát* and *Sohrâb and Rustum*." Arberry, "Hafiz and His English Translators," shares Cannon's view as to the importance of Jones' translation.

47.   Julie Scott Meisami, "Norms and Conventions of the Classical Persian Lyric: A Comparative Approach to the *Ghazal*," *Proceedings of the IXth Congress of the International Comparative Literature Association: Innsbruck 1979*, volume 1 (Innsbruck: Verlag des Instituts für Sprachwissenschaft der Universität Innsbruck, 1981), pp. 203-207, argues sensibly for appreciation of affinities among Augustan love poetry, medieval courtly love verse, Renaissance lyrics, and classical Persian *ghazals*. In the light of orientalist tendencies to consider the *ghazal* an alien verse form and to ignore comparatist

possibilities, Meisami's view provides a helpful starting point in dealing with the Hâfezian *ghazal* in terms of poetry *qua* poetry, as part of a universal phenomenon. She avoids the concomitant dangers of ethnocentrist evaluation through careful application of such terms as "classicist," "courtly love," and "medieval." Culturally speaking, one can make a case for the Achaemenid--Sâsânid ages constituting a "classical" period and Islamic Iran from 751 to the Safavids being a "medieval" period, with a "modern" period thereafter.

48.   Qazvini and Ghani, *Divân-e Hâfez*, no. 3, pp. 3-4; Khânlari, *Divân-e Hâfez*, no. 3, pp. 22-33 (order of bayts: 1, 2, 3, 4, 8, 5, 6, 7, 9); Hillmann, *Unity*, pp. 10-26; and idem, "Hâfez's Turk of Shiraz' Once Again," *Iranian Studies* 8 (1975): 164-182.

49.   Ehsan Yarshater, "The Modern Literary Idiom," *Iran Faces the Seventies* (New York: Praeger, 1971), p. 303.

50.   Idem, "Affinities between Persian Poetry and Music," *Studies in the Art and Literature of the Near East*, edited by Peter Chelkowski (Salt Lake City: Middle East Center at the University of Utah and New York University Press, 1974), p. 75.

51   Ibid., pp. 75-76.

52.   Idem, "Cultural Development in Iran," *Iran: Past, Present and Future*, edited by J.W. Jacqz (New York: Aspen Institute for Humanistic Studies, 1976), p. 416.

53.   J.T.P. de Bruijn, *Of Piety and Poetry: The Interaction of Religion and Literature in the Life and Works of Hakim Sana'i of Ghazna* (Leiden: E.J. Brill, 1983).

54.   Ehsan Yarshater, "Persian Poetry in the Timurid and Safavid Periods," *The Cambridge History of Iran*, volume 6 (Cambridge: Cambridge University Press, 1986), pp. 973-974.

55.   Forugh Farrokhzâd, as reported by interviewer Sadroddin Elâhi, *Immortal Forugh Farrokhzâd*, pp. 110-111.

56.   Nimâ Yushij, *Harfhâ-ye Hamsâyeh* [Words with (My) Neighbor)] (Tehrân: Donyâ, 1978/9, fourth printing), p. 104. Because classical Persian poetry exhibits strict adherence to conventional patterns of rhyme, meter, figures of speech, and the like, modernist critics and readers often question the poetic appeal of much of it. This controversial issue is addressed in Michael Hillmann, "Manûchihrî: Poet or Versifier?" *Edebiyat* 1 (1976): 93-110. Of course, some traditionalist poets and critics hold that the word *she'r* [poetry] should be used simply and exclusively to denote metered speech arranged in lines of verse.

57.   Nâser Khosrow, *Forty Poems from the Divân*, translated with introductions and notes by Peter Lamborn Wilson and Gholam Reza Aavani (Tehrân: Imperial Iranian Academy of Philosophy, 1977). Also idem, *Nâser-e Khosraw's Book of Travels (Safarnama)*, translated by W. M. Thackston, Jr. (Albany, New York: SUNY Press, 1986).

58.   Qazvini and Ghani, *Divân-e Hâfez*, no. 101, pp. 69-70; Khânlari, *Divân-e Hâfez*, no. 97, pp. 210-211.

59.   According to Julie Scott Meisami, "The World's Pleasance: Hâfiz's Allegorical Gardens," *Comparative Criticism* 5 (1983): 172 and 184, note 51, a *rend* is a "drinker of wine, poet, lover, and something of a philosopher as well--who embodies the virtues of independence, honesty, compassion, and total dedication to love, and who has reached the state of contentment denied to the

ascetic and his ilk because of their preoccupation with the affairs of the world. The *rend* . . . celebrates life with wine." She adds: "The *rends* were 'brotherhoods' which practised the virtues connnected with chivalry and courtesy and opposed themselves, through their assumption of the guise of libertinism, to the interests of the religious hierarchy."

60.   Qazvini and Ghani, *Divân-e Hâfez*, no. 26, p. 20; Khânlari, *Divân-e Hâfez*, no. 22, pp. 60-61; Hillmann, *Unity*, pp. 56-64.

61.   Khânlari, *Divân-e Hâfez*, volume 2, p. 1171.

62.   Annemarie Schimmel, *As Through a Veil: Mystical Poetry in Islam* (New York: Columbia University Press, 1982), especially chapters 2 and 3. Also, see the last sentence in footnote 25, above.

63.   A.J. Arberry, *Sufism: An Account of the Mystics of Islam* (London: Allen & Unwin, 1950, subsequently reprinted).

64   Jalâloddin Rumi, *Selected Poems from the Divâni Shamsi Tabriz*, edited and translated by Reynold A. Nicholson (Cambridge: Cambridge University Press, 1977, first published in 1898), #31, pp. 124-127 and 281. Although the poem does not appear in more recent scholarly editions of the *Divân*, it nevertheless represents the mood and views for which Rumi is famous. In addition, according to M.R. Ghanoonparvar, the poem is popular in parts of Iran as accompaniment to Sufi dancing.

65.   Qazvini and Ghani, *Divân-e Hâfez*, no. 142, pp. 96-97; Khânlari, *Divân-e Hâfez*, no. 136, pp. 288-289; Hillmann, *Unity*, pp. 38-46.

66.   Mahmud Shabestari, *Kanz al-Haqâ'eq* [Treasure of Truths], edited by Mohammad 'Ali Safir (Tehrân: Sherkat-e Sahâmi-ye Ofset, 1965), pp. 120-122.

67.   Qazvini and Ghani, *Divân-e Hâfez*, no. 321, p. 219, *bayt* 6; Khânlâri, *Divân-e Hâfez*, no. 316, pp. 364-365, *bayt* 7; Hillmann, *Unity*, p. 44.

68.   Ahmad Shâmlu, "She'ri Keh Zendegi'st" [Poetry Which Is Life], *Havâ-ye Tâzeh* (Tehrân: Nil, 1976, fifth printing), pp. 87-99.

69.   Sadeq Hedayat, *The Blind Owl*, translated by D.P. Costello (London: J. Calder, 1957; New York: Grove Press, 1957, and Evergreen Black Cat Edition paperback, 1969). Scholars have argued over the accuracy and stylishness of Costello's version. According to Peter Avery, in conversation with this writer in January 1989, Costello did not know Persian, but translated from the Russian translation, thereafter seeking clarification of passages from Persianists. In any case, the translation is adequate.

70.   Jalâl Âl-e Ahmad, "Hedâyat-e *Buf-e Kur*" [The Hedâyat of *The Blind Owl*], translated by A. A. Eftekhary," The Hedâyat of *The Blind Owl*," pp. 27-42.

71.   A.R. Navabpour, "A Study of Recent Persian Prose Literature with Special Reference to the Social Background," Ph.D. Thesis, University of Durham, 1981.

72.   Manoutcher Mohandessi, "Hedayat and Rilke, reprinted in *Hedâyat's The Blind Owl Forty Years After*, pp. 118-124. Michael Beard, "Character and Psychology in Hedayat's *Buf-e Kur*," *Edebiyiat* 1 (1976): 207-218; "The Hierarchy of the Arts in *Buf-e Kur*," *Iranian Studies* 15 (1982): 53-67; idem, "Sâdeq Hedâyat's Composite Landscapes: Western Exposure," *Persian Literature*, pp. 323-334; and idem, *A 'Blind Owl' Companion* (Princeton, New Jersey: Princeton University Press, 1990).

73.   Bahram Meghdadi and Leo Hamalian, "Oedipus and the Owl," *The Blind Owl Forty Years After*, pp. 142-152; and Carter Bryant, "Hedâyat's Psychoanalysis of a Nation," ibid., pp. 153-167.

74. Homa Katouzian, in an unpublished essay called *"The Blind Owl*: A Critical Exposition."

75. Sâdeq Chubak, "The Sigh of Mankind" [Ah-e Ensân], translated by Leonard Bogle, *Major Voices in Contemporary Persian Literature*, pp. 73-80.

76. Farhang Jahanpour, "[Book Review:] *Lost in the Crowd* [1985]," *Iranian Studies* 18 (1985): 449.

77. Hamid Naficy, "Iranian Writers, the Iranian Cinema, and The Case of *Dâsh Akol*," *Iranian Studies* 18 (1985): 231-251.

78. M.R. Ghanoonparvar, "Writing as Therapy," *Hedâyat's 'The Blind Owl'* *Forty Years After*, pp. 68-75.

79. Elton Daniel, "History as a Theme of *The Blind Owl*," *The Blind Owl Forty Years Later*, pp. 76-86.

80. Beard, "Psychology and Character," p. 217; M. R. Ghanoonparvar, "Writing as Therapy," pp. 68-75.

81. Beard, "Psychology and Character," p. 216.

82. E.g., Hasan Kamshad, "Historical Self-Analysis,'"*The Blind Owl' Forty Years After*, pp. 15-26; and Ehsan Yarshater, "Sâdeq Hedâyat: An Appraisal," *Persian Literature*, p. 322.

83. Beard, "Psychology and Character."

84. Leonard Bogle, "The Khayyâmic Influence," pp. 87-98.

85. Al-e Ahmad, "The Hedâyat of *The Blind Owl*," pp. 21, 36, and 40.

86. The event was recorded, and an audio cassette tape of it made available to the author by Arshak Tahmasebi.

87. Gholâmhosayn Sâ'edi, "Sharh-e Ahvâl" [Autobiographical Remarks], *Alefbâ*, new series, no. 7 (Fall 1986): 4-5.

88. Nimâ Yushij, "Ay Adamhâ" [Hey, People], *Majmu'eh-ye Asâr--Daftar-e Avval: She'r* [Collected Works--Volume 1: Poetry], edited by Sirus Tâhbâz (Tehrân: Nashr-e Nâsher, 1985), pp. 398-399.

89. Sâ'edi, "The Umbrella" [Chatr] (1959), translated by John R. Perry, *Major Voices in Contemporary Persian Literature*, pp. 148-151.

90. Idem, *Chub'bedasthâ-ye Varazil* [Clubwielders of Varazil] (Tehrân: Morvârid, 1965); translated by Deirdre Lashgari as *Up in Arms in Varazil* (1976).

91. Idem, *A-ye Bikolâh A-ye Bâkolâh* [Short 'A,' Long 'A'] (Tehrân: Nil, 1967); translated by Giselle Kupicinsky as "O Fool! O Fooled!" in *Modern Persian Drama* (Lanham, Maryland: University Press of America, 1987).

92. Idem, "Gâv" [The Cow], *Arash*, no. 7 (Tir 1964): 65-83; reprinted in *Azâdârân-e Bayal* [The Mourners of Bayal] (Tehrân: Nil, 1965), pp. 106-137.

93. Idem, *Gâv: Dâstâni barâye Film* [The Cow: A Screenplay] (Tehrân: Agâh, 1975; first printed in 1971), translated by Mohsen Ghadessy, *Iranian Studies* 18 (1985): 257-323.

94. *Buf-e Kur* [The Blind Owl], directed by Kayomars Derambakhsh (Tehrân: National Iranian Radio and Television, 1974).

95. Michael Hillmann, "Sadeq Hedayat's *The Blind Owl* as an Autobiographical Nightmare," *Irânshenâsi* 1, no. 1 (Spring 1989): 1-21 (English section).

96. Edward Shils, "Intellectuals," *International Encyclopaedia of the Social Sciences* 7 (1968): 399-415. The Persian word generally assumed to be synonymous with "intellectual" is *rowshanfekr*, the term Âl-e Ahmad uses in his writings to mean "intellectual." Literally denoting "bright/clear thought" or "enlightened (as to thought)," the term *rowshanfekr* implies a laudable state.

Consequently, it acquired a special connotation during the post-Mosaddeq pre-Khomayni era, when *engagé*, non-establishment writers and other intellectuals used it as a value-laden label for one of their own. Therefore, such establishment intellectuals as Parviz Nâtel Khânlari (b. 1913), editor of *Sokhan*, University of Tehrân Professor of Persian, and holder of several important government posts during the later Pahlavi era, was not considered *rowshanfekr* by such writers as Al-e Ahmad. On the other hand, in terms of Shils' definition, Khânlari's academic, research and editorial interests in Persian linguistics and literature qualify him as a thoroughgoing intellectual.

In post-Pahlavi Iran, further confusion over the use of the term *rowshanfekr* arose in non-establishment circles because many of their number, who supported the overthrow of the Pahlavi monarchy, supported Ruhollâh Khomayni and the establishment of the Islamic Republic of Iran at least early in 1979. Leading Tudeh Party figures continued their support of the Islamic Repuablic until the time of their own arrest in 1983. In any case, such pro-Khomayni feelings made such individuals no longer *rowshanfekr* in the eyes of anti-Pahlavi, anti-Khomayni intellectuals who felt forced into silence or underground or abroad in the early 1980s. Furthermore, those intellectuals who later recanted their support of Khomayni have found it difficult to regain respect among compeers never inclined to accept a Shi'i cleric as a national leader.

97.   Farzaneh Milani, "Power, Prudence, and Print: Censorship and Simin Dâneshvar," *Iranian Studies* 18 (1985): 325-347, discusses "the pronounced aversion of Iranian writers and poets toward giving detailed biographical data on themselves," as does Michael Hillmann, *A Lonely Woman: Forugh Farrokhzâd and Her Poetry* (Washington, D.C.: Mage Publishers and Three Continents Press, 1987), pp. 148-154.

98.   Biographical data in this chapter come mainly from such readily available and translated works as Jalâl Âl-e Ahmad, *Gharbzadegi* [Weststruckness] (Tehrân, 1962/1964), and much reprinted and translated, e.g., *Gharbzadegi* [Weststruckness], translated by John Green and Ahmad 'Alizadeh (Costa Mesa, California: Mazdâ Publishers, 1982); idem, *Khasi dar Miqât* [Lost in the Crowd] (Tehrân: Nil, 1966), reissued in 1978, and translated by John Green et al., *Lost in the Crowd* (Washington, D.C.: Three Continents Press, 1985); idem, "Masalan Sharh-e Ahvâlât" [An Autobiography of Sorts], *Jahân-e Now* 24, no. 3 (1969): 4-8, and much reprinted, and translated in *Iranian Society: An Anthology of Writings*, compiled and edited by Michael C. Hillmann (Costa Mesa, California: Mazdâ Publishers, 1982), pp. 14-19; idem, "Pir'mard Cheshm-e Mâ Bud" [The Old Man Was Our Eyes], *Arash*, no. 2 (Day 1961): 65-75, and translated in *Iranian Society*, pp. 99-110; and idem, "Samad va Afsâneh-ye 'Avâm" [Samad and the Folk Legend], *Arash*, no. 18 (Azar 1968), pp. 5-12, translated in *Iranian Society*, pp. 134-142.

99.   Simin Dâneshvar, "Ghorub-e Jalâl" [Jalâl's Sunset], *Arash*, no. 31 (Shahrivar 1981): 47-61; reprinted in idem, *Ghorub-e Jalâl* (Tehrân: Ravâq, 1982): 28-48. Translated by Farzaneh Milani and Jo-Anne Hart as "Jalâl's Sunset," *Iranian Studies* 19 (1986): 47-63. Maryam Mafi's translation appears under the title of "The Loss of Jalal" in Simin Daneshvar, *Daneshvar's Playhouse* (Washington, D.C.: Mage Publishers, 1989), pp. 133-153.

100.   Shamsoddin Al-e Ahmad, "Jalâl Shahid Shod yâ beh Marg-e Tabi'i Mord . . . Shams: Jalâl-râ Koshtand" [Was Jalâl Martyred or Did He Die a Natural

Death?. . . Shams: Jalâl Was Murdered], *Javân*, no. 27 (15 Tir 1979): 24-25, most of which is translated in *Iranian Society*, pp. 146-148.

101. Reza Baraheni, *The Crowned Cannibals: Writings on Repression in Iran* (New York: Random House Vintage Books, 1977), p. 124. Also, idem, *God's Shadow Prison Poems* (Bloomington, Indiana: Indiana University Press, 1976), p. 5, asserts that Al-e Ahmad was assassinated.

Baraheni's claim that the government liquidated dozens of writers during the reign of Mohammad Rezâ Shâh Pahlavi (ruled 1941-1979) is false, as are numerous other assertions in *The Crowned Cannibals*, a volume intended more as polemic than as contemporary history. Of course, exaggeration for the sake of buttressing arguments and views was a common tactic of anti-establishment Tehrân writers during the later Pahlavi years, Al-e Ahmad prominent among them in this regard. Baraheni's case, with respect to the nature of Al-e Ahmad's death, is particularly illustrative. For while he has argued in the English-speaking world that Al-e Ahmad was assassinated, he has voiced a different (and subtly self-serving) view in Iran. In "Jalâl az Didgâh-e Rezâ Barâheni" [Jalâl from the Perspective of Rezâ Barâheni], *Mi'âd bâ Jalâl* [Rendezvous with Jalâl], edited by Mehrdâd Jahâni (Tehrân: Ravâq, 1983), pp. 101-102, Baraheni answers a question about Al-e Ahmad's death with these words: "Jalâl viewed death in the form of martyrdom, and he expected to become a martyr; but he was not martyred . . . . People have a halo who achieve martyrdom . . . Jalâl spoke of martyrdom but did not become a martyr . . . Opposition in the age of eastern strangulation throws the dissident into the path of martyrdom. And Jalâl, the most forceful oppositionist of his age, was not martyred. But after his death, many of his supporters believed that he had been assassinated. The situation was this: Jalâl had never even been jailed. The one or two times he was questioned it was without torture. And it was not even within the confines of SAVAK. Despite these facts, everyone has a feeling of martyrdom concerning Jalâl. To a point, Jalâl himself is responsible for the spreading of this illogicality. Jalâl believed that suspicious deaths had to be put at the government's doorstep . . ."

102. Simin Dâneshvar, "Jalâl az Didgâh-e Simin Dâneshvar" [Jalâl from the Perspective of Simin Dâneshvar], *Rendezvous with Jalâl*, p. 27.

103. As for suspicions about the death of the one literary figure mentioned, Gholâmhosayn Sâ'edi, *Alefbâ*, new series, no. 7 (Fall 1986): 85, opines: "This business of SAVAK killing Samad has no truth in it, in my view. Samad fell into the Aras River and drowned . . . In fact, Al-e Ahmad put this rumor into everyone's mouth. One of the chief traits of Jalâl Al-e Ahmad--and I'm not saying it is good or bad, perhaps it's very good--was his readiness to create and nurture myths. By creating a myth, he could, for example, cause the enemy greater fear."

104. According to Eslâm Kâzemiyeh, in conversation with the author in Paris in June 1984.

105. According to Ne'mat Mirzâzâdeh, in conversation with the author in Paris in June 1984.

106. Ibid.

107. Materials not listed in John Green's "Bibliography" in *Lost in the Crowd*, pp. 152-155, will appear in this writer's forthcoming biographical study called *An Iranian Mullah's Son: The Life and Times of Jalâl Al-e Ahmad*.

108. Ahmad Shâmlu, "Sorud barâye Mard-e Rowshan keh beh Sâyeh Raft" [Anthem for the Bright Man Who Went into the Shadows], *Shekoftan dar Meh*

[Blossoming in Mist] (Tehrân: Ketâb-e Zamin, 1970), pp. 29-32; translation by Esmâ'il Kho'i, *Major Voices in Contemporary Persian Literature*, pp. 187-188.

109.   Al-e Ahmad depicts this event in a short story called "Jashn-e Farkhondeh" [The Joyous Celebration], first published in *Arash*, no. 1. (October/November 1961) and reprinted in *Panj Dâstân* [Five Stories] (Tehrân, 1971), pp. 25-44; it is available in Minoo S. Southgate's translation in *Modern Persian Short Stories*, pp. 19-33. Simin Dâneshvar verifies the autobiographical accuracy of most of Al-e Ahmad's stories in "Showharam Jalâl" [My Husband Jalâl], *Jalâl's Sunset*, p.12.

110.   Al-e Ahmad depicts this event in a short story called "Khâharam va 'Ankabut" [My Sister and the Spider], which was published in *Five Stories*, pp. 45-66, reprinted in *Ferdowsi*, special issue, no. 1006 (18 Mordâd 1971): 44-47, and which appears in a translation by A.R. Navabpour and Robert Wells in *Iranian Society*, pp. 20-33.

111.   Gholâmhosayn Sâ'edi, in several conversations with the author in Gallieni (Paris) during June 1984. Unless otherwise noted, all views attributed to Sâ'edi derive from these conversations.

112.   Rezâ Barâheni, "Jalâl from the Perspective of Dr. Rezâ Barâheni," pp. 92-104.

113.   *Ferdowsi*, no. 829 (11 Mehr 1967): 8. Al-e Ahmad had grounds for his suspicions about America: the American government, as Kermit Roosevelt outlines in *Countercoup: The Struggle for the Control of Iran* (New York: McGraw-Hill, 1979), had successfully plotted the overthrow of the legally elected and constituted government of Iran in August 1953, when it forced the ouster of Mohammad Mosaddeq in favor of Mohammad Rezâ Pahlavi. It will be generations before Iranian intellectuals will forgive America for that action.

114.   Mahmud Azâd Tehrâni, as quoted in *Bâmshâd*, no. 94 (16-23 Mehr 1968): 27.

115.   Jalâl Al-e Ahmad, *Sangi bar Guri* [A Stone on a Grave] (Tehrân: Ravâq, 1981), p. 70.

116.   Rezâ Barâheni, Jalâl from the Perspective of Dr. Rezâ Barâheni," p. 96.

117.   E.g., Ebrâham Golestân, as expressed in numerous conversations with the author in London during the spring of 1982.

118.   Simin Dâneshvar, "Pâ-ye Sohbat-e Simin-e Dâneshvar" [Talking with Simin Dâneshvar] (an interview conducted by Farzaneh Milani), *Alefbâ*, new series, no. 4 (Fall 1983): 153-154.

119.   Afshin [pseudonym], "Gharbzadegi yâ 'Arabzadegi" [Weststruckness or Arabstruckness], *Ferdowsi*, no. 787 (3 Abân 1966): 12-14; no. 788 (10 Abân 1966): 6-7.

120.   Feraydun Adamiyat, "Ashoftegi dar Fekr-e Târikhi" [Confusion in Historical Thinking], *(Zamimeh-ye) Jahân-e Andisheh* (Khordâd 1981). 22p.

121.   *Irân va Jahân* 3, no. 11 (11 October 1982): 8

122.   Ahmad Shâmlu, in a personal written communication to Leonardo P. Alishan in 1986.

123.   Simin Dâneshvar, *Jalâl's Sunset*, p. 47.

124.   E.g., Brad Hanson, "The 'Westoxication' of Iran: Depictions and Reactions of Behrangi, Al-e Ahmad, and Shari'ati," *International Journal of Middle Eastern Studies* 15 (1983): 1-23,

Roy Mottahedeh, *The Mantle of the Prophet: Religion and Politics in Iran* (New York: Simon and Schuster, 1985), pp. 287 ff, begins his sketch of Al-e

Ahmad's career with the assertion that the latter "returned to religion in the sixties." Hamid Algar, "Introduction," *Occidentosis: A Plague from the West*, translated by R. Campbell (Berkeley: Mizan Press, 1984), pp. 9-24, likewise asserts Al-e Ahmad's "ultimate return to Islam," but notes that "the sense in which he rediscovered Islam after the writing of *Gharbzadegi* requires careful definition; it is certainly not a straightforward return to guidance from one formerly erring but now penitent." Algar adds that "there is no clear sign that Al-e Ahmad foresaw, or would have supported, a revolution led and directed by the *ulama*."

In a review of John Green's translation of *Lost in a Crowd*, William L. Hanaway, Jr., *World Literature Today* 60 (1986): 515-516, asserts: "Al-e Ahmad . . . never succeeded in coming to terms with religion, as much as he seems to have wanted to . . . . Al-e Ahmad was not a believer and wondered why he was doing it [making a religious pilgrimage to Mecca] . . . . The book should be read by all who still believe that at the end of his life the author thought religion to be the solution to Iran's problems." In a conversation with this writer in Gallieni (Paris) in June 1984, Gholamhosayn Sâ'edi claimed that Al-e Ahmad definitely did not believe in God and that the two of them drank alcoholic beverages to excess the evening before Al-e Ahmad set out for Mecca.

125. Mohammad Rezâ Pahlavi (1919-1980), as quoted by Oriana Fallaci, *Interview with History*, translated by John Shepley (New York: Liveright, 1976), pp. 272, states his unequivocal belief in the superiority of men. Consequently, his regime's efforts in behalf of women's rights must be judged as part of the policy of Westernization and as orchestrated evidence of the "progressiveness" of that regime, and not as a program inspired by any principle of equality of the sexes.

126. Ruhollâh Khomayni, as quoted in *Sayings of the Ayatollah Khomeini*, translated (from Persian into French) by Jean-Marie Xaviere, translated (from French into English) by Harold I. Salemson and edited by Tony Hendra (New York: Bantam Books, 1980), p. 109. A more literal translation, presented in the broader context of Khomayni's general views appears in idem, *A Clarification of Questions*, translated by J. Borujerdi (Boulder, Colorado: Westview Press, 1984), p. 323, #2459: "It is recommended that one hurries in giving a husband to a daughter who has attained puberty, meaning that she is of the age of religious accountability. His Holiness Sâdeq [the sixth Shi'i Emâm], salutations to him, said that it is one of man's good fortunes that his daughter does not see menses in his own house." In a review of *A Clarification of Questions*, Hamid Algar, *International Journal of Middle East Studies* 19 (1987): 245-246, argues that the book is not particularly representative of Khomayni's distinctive approach to theology and that the translation is seriously flawed by being mechanically literal.

Khomayni's views on women are discussed by Amir Taheri in *The Spirit of Allah: Khomeini and the Islamic Revolution* (Bethesda, Maryland: Adler & Adler, 1986), p. 35, where it is asserted that Khomayni's mother and sister were married at nine years of age and that he married his wife when she was ten and he twenty-seven. Shireen Mahdavi presents a feminist overview of the issue in "The Position of Women in Shi'a Islam: Views of the 'Ulama," *Women and the Family in the Middle East: New Voices of Change*, edited by Elizabeth Warnock Fernea (Austin, Texas: University of Texas Press, 1985), pp. 255-268. Fazlur Rahman, "The Status of Women in Islam: A Modernist Interpretation," *Separate Worlds*, edited by Hanna Papanek and Gail Minault (Columbia, Missouri: South Asia Books, 1982), pp. 285-310, reveals how some Western-educated Moslem intellectuals defend the continuation of traditional subordination of women to men.

127. Ali Shari'ati, *Fâtemeh Fâtemeh'ast* [Fâtemeh Is Fâtemeh], translated by Laleh Bakhtiyar (Tehrân: The Shariati Foundation, 1981).

128. Mohammad Ishaque, *Four Eminent Poetesses of Iran* (Calcutta: The Iran Society, 1950), treats the four most famous poetesses prior to Forugh Farrokhzâd: Râbe'eh, Mahsati, Qorratol'ayn, and Parvin E'tesâmi. For information on Qorratol'ayn and E'tesami, see footnotes 134 and 136, respectively. But virtually nothing is available in English on pre-Qâjâr, female literary figures. Mahsati is the subject of Friedrich Max Meier's *Die Schöne Mahsati* (Wiesbaden: Franz Steiner, 1965).

129. Heshmat Moayyad, "Parvin's Poems: A Cry in the Wilderness," *Islamwissenschaftliche Abhandlungen Fritz Meier*, edited by Richard Gramlich (Wiesbaden: Franz Steiner, 1974), p. 164, observes: "The very few preserved fragments of poetry which are ascribed to certain names of women [in premodern Iranian history] are not sufficient to secure a place of honor to any of them." Farzaneh Milani, "Forugh Farrokhzâd: A Feminist Perspective," *Bride of Acacias: Selected Poems of Forugh Farrokhzâd*, translated by Jascha Kessler with Amin Banani (Delmar, New York: Caravan Books, 1982), pp. 141-142, argues that a deliberate suppression of women's accomplishments throughout Iranian history accounts for the paucity of women's names in any Iranian pantheon. Joanna Russ, *How to Suppress Women's Writing* (Austin, Texas: University of Texas Press, 1983), reviews universal ways in which either women have been denied access to opportunities or women's accomplishments are routinely not given their due.

130. John D. Yohannan, editor, *Joseph and Potiphar's Wife in World Literature: An Anthology of the Story of the Chaste Youth and the Lustful Stepmother* (New York: New Directions Books, 1968), provides Genesis and Koranic accounts, along with an abridgment of the culminating Persian redaction by Jâmi (1414-1492) called *Joseph and Zolaykhâ*, in which Potiphar's wife becomes much more than a stereotypically weak female smitten by Joseph's perfect beauty.

131. Bapsy Pavry, *The Heroines of Ancient Persia, Stories Retold from the Shâhnâmeh of Ferdowsi* (Cambridge, England: Cambridge University Press, 1930), presents romantic images of legendary Iranian women.

132. In an unpublished essay, Leonardo P. Alishan traces from pre-Islamic Iran to the present the association of femaleness with the earth as material and evil in contrast with spirituality associated with maleness. Idem, "Forugh Farrokhzâd and the Forsaken Earth," *Forugh Farrokhzâd A Quarter-Century Later*, compiled and edited by Michael Hillmann, *Literature East and West* 24 (1988): 105-114, reviews literary representations of this view from Rudaki (d. 940/1) to Golshiri (b. 1937).

133. Tâjossaltaneh's memoirs are available in Persian: *Khâterat-e Tâjossaltaneh* [Memoirs of Tâjossaltaneh] (Tehrân: Nashr-e Târikh-e Irân, 1982).

134. In an unpublished paper delivered at Farrokhzâd week at The University of Texas in Austin in February 1987 called "Feminist Consciousness in Iranian Poetry from Qorratol'ayn to Forugh Farrokhzâd," Mohammad Valadi questions

conventional views on the part of admirers and detractors alike concerning Qorratal'ayn's personality and achievements.

135. The basic Persian sources are Tal'at Bassâri, *Zandddokht, Pishâhang-e Nehzat-e Âzâdi-ye Bânovân-e Irân* [Zanddokht, Precursor of the Freedom Movement of the Women of Irân] (Tehrân: Tahuri, 1968); and *Divân-e Zhâleh Qâ'em'maqâmi* [Collected Poems of Zhâleh Qâ'em'maqâmi], edited by (her son) Hosayn Pezhmân Bakhtiyâri (Tehrân: Ebn-e Sinâ, 1967).

136. Parvin E'tesâmi, *A Nightingale's Lament (Selected Poems)*, translated by Heshmat Moayyad and Margaret Madelung (Costa Mesa, California: Mazdâ Publishers, 1985).

137. Dâneshvar, "Talking with Simin Dâneshvar," p. 154.

138. The first two chapters of Hillmann, *A Lonely Woman*, review Farrokhzâd's life, while the third chapter outlines specific aspects of the oppression of women in Iran as described by Iranian women themselves. Azar Tabari, "The Enigma of the Veiled Iranian Woman," *MERIP Reports*, no. 103 (February 1982): 22-27, describes the inferior status of Iranian women in the context of Islamic dogma. In a brief article called "Farrokhzâd, Bonyângozâr-e Maktab-e Mo'annas-e She'r-e Fârsi" [Farrokhzâd, Founder of the Feminine School in Persian Poetry], *Ferdowsi*, no. 950 (27 Bahman 1970): 20, Rezâ Barâheni asserts that Farrokhzâd singlehandedly brought the feminine gender into Persian literature. In another essay called "Women and Their Position in Masculine History," *The Crowned Cannibals*, pp. 45-64, Barâheni vividly outlines the oppression of women in Iranian culture.

139. Forugh Farrokhzâd, "Towzih" [Explanation], *Asir* [(The) Captive], (Tehrân: Amir Kabir, 1956, second printing), p. 159, discussed in Hillmann, *A Lonely Woman*, pp. 73-74.

140. Ibid., pp. 73 ff. E.g., Farzaneh Milani in written comments to a draft of part of *A Lonely Woman*.

141. Farrokhzâd is the most translated modernist Persian poet. Versions of nearly twenty of her poems appear in *Forugh Farrokhzâd A Quarter-Century Later*.

142. Composed in Tehrân in the spring of 1955, "Halqeh" [The (Wedding) Band] was published in *Asir* [The Captive] (Tehrân: Amir Kabir, 1955), pp. 149-150.

143. "Sorud-e Paykâr" [Call to Arms or Battle Cry] was first published in *Nabard-e Zendegi* 1, no. 1 (Farvardin 1955): 51. Farrokhzâd chose not to include the poem in any of her collections of verse.

144. "Beh Khâharam" [To My Sister] appears in *Tazkereh-ye Sho'arâ-ye Mo'âser-e Irân* [An Anthology of Contemporary Poets of Iran], 2 volumes, compiled by Sayyed 'Abdolhamid Khalkhâli (Tehrân: Tahuri, 1955 and 1958) 2: 246-250. Farrokhzâd chose not to include the poem in any of her collections of verse.

145. "'Arusak-e Kuki" [The Windup Doll] was composed in 1960 or 1961 and published in *Another Birth*, pp. 71-75.

146. Undated, "O Jewel-studded Land" [Ay Marz-e Porgohar] was published in *Another Birth*, pp. 1148-157. The translation here owes much, including the quotation of numerous phrases, to the version by Jascha Kessler with Amin Banani in *Bride of Acacias: Selected Poems of Forugh Farrokhzâd*, pp. 82-86.

147. Composed in Tehrân in mid-summer 1954, "Asir" [(The) Captive] was the title poem of Farrokhzâd's first collection, *The Captive*, pp. 33-35.

148. "Gonâh" [(The) Sin], *Divâr* [(The) Wall] (Tehrân: Amir Kabir, 1956), pp. 11-15. The Persian text is also presented, along with commentary, in Hillmann, *A Lonely Woman*, pp. 77-78. Zjaleh Hajibashi, "Redefining 'Sin'," *Forugh Farrokhâd A Quarter-Century Later*, pp. 67-71, offers an analysis of the poem.

149. Composed in mid-summer 1955, "She'ri barâyeh To" [A Poem for You] appears in Farrokhzâd's third collection of verse, *'Esyân* [Rebellion] (Tehrân: Amir Kabir, 1958), pp. 55-60.

150. Idem, *Harfhâ'i ba Forugh Farrokhzâd: Chahar Goft va Shonud* [Conversations with Forugh Farrokhzâd: Four Interviews] (Tehrân: Morvârid, 1977), pp. 37-38.

151. Farzaneh Milani, "Forugh Farrokhzâd: A Feminist Perspective," Ph.D. Dissertation, University of California, Los Angeles, 1979, pp. 156-159.

152. "Vahm-e Sabz" [Green Delusion] was first published as "Owhâm-e Bahâri" [Springtime Delusions] in *Ketâb-e Hafteh*, nos. 23-24 (27 Esfand 1962): 330-332, and reprinted in a slightly altered final form in *Another Birth*, pp. 117-122.

153. "Fath-e Bâgh" [Conquest of the Garden] is dated Spring 1962 and was first published in *Kayhân-e Hafteh*, no. 36 (24 Tir 1962): 136-141. It then appeared in *Another Birth*, pp. 125-129, which is the text used as the basis of the translation here. Ardavan Davaran, "'The Conquest of the Garden': A Significant Instance of the Poetic Development of Forugh Farrokhzâd," *Another Birth: Selected Poems of Forugh Farrokhzâd* (Emeryville, California: Albany Press, 1981), pp. 117-124, presents an insightful analysis of the poem, as does Farzaneh Milani, "Nakedness Regained: Farrokhzâd's Garden of Eden," *Forugh Farrokhzâd A Quarter-Century Later*, pp. 91-104.

154. Undated, "Tavallodi Digar" [Another Birth] is the title poem of *Another Birth*, pp. 164-169. The translation here is by Karim Emami who, as reported in "On Translating a Persian Poem," *Kayhan International*, 27 January 1966, p. 5, reprinted in *Forugh Farrokhzâd Twenty Years Later*, pp. 73-78, collaborated with the poet on it. The poem is explicated in Hillmann, *A Lonely Woman*, pp. 110-19, and by M.R. Ghanoonparvar in *Forugh Farrokhzâd A Quarter Century Later*, pp. 79-89.

155. "Tanhâ Sedâ'st Keh Mimânad" [It Is Only Sound That Remains] was first published in *Arash*, no. 11 (Azar 1966): 99-102, and then anthologized in Farrokhzâd's fifth, final, and posthumously published collection called *Imân Biyâvarim beh Aghâz-e Fasl-e Sard* [Let Us Believe in the Beginning of the Cold Season] (Tehrân: Morvârid, 1974), pp. 76-81.

156. Esmâ'il Fasih, *Sorayyâ dar Eghmâ*, 3rd printing (Tehrân: Nashr-e Now, 1985); translated as *Sorayya in a Coma* (London: Zed Press, 1985); and reviewed by A.R. Navabpour, *Iranian Studies* 18 (1985): 427-432.

157. Nimâ Yushij, "Ay Shab" [O Night], *The Collected Works of Nimâ Yushij*, pp. 36-38.

158. Nâder Nâderpur, "Khun va Khâkestar" [Blood and Ashes], translated by Michael Hillmann from a handwritten text supplied by the poet, *False Dawn: Persian Poems--Literature East & West* 22 (1986): 74-76. The Persian text is available in Nâderpur, *Khun va Khâkestar* (Los Angeles: Ketâb Corp., 1989).

159. Montesquieu, *The Persian Letters,* translated by J. Robert Loy (New York: The World Publishing Company [Meridian Books], 1972), p. 88.

160. Taheri, *The Spirit of Allah*, pp. 59-60.

161. Jalâl Âl-e Ahmad, "Tajhiz-e Mellat" [The Mobilization of Iran (literally: the nation)], translated by David C. Champagne, *Major Voices in Contemporary Persian Literature*, pp. 61-70.

162. Gholamhosayn Sâ'edi "Dandil" [Dandil], translated by Hasan Javadi, *Dandil: Stories from Iranian Life* (New York: Random House, 1981), pp. 1-28.

163. Michael Hillmann, "Revolution, Islam and Modernist Persian Literature," *Iran: Essays on a Revolution in the Making*, edited by Ahmad Jabbari and Robert Olson (Costa Mesa, California: Mazdâ Publishers, 1981), pp. 121-142.

164. Jalâl Âl-e Ahmad, "Samad and the Folk Legend," translated by Leonardo P. Alishan, *Iranian Society*, pp. 134-142; Samad Behrangi, "From *An Investigation of Educational Problems in Iran*," *Major Voices in Contemporary Persian Literature*, pp. 196-206; idem, *The Little Black Fish and Other Modern Persian Short Stories*, translated by Eric Hooglund and Mary Hegland (Washington, D.C.: Three Continents Press, 1976).

165. "A Biobibliographical Sketch," *On the Sociology of Islam: Lectures* by Ali Shari'ati, translated by Hamid Algar (Berkeley: Mizan Press, 1979), pp. 11-38, is a handy, if sketchy, treatment of the career of this influential reformer, whose chief works have been published in Persian in thirty-four volumes. Shari'ati's significance is treated in Ervand Abrahamian, "'Ali Shari'ati: Ideologue of the Iranian Revolution," *MERIP Reports*, no. 102 (January 1982): 24-28.

166. According to his son Sheraguime Youchidje, in conversation with the author in Austin, Texas during August 1985. In a letter to the author dated 27 July 1987, Ebrahim Golestan offers a contrary view of Nimâ's use of opium: "His was a way of passing time, and pleasure, like so many others in this country." But I never saw or heard of a happy opium addict in Iran.

167. According to Mottahadeh, *The Mantle of the Prophet*, p. 164: Classical "Persian poetry came to be the emotional home in which the ambiguity that was at the heart of Iranian culture lived most freely and openly." Taheri, *The Spirit of Allah*, p. 59, observes that "some Iranian thinkers" see Moslem Iranian culture as the backdrop to "our national multiple schizophrenia."

168. Jalâl Âl-e Ahmad, "Hâfez," *Farhang-e Jalâl Âl-e Ahmad* [A Jalâl Âl-e Ahmad Dictionary], compiled by Mostafâ Zamâni Niyâ (Tehrân: Pâsârgâd, 1984/85, second printing), p. 374; idem, *Dar Khedmat va Khiyânat-e Rowshanfekrân* [On the Good Offices and Treasonable Activities of Intellectuals] (Tehrân: Ravâq, 1977), pp. 176-177.

169. Mohammad 'Ali Jamâlzâdeh, "Persian is Sugar" [Fârsi Shekar'ast], translated by S.M. Moosavi et al., *Major Voices in Contemporary Persian Literature*, pp. 13-20.

170. Ahmad Shâmlu, "Dar In Bonbast" [In this Dead End], *Iran Sun* (November 1979): 45; reprinted in idem, *Tarâneh'hâ-ye Kuchek-e Ghorbat* [Little Songs of Alienation] (Tehrân: Mâzyâr, 1980), pp. 30-32. In "Ahmad Shâmlu: The Rebel Poet in Search of an Audience," *Iranian Studies* 18 (1985): 401 ff., Leonardo Alishan briefly discusses "In This Dead End" and other poems "written during and on exile" in the context of Shâmlu's post-Pahlavi career. In "Poetry against Piety: The Literary Response to the Iranian Revolution, "*World Literature Today* 60 (1986): 253, Ahmad Karimi-Hakkak characterizes "In This Dead End" as the expression of "the poet's sense of an impending danger threatening basic and native social values," culminating "in the feast of Satan,

celebrating the demise of intellectual dreams." Karimi-Hakkak's brief essay is of further interest because of his attempt to explain how it happened that secular minded Iranian writers supported the Khomayni movement, at least through early 1979.

171. Leonardo P. Alishan, "From The Waste Land to the Imam," *Iranian Studies* 15 (1982): 181-210. Farzaneh Milani, "Conformity and Confrontation: A Comparison of Two Iranian Women Poets," *Women and the Family in the Middle East*, pp. 317-330; and Tâhereh Saffârzâdeh, "Goftogu bâ . . . Shâ'er-e Enqelâbi" [A Conversation with . . . a Revolutionary Poet], *Ettelâ'ât*, no. 182945 (11 October 1989): 8-9 and 17.

172. E.g., "The Poets," *Holy Qur'an*, translated by M.H. Shakir (Elmhurst, New York: Tahrike Tarsile Qur'an, Inc., 1984, third printing), p. 363, #224: "And as to the poets, those who go astray follow them." Shahrokh Meskoub, *(Iranian) Nationality and (the Persian) Language* (Washington, D.C.: Mage Publishers, 1990), discusses the antipathy of Shi'i clerics toward imaginative literature.

173. Paul Sprachman, "Ebrahim Golestan's *The Treasure*: A Parable of Cliché and Consumption," *Iranian Studies* 15 (1982): 155-180, discusses Golestân's novel and film called *Asrâr-e Ganj-e Darreh-ye Jenni* [The Secrets of the Treasure of the Possessed Valley], which satirizes Pahlavi Iran.

174. Some critics operating in an environment which asserted social commitment in literature [*ta'ahhod-e adabi*] as a criterion for literary excellence are particularly negative about Jamâlzâdeh's works because of his long separation from Iran. For example, Rezâ Barâheni, *Qesseh'nevisi* [Fiction-writing] (Tehrân: Ashrafi, 1969), p. 528, asserts that Jamâlzâdeh is just "an old man parading his memories of Iran from thirty years ago." Michael Hillmann's review of *Once upon a Time*, translated by Heshmat Moayyad and Paul Sprachman (New York, New York: Bibliotheca Persica, 1985), *Journal of Near Eastern Studies* 47 (1988): 311-313, reviews the issue.

175. According to Goli Taraqqi, in conversation with the author in Paris in the spring of 1982.

176. Sohrâb Sepehri, "Water's Footsteps: A Poem," translated by Karim Emami, *Iranian Studies* 15 (1982): 97-116. Idem, Dâryush Ashuri, and Hosayn Ma'sumi Hamadâni, *Payâmi dar Râh: Nazari beh She'r va Naqqâshi-ye Sohrâb Sepehri* [A Message along the Way: A Look at the Poetry and Painting of Sohrâb Sepehri] (Tehrân: Tahuri, 1981), offer detailed critiques of Sepehri. The volume also includes a bibliography of materials in English on the poet-painter published in Iran. Layli Golestân, compiler, *Sohrâb Sepehri, Shâ'er, Naqqâsh* [Sohrâb Sepehri, Poet, Painter] (Tehrân: Amir Kabir, 1980), includes twenty-eight color plates of his paintings. Other treatments include: Faraj Sar-e Kuhi, "'Arefi Gharib dar Diyâr-e 'Asheqân" [A Strange Gnostic in the Realm of Lovers], *Adineh*, no. 11 (15 Ordibehesht 1987): 40-44; and Hosayn Ma'sumi Hamadâni, "Sepehri va Moshkel-e She'r-e Emruz" [Sepehri and the Problem of Today's Poetry], *Kayhân-e Farhangi* 3, no. 2 (May 1986): 23-27.

177. In a review of *A Lonely Woman* in *Forugh Farrokhzâd A Quarter-Century Later*, pp. 51-52, William L. Hanaway, Jr., writes: " Because . . . Hillmann believes . . . that Farrokhzâd rejected the mold that patriarchy fashioned for her, he claims that she is a twentieth-century Sohrâb who followed in an important line of reforming voices throughout Iranian mythology and history. Here he has misinterpreted the mission of Sohrâb and inadvertently

identified Farrokhzâd with the wrong party. While it is true that Sohrâb was killed in error by his father Rostam, it was not because Sohrâb rejected the patriarchal mode. Quite the contrary: Sohrâb's goal was to overthrow the foolish King Kâvus and install Rostam on the throne. He had no intention of changing the system of monarchy, but only to substitute one all-powerful ruler for another. Quite clear also is his own desire to rule in Turân after deposing Afrâsiyâb. Thus to equate Farrokhzâd with Sohrâb is to suggest that she was a monarchist and upholder of patriarchy, willing to change the actors but unwilling to tamper with the system itself. This is, of course, quite incorrect."

My reading of Sohrâb's character and aims (as outlined above in chapter 1) is quite different. Motivated by love and a belief that merit should be rewarded, Sohrâb seeks to place on the throne a man who, in his view, deserves to be there: his own father. He plans to share in the rule of the Iranian empire and to install his mother as queen. As an actor in a monarchical age in a narrative composed in another monarchical age. Sohrâb necessarily envisions justice and reforms within the contexts and world view familiar to him. Nevertheless, his belief that the younger generation, not in power, should have a voice in who rules and that only one who deserves to rule should be king make him, in my mind a kindred spirit and mythological forbear to Farrokhzâd.

178.   Jalâl Al-e Ahmad, *Lost in the Crowd*, pp. 105-106. Idem, *Kârnâmeh-ye Seh Sâleh* [Three-year Report] (Tehrân: Zamân, 1966), p. 164.

179.   Mehdi Akhavân-e Sâles, "Zemestân" [Winter], *Zemestân* [Winter] (Tehrân: Morvârid, 1975, fourth printing), pp. 97-99.